The
Changing Society
of
CHINA

by *CH'U CHAI* and *WINBERG CHAI*

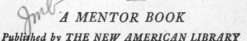

A MENTOR BOOK
Published by THE NEW AMERICAN LIBRARY

To DAVID J. STERN

FIRST PRINTING, FEBRUARY, 1962

MENTOR TRADEMARK REG. U.S. PAT. OFF. AND FOREIGN COUNTRIES
REGISTERED TRADEMARK—MARCA REGISTRADA
HECHO EN CHICAGO, U.S.A.

Library of Congress Catalog Card No. 62-9702

MENTOR BOOKS *are published by*
The New American Library of World Literature, Inc.
501 Madison Avenue, New York 22, New York

PRINTED IN THE UNITED STATES OF AMERICA

CHINA
Never Changed

FOR THOUSANDS OF YEARS CHINA ENJOYED A STABLE CULTURE. WHEN EUROPEANS FIRST PENETRATED THAT VAST COUNTRY, THE INHABITANTS REGARDED THE FOREIGNERS AS BARBARIANS BECAUSE THEY DID NOT HAVE THE ADVANTAGE OF CHINA'S ANCIENT HERITAGE AND TRADITION.

CHINA CONTINUED AS AN AUTONOMOUS STATE UNTIL THE OPIUM WAR OF 1839. AT ITS CONCLUSION WESTERN POWERS MADE TREATIES WITH THE CHINESE GOVERNMENT THAT ALLOWED AN EXPANSION OF EUROPEAN TRADE THROUGHOUT THE COUNTRY. CHINA'S SPLENDID ISOLATION WAS ENDED.

This fascinating book has a breadth and scope as large as China itself. The authors consider the Chinese personality; China's philosophy, art, literature, and religion; the complex relation of its past to its present. They show how an effort to reconcile Eastern tradition with Western industrialization gave birth to revolutionary factions—the collapse of the Manchu dynasty; the rise of the Nationalist party and Sun-Yat-sen; the rise and fall of Chiang Kai-shek.

Today the mainland of China is ruled by the Communist party and Mao Tse-tung, who gained his power by leading the vast peasant population in uprising and reform. China, remote and isolated for centuries, is now engaged in a social upheaval that may change the face of the world.

MENTOR Books of Related Interest

Contents

Introduction

CHAPTER I. THE BACKGROUND

1. Geographic Background   11
2. Historical Experience   16
3. An Estimate   20

CHAPTER II. THE CHINESE PEOPLE

1. Ethnic Origins   26
2. Racial Amalgamation   30

PART I: Social and Political Institutions

CHAPTER III. THE FUNDAMENTAL CONCEPTIONS

1. The National or Racial Conception   34
2. The Religious Conception   36
3. The Political Conception   38
4. The Humanistic Conception   40

CHAPTER IV. THE CHINESE GOVERNMENT

1. The Structure of the Imperial
   Government   42
2. The Structure of the Nationalist
   Government   50
3. The Structure of the Communist
   Government   56

CHAPTER V. THE CHINESE SOCIETY

1. Agrarian Society and Economy   61
2. Structure of Chinese Society   66
3. Secret Societies   71

CHAPTER VI. THE CHINESE FAMILY

1. The Function of the Family in Chinese
   Civilization   74
2. The Ethical Basis of the Chinese Family   76
3. The Cult of Ancestor Worship   78
4. The Institution of Marriage   81
5. The Family Reform   83

CHAPTER VII. THE PEOPLE'S COMMUNES

1. The Communist Agrarian Policy   87
2. What Is a People's Commune?   92
3. The Prospects   97

CHAPTER VIII. CHINESE LAW

1. The Conception of Law: Li versus Fa   101
2. The Codification of Law   104
3. The Administration of Law   107

PART II: Chinese Thought and Learning

CHAPTER IX. THE SPIRIT OF CHINESE CULTURE

1. Cosmic Conception   110
2. Life Attitude   118
3. Conclusion   124

CHAPTER X. THE DEVELOPMENT OF CHINESE PHILOSOPHY

1. "A Hundred Schools Contend"   126
2. The Revival of Learning   132
3. Introduction of Buddhism   134
4. The Rise of Neo-Confucianism   136
5. The New Culture Movement   139

CHAPTER XI. CHINESE RELIGION

1. The Three Great Traditions   142
2. The Popular Beliefs   145

CHAPTER XII. CHINESE LITERATURE

1. Literature and Philosophy   151
2. The Character of Chinese Literature   153
3. The Literary Revolution   163

CHAPTER XIII. THE CHINESE LANGUAGE

1. The Origin and Development of the Chinese Language   167
2. The Classification of Dialects   169
3. The Evolution of Chinese Characters   171
4. The Language Reform   174

CHAPTER XIV. THE BASIC IDEALS OF CHINESE ART

1. Formalism—The Perfection of Form   177
2. Symbolism—The Economy of Means   179
3. Naturalism—The Beauty of Nature   181
4. Romanticism—The Spirit of Creation   184

PART III: Reform and Revolution

CHAPTER XV. SOCIAL CHANGES IN THE PAST HUNDRED YEARS

1. Western Encroachments — 187
2. Collapse of the Imperial Rule — 189
3. Breakdown of Agrarian Economy — 192
4. Traditionalism versus Modernism — 194

CHAPTER XVI. K'ANG YU-WEI AND THE REFORM MOVEMENT

1. K'ang's Political Views and Activities — 196
2. K'ang's Writings and Philosophy — 199

CHAPTER XVII. SUN YAT-SEN AND THE NATIONALIST REVOLUTION

1. The Evolution of the Kuomintang (Nationalist Party) — 205
2. The Political Doctrines of Sun Yat-sen — 208

CHAPTER XVIII. CHIANG KAI-SHEK AND NATIONALISM

1. The Nationalist Collapse on the Mainland — 214
2. The Political Thought of Chiang Kai-shek — 217

CHAPTER XIX. MAO TSE-TUNG AND COMMUNISM

1. The Rise of Chinese Communism — 222
2. Mao Tse-tung's Early Activities and Writings — 225

CHAPTER XX. THE CHANGING CHINESE IN A CHANGING SOCIETY

1. The Chinese Type of Humanity — 230
2. The Communist Type of Humanity — 232

Selected Bibliography — 237

Chronological Table — 244

Index — 250

Administrative Divisions of China

Foreword

China until very recently has been of relatively little interest to the average American. While the differences between East and West have frequently been exaggerated, mutual understanding and appreciation have always been difficult to achieve because of the formidable barriers of geography, language, divergent traditions, and conflicting objectives. To an important degree this failure in understanding has caused many disagreements, conflicts, and even wars.

Therefore, the critical problem of our time is the relation between the Western world and China, which is crucial for world peace and prosperity. The establishment of closer relations calls for sympathetic and sound understanding as well as for critical and objective knowledge of the people, their culture, and their current problems.

The purpose of this book, then, is to offer to the layman a deeper understanding of what China was in the past, what China is today, and what China will be in the years to come. Although each chapter is a unit devoted to a single subject that can be read without reference to the other chapters, it is advisable for the reader to begin with the first chapter and go through the entire book. An extensive bibliography has been included for those who may wish to make further studies on this subject.

In preparation for the writing of this volume, we wish to express our gratitude to our colleagues and students for their support and encouragement. We are also indebted to the editors of the New American Library. Our thanks are also due to Mrs. May Ann Tsao Chai for her valuable assistance in many ways.

Ch'u Chai
Winberg Chai

Introduction

CHAPTER I.   THE BACKGROUND

1. Geographic Background

Chinese history runs back as far as the histories of Egypt, Babylonia, and India, but its continuity has been far less disturbed by foreign conquests. Chinese culture has been isolated in its development, and is different in character from the cultures of Egypt, Babylonia, and India. The geographic background of Chinese culture will help to explain this difference.

The natural environment forms the background of all human existence and constantly conditions all human institutions. Human culture originated in the place where population aggregated in a considerable number and maintained permanent relations. An area irrigated by rivers and protected by natural barriers was required by primitive men to support a large population and to bring about those relations among men. In looking at the map of the world, we shall find comparatively few places that fulfill these requirements. It is therefore no accident that all early known civilizations developed along the Nile Valley in Egypt, the Tigris-Euphrates valleys in Babylonia, and the Ganges in India. In the origin of civilization, geography played an important part.[1] The earliest civilizations may be regarded as "fluvial," centering along the banks of rivers and in fertile river valleys. Then European civilization became "thalassic," focusing

[1] This is not the view of Toynbee. See his *Civilization on Trial*, New York, Oxford Univ. Press, 1948, p. 11.

in the Mediterranean, and finally "oceanic," utilizing the great oceans as bonds of contact between East and West.[2]

There is a traditional belief that Chinese civilization originated in the Hwang Ho (Yellow River) valley, but in fact the Hwang Ho itself is not suitable for irrigation or communication. The earliest sites of Chinese civilization were not upon the Hwang Ho itself, but upon its tributaries. At the confluence of the Hwang Ho and its tributaries, there are many different alluvial deltalike tracts of land, for which the Chinese character is *jui* (　汭　), such as the Wei Jui, the Ching Jui, the Lo Jui, and others.

Important culture sites in ancient China were located, for example, in the northwest areas which contain various alluvial tracts of land formed by the Hwang Ho and its tributaries. The Yü culture (2255–2205 B.C.) had its origin in the southwest of Shansi, on the northeast bank of the Hwang Ho, into which the Fen River flows. Next, the Hsia culture (2205–1766 B.C.) had its origin in the northwest of Honan, on the south bank of the Hwang Ho, into which the Yi River and the Lo River flow. And the Chou culture (1122–255 B.C.) had its origin in the east of Shensi, on the west bank of the Hwang Ho, into which the Wei River flows.

These *jui*, or deltas, formed a number of land units of various sizes and of various formations, separated from one another by natural barriers or broad rivers or high mountains, or joined by river systems or valleys. Some units were distinct, with natural boundaries on all sides, and other natural boundaries were indistinct or broken in places. In either case, the fords of the Hwang Ho in such districts as Ho Tsin, Ling Tsin, and Ping Lu in Shansi were the means of transportation and communication among these deltas. Chinese history records that the Hsia people came from the Lo River valley northward across the Hwang Ho, then by Mao Tsin in the district of Pin Lu and further east by Meng Tsin to meet the Yü people in the Fen River valley. As a consequence, the Yü and Hsia cultures were closely connected. The Chou people seem to have come from the west in central Shensi and, harassed by the nomadic tribes, made frequent moves. According to the *Shih Ching*, or *Book of*

---

[2] The early cultures of India were also mainly fluvial; large numbers of inhabitants congregated along the riverbanks.

Odes, they first lived in the district of Tai, then moved to Ping, then to Chi, then to Feng Hao, and finally settled in the Wei River valley. Here they cleared the rich alluvial land and came into contact with the inhabitants of the Fen River valley on the east bank of the Hwang Ho. The three great cultures were thus blended into one at a very early period, and helped to develop the consciousness of unity that encouraged the formation of a united state with great territorial expansion. This was the so-called western center of Chinese culture. Here the Yang Shao culture [3] originated and flourished.

In ancient days, the Hwang Ho flowed through the eastern part of Honan as far as the district of Cheng, and thence it turned northward under the Ta P'ei Mountain and along the Taiheng Range before entering the sea at the Po Hai Bay near Tientsin. The ancient capital of the Shang, or Yin, dynasty (1766–1122 B.C.) was in the district of An Yang in Honan, where the Chang River and the Huan River flow into the Hwang Ho. During the past fifty years, tortoise shells, animal bones, pottery articles, stone implements, and bronze objects have been successively unearthed on the "Ruins of Yin," the original site of the capital of the Shang (Yin) dynasty. A majority of these materials have proved to be the relics of that remote dynasty.

The Shang people originally lived near Kuei Teh in Honan, which is beyond the Hwang Ho. In ancient times, there were in that region many marshes and small rivers. The early culture of the Shangs probably originated near these marshes and rivers, where they farmed the fertile soil and raised cattle and sheep on the rich grasslands. So far as we know, these marshes and rivers lay in ancient times between the Huai River and the Chi River; that is, the plains of what is now northern Honan, southern Hopei, and southwestern

[3] The Yang Shao culture takes its name from a prehistorical settlement in the west of Honan. In 1921 J. G. Anderson discovered neolithic remains at the village site of Yang Shao Ts'un in western Honan, and in the course of the next year or so located dozens of others over a large area extending from Kansu to southern Manchuria. Typical of this culture is its wonderful handmade pottery of hard-baked red or brown color with black, purple, white, and red designs. Hence Yang Shao is also known as the Painted Pottery culture.

Shantung. The most remote area of the Shang sites was not much over one hundred miles from the Hwang Ho.

During the first three hundred years following the founding of the kingdom sometime between the eighteenth and seventeenth centuries B.C., the Shangs were forced by the floods of the Hwang Ho to move their capital. It was not until the fourteenth century B.C. that King Pan Keng moved the capital to An Yang in northern Honan, where a permanent site was found. An Yang, which was then known as Yin, remained the royal capital for about 270 years. This was the so-called eastern center of Chinese culture, which evidently descended from the Lung Shan culture [4] that originated and flourished in the alluvial plains of East China.

These two cultures had, even in prehistoric days, each been influenced by the other. It seems that the Shang people had dominated in the west as far as the Wei River valley in other words, they had long been in contact with the Chou people. Eastward their power extended to the sea coast of North China, including the lowlands of the Chi River in Shantung; northeastward, to the Liao River in Hopei; southward, to the Huai River in Anhwei; and southeastward, to the Han River in Hupeh. It is believed that the Shang culture even penetrated into the regions south of the Huai and Han rivers and north of the Yangtze. Though outside the Hwang Ho valley, these regions were already influenced by the Chinese culture as early as the Shang (Yin) dynasty, of which we have knowledge from the classics and the excavations and the documents they have brought to light. In the beginning of the Chou dynasty, the Yangtze valley and the lands near the Han, the Huai, the Chi, and the Liao all had become integral parts of the Chinese cultural entity.

From this short sketch of the physical environment, we may note the major reason for the differences between Chinese culture and the cultures of Egypt, Babylonia, and India. As mentioned above, all early known civilizations developed

---

[4] The Lung Shan culture, also known as the Black Pottery culture, was discovered at a place called Ch'eng Tzu-yai in the district of Lung Shan in Shantung by the Chinese archaeologist Wu Chin-ding in 1928. This culture is distinguished by a black pottery of exceptionally fine quality and has been regarded as one of direct predecessors of the later Chinese civilization.

in river valleys. In the case of Egypt and Babylonia,[5] the rivers have only a few tributaries over a small area. The case of India is slightly different. In the alluvial plain watered by the Indus and four of its tributaries, India developed its first real civilization; after the Indo-Aryan people invaded India, they spread eastward until the Epic Age (1000–500 B.C.), when they created kingdoms along the Ganges valley. Like Egypt, Babylonia, and India, China first developed a fluvial civilization. However, in China the major rivers have many tributaries which act as waterways over a vast area. The three great rivers drained the three natural divisions of China—the Hwang Ho in North China, the Yangtze River in Central China, and the Pearl River in South China. Besides, there are many small rivers and streams, such as the Shu Stream near the Fen River, the Yi Stream near the Lo River, the Feng and the Hao streams near the Wei River. All these rivers and streams were famous in ancient Chinese history. It is an important fact that the agrarian culture of ancient China owed its origin to a vast area intersected by many rivers with numerous deltas for human habitation. These deltas were scattered far and wide; they were protected by natural barriers and developed different cultures. However, because of the many important rivers, the independent cultures became amalgamated through constant contacts and constant migrations. It is therefore not surprising to learn that China has long been more homogeneous—politically, culturally, and racially—than many other areas of comparable size.

Climate is another important factor in cultural development. None of the great civilizations appears to have originated within 25° of the equator.[6] Egypt, Babylonia, and the Indus region are not exceptions to this rule, lying in latitudes of 25° to 35°, where the bounty of nature furnishes food in abundance and gives leisure for social development. China, in contrast, is located on the eastern side of the Eurasian continent, and Chinese culture originated in a

[5] Ancient Egypt was situated in the narrow Nile valley, in the 800 miles between the second cataract and the Delta. The culture of old Babylonia originated in a rich plain, extending about 170 miles north of the Persian Gulf between the Tigris and the Euphrates rivers.

[6] See Ellsworth Huntington, *Mainsprings of Civilization,* New York, New American Library, 1959, Chap. 15.

region which has a continental climate—very hot in summer and considerably cold in winter. From the *Book of Odes*, we learn that the climate, agricultural products, and the life of peasants described in the Chou period bore much resemblance to those of the present day. So the Chinese people began to build their culture under more difficult circumstances, and consequently had to work harder than their rich neighbors in Egypt, Babylonia, and India in order to prepare shelter, clothing, and fuel to protect themselves against the cold and moisture of winter.

The preceding discussion makes clear three points, and we need only to review them briefly. First, most ancient cultures emerged in deltas, which were fit to be the homes of small, distinct units, but attempts to maintain united nations of great size in these places did not succeed. Chinese culture arose in a vast area which encouraged the formation of one united nation with great territorial expansion. Second, cultures springing from small areas were compelled to wage defensive wars against outside invaders, and in the end were either cut short or gradually declined. Chinese culture, arising in a vast area, soon achieved an internal unity that enabled it to tame the great wilderness and resist dangers from without, and hence suffered fewer invasions and interruptions to its continuity. Third, cultures which originated in warm climate and fertile soil tended to stagnate and decay. Chinese culture, developing in a comparatively cool climate and a vast area, maintained itself by promoting a social system which placed value on foresight and thrift. China has good reasons to be proud of her culture, which emerged from the ancient world and during the Ch'in (255–206 B.C.) and Han (205 B.C.–A.D. 220) dynasties, unified a vast nation, extending from the Hwang Ho basin down to the Yangtze valley, at a time when the ancient cultures of Egypt, Babylonia, and India had already ceased to dazzle the eyes of the world and been swamped by other cultures.

2. Historical Experience

There were great cultures in ancient Egypt, Babylonia, and India, which had produced considerable achievements in the arts and in the rudiments of science, but as their intellectual vigor waned they had left their places to other peoples. Even today, Chinese culture and European culture are the two pillars of human civilization. These two great cultures, however widely separated, are not indifferent to each other: this is a century that East and West join hands in cultural collaboration.

European culture owes its origin to Greece, where we can find all the characteristic features of Europe. The mountains and the sea break up this area into numerous valleys and islands, easily defended, and yet, because of the sea, not isolated. Special attention deserves to be paid to this geographic background, which not only determined the basic character of Greek culture, but also played a considerable role in shaping its development.

Greek culture flourished during the period of the Chou dynasty in China. This period in China, as in Greece, was an age of great mental activity, in which all kinds of original ideas spread unchecked. The Chou period produced such great classics as the *Shu (History)*, *Shih (Odes)*, *Yi (Change)*, *Li (Ceremonies)*, and *Ch'un Ch'iu (Spring and Autumn Annals)*, which have molded Chinese thought right up the twentieth century. China's great philosophers, such as Lao Tzu, Confucius, Mo Tzu, Mencius, Chuang Tzu, and Han Fei Tzu, all belonged to this time. And again, the Chou period was an age of intense political activity. The vast domain of China was then divided into a number of feudal states, which were later engaged in frequent civil wars, but the Chinese people were of one blood, were possessed of a common civilization, and were united by a common language.

In Greece, similar conditions prevailed. However, there is an important difference. Greek geographical conditions broke the country into semi-independent city-states and the Greek political system bred intercity jealousies and frequent civil wars. Therefore, the Greek city-states, though sharing a common culture, were never united as one political entity; they remained as independent city-states, each of which was a separate unit. This lack of unity was the weakness that was one day to prove fatal. The Chinese feudal states, in contrast, were only the fragments of an empire, the Royal House of the Chous. Confucius seemed to allude to this in a beautiful passage in which he compared the Royal House of Chou—the central government—to the polar star, which sits unmoved on its central throne, while all the constellations—the vassal states—revolve around it. Feudalism, as it existed in the Chou period, was in fact a step toward the centralization of national strength. When the Chous took power they distributed their people to different parts of China as armed settlers. So China during the Chou period was virtually a united nation. Unity was what was lacking in Greek politics. Political conditions account in the main for the cultural difference between China and Greece.

The unity of Greece was brought about by the conquest of Rome during the time when China became a united nation under the emperors of the Ch'in and Han dynasties. During the four hundred years of the Han dynasty, as we shall see, many of the features that distinguish modern civilization were firmly established. In the same measure that Western civilization springs from Greece and Rome, oriental civilization owes its primary inspiration to China during the Han period.

Rome, starting as a city-state, extended her power by alliance and conquest over surrounding cities. It was conquest and expansion that led to the emergence of a new form of state—a great empire, vast in area, centralized in organization, and uniform in law. The Roman world-state gave the Westerners a conception of one universal culture based on peace and order, which they had never had before. So when Rome succeeded Greece, not only was the political structure changed from city-states to empire, but Greek culture was replaced by Roman culture as well. Up to the period of the Han dynasty, the Chinese people had been in possession of China for more than two thousand years. Chinese culture still persisted, and her ancient tradition had not changed; there was only a change in internal political structure—that is, from feudalism to a provincial system. In Western history, when Rome took on importance politically and culturally, she appeared as an entirely new entity and incorporated Greek culture into her own, while in China the rise and fall of dynasties were changes only in political structure, and not in culture.

And again, we may compare the Middle Ages in Europe after the fall of Roman Empire with the period of the Six Dynasties (A.D. 220–580), which succeeded the Han dynasty in China. In the midst of cruel invasions and bloody battles, new religions—Buddhism and Christianity—gave men a feeling of hope and spiritual assurance to offset the uncertainty and insecurity in the world about them. In Europe and in China, during these centuries of destruction, monasteries became cultural depositories where artistic and literary traditions were preserved and continued. However, there is a marked difference. The fall of the Roman Empire, like the decline of Greek culture, was brought about by a foreign invasion. The invasion of the Teutonic barbarians was at first marked by considerable destruction. Not only did the political structure of Europe undergo a total change, but also Roman civilization and tradition seemed completely lost. The fall of the Han dynasty was not caused by foreign invasions; there was only a slight change in political structure, and Chinese culture still persisted. Even when Tartar tribes invaded northern China in the fourth century, Chinese traditions and institutions still predominated. As these northern barbarians lived within the boundaries of the Chinese nation and under the influence of Chinese culture, they had already been assimilated into the Chinese race. For this reason, their revolts might be regarded as political *coups d'etat* rather than as a foreign invasion. In Europe, the Teutonic tribes came as a new people and absorbed the Romans; whereas in China, during the period of Six Dynasties, the Chinese people remained as the foundation of society, and the Tartar newcomers played the role of a minority.

The Teutonic invaders destroyed the foundation of the social order and released new and terrifying forces, the results of which were modern civilization and modern states. While these changes were in progress such social and political life as existed was of the peculiar transitional form known as feudalism. The European feudalism which succeeded the fall of Roman Empire differed from the Chinese feudalism of the Chou period. Feudalism in ancient China was a necessary step in the progress of Chinese culture toward a united nation, while European feudalism was a transitional political system which brought a measure of order to the chaos that engulfed Europe after the collapse of the Roman Empire. The progressive force making for unity in Europe was not feudalism, but Christianity. The only institution that retained its unity during the Middle Ages was the church. Growing up on the ruins of the Roman Empire, the church adopted an imperial organization which was far more united and efficient than any possessed by its competitors, and its power was further strengthened by the superstitious reverence in which it was held by the Teutonic barbarians. Greece, Rome, and Christianity were the three forces which made up the fabric of Western civilization.

During the period of Six Dynasties, Buddhism, as introduced from India, offered new notions and new ideals with which the old Chinese culture had to contend. However, Buddhism did not permeate Chinese culture so deeply and thoroughly as Christianity did in Europe. The reason is that Christianity came to Europe as a new force after the decay of Roman culture, while Buddhism came to China as a foreign creed and was finally absorbed by Confucian philosophy, losing its original character.

By the end of the Middle Ages in Europe, the Renaissance marked the emergence of modern civilization and modern states, which appeared as entirely new entities, independent of the traditions of ancient Greece and Rome. In Western history the center of culture shifted from one place to another. But in Chinese history, the foreign invasions did not create a marked break or change in the continuity and unity of Chinese culture and civilization. During the 631 years from 1280 to 1911, China was under alien rulers—first the Mongols, and later the Tungus Manchus—for 355 years. But though the aliens dominated the Chinese politically, the Chinese dominated them culturally.

3. An Estimate

To the Chinese, who became a vast and united nation at a very early period, internal problems are more important than external ones, and their attitude is comparatively "introvert", looking inward upon themselves. On the contrary, Europe as a whole is adapted to a number of small states; all attempts to maintain a continental empire in Europe have failed. The continent of Europe even today is still merely a geographical expression, whereas in China there is one written language, one culture, and one nation. Hence to the Westerners external problems are more important than internal ones, and their attitude is comparatively "extrovert," looking outward upon the external world. As a result, geographical discoveries and scientific inventions have thoroughly energized the culture of the West and carried it to the ends of the earth. It is because the Chinese are "introvert" that they emphasize the continuation of life in time and cling to the heritage of their traditions. As a result, Chinese culture is unique in its continuity, and its remarkable characteristic is a capacity for change without disruption. In its development Chinese culture has absorbed many heterogeneous elements through an assimilating power that testifies to its marvelous vitality. It has also undergone some modifications in consequence of alien influences, but such modifications have not affected its main stream, which remains fundamentally and characteristically Chinese.

Next, the difference in respective economic conditions between China and the West has a bearing on the cultural differences. Since China is a continental country, the Chinese people have to make their living by agriculture. Even today the portion of the Chinese population engaged in farming is estimated at 75 to 80 per cent. Chinese culture since the early days has been based on agriculture. From the Western viewpoint cultural progress proceeds from agrarian civilization to commercial civilization, whereas from the Chinese viewpoint human civilization will never cease to be agrarian in character. Westerners regard civilization as changing and progressive, while the Chinese consider civilization as static and growing. One reason for the different views is that the Chinese *were* farmers and the way of life of the farmers is to follow nature, so they desire no change; whereas the Westerners *were* merchants and the way of life of merchants is to look for novelty and change. It is therefore not surprising that China failed to have the scientific and industrial revolutions that transformed and modernized European nations. In China there were many noteworthy industrial inventions, but the Chinese failed to profit by them and often discouraged mechanical production.

In this connection, it is interesting to note the distinction Confucius made between the wise and the good. He said:

> The wise take delight in water; the good take
>   delight in mountain.
> The wise move; the good stay still.

The wise find enjoyment; the good enjoy a full
span of life.[7]

In this passage there is something which suggests the difference between the Western way and the Chinese way—the way of the wise and the way of the good.

And again, we may point out that life-ideal is another reason for the difference between Chinese culture and Western culture. The Westerners are impressed by the antagonism of the different factors in the world: the antagonism of human versus divine; of ideal versus real, of society versus individual, of authority versus liberty, and so forth. The Chinese, in contrast, are impressed not by the antagonism, but by the continuity of the world. To the mind of the Chinese, society and the individual are not antagonistic to each other; they are simply a continuous whole. "Liberty" is an all-important word in the West, for it is the essence of Western civilization. Another significant word in Western civilization is "organization," for it was most needed in the formation of the modern state. While Greek civilization, demanding reason and personal freedom, represents "liberty," the Roman Empire and Christianity, emphasizing authority and discipline, represent "organization." These two words represent the two main trends in Western civilization. Because of the antagonism between society and the individual, Westerners demand liberty as well as organization. The Chinese, however, are not interested in these two concepts. Because they look inward, the Chinese regard society and individual as one whole. Although the whole is formed of many minor selves, yet the minor selves are not antagonistic to the whole; on the contrary, they form a part of it, just as the growing and expanding roots merge into the whole. In the *Ta Hsueh*, or *Great Learning*,[8] we read that by cultivating oneself, one can regulate the family; by regulating the family, one can govern the state; by governing the state, one can pacify the world. The converging series grows by stages, expands by stages, and accomplishes by stages. However widely the branches may extend, the quality of their fruit is determined

---

[7] *Analects,* VI, 21.

[8] The *Ta Hsueh,* originally a chapter of the *Li Chi* (*Book of Rites*), was attributed to Tseng Tzu, one of the disciples of Confucius. See its opening section.

by the common root. Thus the self is not antagonistic to the family, to the state, or to the world, for the self merges into the whole. This is the Chinese philosophy of life. If we look at Chinese culture from the perspective of Greek-Roman-Christian civilization, we shall not be able to see its real meaning and value.

Finally, there is the difference between the religious beliefs of East and West. According to Westerners, the universe is composed of pairs of opposites and contradictories; hence they draw a clear distinction between heaven and earth, heaven being a spiritual world separated from the earth by a vast distance of space. They further believe that man consists of soul and body, the soul making contact with the spiritual world of reason and the body making contact with the material world of the senses. By making this sharp distinction between the spiritual and the material, they opened the door to complete skepticism as regards the universe. As a result, science and philosophy are interactive from the Western standpoint, and it is not surprising that some of the great philosophers were at the same time men of science.

Chinese thinkers, however, for centuries have believed that what happens in the universe is a continuous whole, a chain of natural sequence. This is the conception that confirms and perpetuates the fusion of heaven and earth, between which, as they affect the daily life and conduct of the people, the distinction is in practice hard to draw and harder to maintain. It has been generally accepted that the mind of the Chinese is filled with romance and poetry, so that for them the invisible world is peopled with fairies and all kinds of gods; but to the Chinese the invisible world is not a kingdom in heaven but a paradise on earth. This earthly paradise can be reached by the following steps: first, by manifesting virtuous influence; second, by writing literary masterpieces; and third, by undertaking great deeds. The Chinese have seldom been preoccupied with a heavenly kingdom outside the human world. In the West, the desire for immortality crystallized into religion, whereas in China it became ethics. Religion and ethics are interactive from the Chinese standpoint, and it is no wonder that Chinese philosophy has from the outset emphasized the moral qualities of man, rather than his intellectual and material qualities. The sense of duty is stronger in China than the love of liberty. In the West, duty and privilege are opposites, whereas in China they are merged together, forming the identification of nature (liberty) with destiny (duty) as well as the union of Heaven with Man.[9] The Chinese conceive the universe as a harmonious whole in which "all things are in harmony and in accordance."

Without further comment, we conclude that in China one discerns a unity of thought unknown in the Western world. Modern science gives us freedom to study the specific, but deprives us of the vision to see human life in its unity. It is the spirit of unity that combines art, religion, philosophy, and literature, as well as social and political institutions, within the House of Chinese Culture. A sense of this unity is in fact what we call the fundamental spirit of Chinese culture,[10] and the most characteristic features of Chinese culture may be illustrated, as different in type, origin, and constitution from other great cultures, by reference to this fundamental spirit.

[9] In Chinese philosophy ethics takes the place of epistemology. Only the Taoist philosophers were gripped by insatiable curiosity about the facts and laws of nature. The speculation of Taoists might have led to the development of physical sciences, had the Chinese mind not been so exclusively interested in human affairs. Instead, Taoist speculation turned to *artistic* comprehension rather than *scientific* understanding of nature.

[10] In an article by Ch'u Chai it is pointed out that the fundamental spirit of Chinese culture "may be looked at from two points of view: that of cosmic conception and that of attitude toward life. In the former the spirit of Chinese culture is manifested as a continuous whole, like a chain of natural sequences. In the latter the spirit of Chinese culture is manifested in the union of the individual with the whole." See "The Spirit of Chinese Culture," *Social Research*, Vol. XXIV, No. 1, 1958.

CHAPTER II.   THE CHINESE PEOPLE

Before speaking of the Chinese people, we must consider two important facts. First, Chinese culture was created by the Chinese people—that is, by the Chinese nation, for the nation and the people became identified in very early times. Second, Chinese culture has continued along its path for four or five thousand years with occasional expansions, but without fundamental changes. The first fact may lead some people to think Chinese culture oversimple, while the second fact may make some people regard the Chinese as overly conservative. But the Chinese have not been stationary through the long past of their national life, which witnessed the rise and fall of so many glorious cultures in other parts of the world. Their culture has advanced from age to age with a stately progress, recording, in each of its great epochs, a decided gain. As a result, Chinese culture is as rich and vital as any other great culture in the world.

We shall make a brief survey of two important areas, an understanding of which is indispensable to the understanding of Chinese culture. Yet no writer on Chinese culture appears to have grasped the significance of either of them. They are:

1. The origin of the Chinese people.
2. The formation of the Chinese people.

A brief survey of their ethnic origin will justify us to conclude that the Chinese are autochthonous and their civilization indigenous. The second survey, which deals with racial intermixture and amalgamation, will prove that the Chinese nation is a unit and through all its members there sweeps the mighty tide of a common life.

25

1. Ethnic Origins

The subject of Chinese ethnic origins is, to say the least, a thorny one. Theories advanced by Western scholars have been many and ingenious. Some [1] have insisted upon the indigenous character of the Chinese people and their civilization, regarding the northwest provinces and the valley of the Hwang Ho as their home from times immemorial. Others [2] are inclined to suggest various places, chiefly Egypt and Babylonia, as the points from which either the Chinese people or their civilization began a migration to China. Chinese writing has been compared with both Egyptian hieroglyphics and Babylonian cuneiform characters, with the conclusion that it was borrowed from one or the other. However, this theory is based merely on chance resemblances owing to coincidental similarities between the manners and customs of different peoples at different times and in different places. Different peoples sometimes happen to think in the same way about the same object, and arrive at similar signs.

Chinese culture can be traced in an unbroken historical line to the Hsia dynasty and in legend to the periods of Shen Lung and Huang Ti in the third millennium B.C. It is true that many details of this continuity are still lacking, but enough is known, from ancient records and archaeological

[1] For instance, John Ross, in his *The Origin of the Chinese People*; Herbert Allen Giles, in his *History of Chinese Literature;* and Friedrich Hirth, in his *The Ancient History of China to the End of the Chou Dynasty.*

[2] There are the old theories of the eighteenth century that the Chinese were connected with Egypt; the theory of Terrian de la Couperie that associates the Chinese with Babylonia. Later C. J. Ball endeavored to support this view from linguistic considerations. More recently E. T. Williams, in his *China, Yesterday and Today,* maintained that Central Asia was the source for the cultures of both Eastern and Western Asia. As to the origins of the Chinese people and civilization, read Li Chi's *The Beginnings of Chinese Civilization,* Seattle, Univ. of Washington Press, 1957.

information,[3] to establish some general facts concerning the origins of the Chinese people.

The ancient Chinese were mentioned in such ancient records as those of the Hua or Hsia people. Hua and Hsia may be the names of places where the ancient Chinese lived. In the *Chou Li,* or *Ritual of Chou,* and the *Kuo Yu,* or *Records of Ancient States,* both composed about the fourth or third century B.C., Hua is the name of a mountain, probably the modern Sung Mountain in Honan, and Hsia is the name of a river, probably the modern Han River in Hupeh. Thus the Hua-Hsia people were probably the ancient Chinese who originally lived in the area extending from a point southwest of the Sung Mountain to the north bank of the Han River. This was the land where the Yang Shao culture, also known as the Painted Pottery culture, originated and flourished. The Hua-Hsia people invented the elements of civilization, such as clothing, the preparation of food, marriage, and a state system; they brought China, as early as the second millennium B.C., to an astonishing high cultural level, and finally founded the Chung-hua nation, by assimilating various tribal stocks who were scattered east of the Pamirs, along the valleys of the Hwang Ho, Huai, Yangtze, Amur, and Pearl rivers.

The Hua-Hsia people formed the main part of the Chinese people, and China's ancient history is centered around their activities. If we trace still further back, all the legends of Shen Nung (? 2737 B.C.) and Huang Ti (? 2697 B.C.) had their origins in the same region.[4] According to the legends, there existed in eastern Honan, extending to the Huai River valley, the clan of Chi under the chieftain Huang Ti, and in

---

[3] The first three volumes of the *Chronicle* of Sze-ma Ch'ien give us a detailed account of facts relating to the genealogy, reigns, and personalities of the ancient period. The *Bamboo Annals* and *Ancient Genealogy* contain a vast amount of historical data of the same era. These books are regarded as the most dependable records of China's antiquity, as supported by the archaeological discoveries made in recent excavations.

[4] Fuhi (? 2852 B.C.), Shen Nung, and Huang Ti were traditionally regarded as the three pioneers of Chinese culture. Fuhi is the supposed inventor of pictorial writing and founder of marriage; Shen Nung is the reputed father of agriculture and of the healing art, while Huang Ti is credited with inventing the famous "south-pointing chariot," and his wife, "The Lady of Si Ling," with being the breeder of silkworms.

western Honan, extending to the Han River valley, the clan of Chiang under the chieftain Shen Nung. The Chi and Chiang clans were the two important branches of the Hua-Hsia people. In prehistoric days, the people had clan names to show their locality and profession, and family names to show their lineage. The clan was a form of social organization, in which all were related and worked together. Neighboring clans formed the tribe, which was led by a chief, and the tribes in turn formed the tribal alliance. Both the chiefs of tribes and those of tribal alliance were elected.[5] The ancient Chinese seem to have developed the tradition of not marrying with the members of the same clan, and this tradition helped the early amalgamation of tribes and races in China. Says the *Book of Odes:* "Being of one large family, they are no strangers to one another"; that is, the various clans were knitted together by marital ties.

These two ancient clans—Shen Nung and Huang Ti—had marriage connections. Later, they warred against each other. From the ancient records, we learn that Huang Ti fought against the descendants of Shen Nung in the plain of Pan Chuan, which is believed to be somewhere near the modern district of Chieh in southern Shansi. This would suggest that the two clans extended their power northward across the Hwang Ho until they approached the district of Chieh, where there is a famous salt lake. This was the salt lake that was sought by all the clans in North China in the early days, for the clan which occupied the salt lake became the leader of the others. It seemed that the clan of Huang Ti won the victory over that of Shen Nung and became the leader of the various clans. Then the ancient Chinese people extended their power westward to the Wei River valley, and thus the mountain in Shensi was given the name of Hua, which has remained until today. They also expanded northward to the Fen River valley, so that southern Shansi was also known as

---

[5] It seems probable that Huang Ti handed over the leadership to Yao (? 2357–2258 B.C.), a chieftain of the clan in southern Shansi, by the voice of the clans. Yao, in turn, called on the clans to name a successor, when Shun (? 2258–2205 B.C.), a chieftain of the clan in eastern Honan, was chosen. Again, Shun transmitted the leadership to an able minister, the Great Yu. Yu departed from these illustrious precedents, and founded the first hereditary dynasty, known as the Hsia dynasty (? 2205–1766 D.C.)

the land of Hsia. In view of these known migrations of the ancient Chinese people, there is no reason to suppose a difference of race or the immigration of a race from Central Asia.

During the last fifty years, archaeology has unearthed important information confirming the continuity of the Chinese people and their culture. Physically, the neolithic people of North China were of the same stock as modern northern Chinese. A kindred physical type was found in South China. According to anthropologists, the Peking Man, who lived in North China about 500,000 years ago, already possessed certain characteristics peculiar to the Chinese race. The Upper Cave Man, who lived about 50,000 years ago, also in North China, was like the modern Chinese in appearance and more advanced in culture than his ancestor of 450,000 years earlier. Studies of the Peking Man and the Upper Cave Man reveal that they were ancestors of the neolithic men in North China.

The Peking Man and the Upper Cave Man belonged to the Paleolithic Age. They lived in caves; they were hunters, already in possession of very simple implements and also of the art of making fire. The old stone-age communities seem to have lasted a considerable time, and to have been spread not only over North China but also over Mongolia and Manchuria. The difference between the Paleolithic Age and the Neolithic Age is that the neolithic people knew how to grind and polish sharp cutting instruments made of chipped stones. The neolithic people were cattle breeders, and to some extent they were also farmers. We have a great deal of evidence that the neolithic people were widely scattered over China, living mainly on hunting, fishing, cattle breeding, and a little farming. They used stone knives, axes, spears, and bows and arrows; they wove baskets and cloth, and they made a good deal of pottery. However, the neolithic people of the various parts of China were far from being uniform; there were various separate cultures, the most important of which, we have noted in the preceding chapter, were the Yang Shao Culture in the west and the Lung Shan Culture in the east. These various cultures, at a certain stage in their development, came into contact with one another and became amalgamated. This explains why the Chinese people are homogeneous in physical appearance and in culture.

To recapitulate briefly, from what is recorded in early Chinese historical records, as evidenced by the archaeological discoveries, we are convinced that the Chinese people are autochthonous and their civilization is indigenous. We can say with certainty that the culture originated in the alluvial tracts of lands which were formed by the Yellow River and its tributaries, and was not just pre-Chinese, but was in fact the early Chinese civilization. Then this culture spread eastward into the coastal plain and southward toward the Yangtze River valley, taking over other early neolithic settlements and absorbing the aboriginal tribes. Whatever the origin of these aboriginal tribes, it was in the Chinese soil that they were rooted, and by the Chinese people that they were absorbed.

2. Racial Amalgamation

In the process of their growth, the Chinese people have absorbed many a heterogeneous element, which has always been transformed into their own substance by an assimilating power that asserts the marvelous energy of the Chinese culture. It is well said that the Chinese people are a great river system formed by one main river with many tributaries flowing into it along its course.

It is possible to divide the formation of the Chinese people into four approximate periods:

First, from the earliest times to the end of the Chou dynasty (255 B.C.) is the period of the foundation of unity and amalgamation of races in China. During this period the Hua-Hsia people formed the main stream and were joined by many lesser races or tribes, from whom they were distinguished chiefly by a knowledge of letters and by the possession of a higher civilization. This incipient culture gave the Hua-Hsia people an immense advantage over the barbarous tribes who surrounded them on every side. These tribes were grouped under several comprehensive terms: those on the east were the Yi, a race of archers; those on the north, the Ti, a race of dog-using nomads later known as Hsiung Nu, who were China's most dreaded adversary; on the west, the Jung (Spearmen) or the Ch'iang (Goat-men), later known as

San Miao, ancestors of the Tibetan tribes; and those on the south, called the Man(a composite of "silk" and "worm," implying that the southern barbarians, even at this early period, were not ignorant of silkworm culture), a race of mixed origin. Most of these tribes were gradually absorbed and assimilated to become a greater Chinese race, constituting the Chinese of the Ch'in (255–206 B.C.) and the Han (205 B.C.– A.D. 220) dynasties. The greatness of these two dynasties lay in their successful amalgamation of various races.

The second period began at the end of the Han dynasty and ended in the Six Dynasties (220–580). The peoples occupying the vast region of North China—diverse in language, but similar in nomadic habits—were in this period combined under the hegemony of the Hsiung Nu or Huns, forming a confederation, or an empire, rather than a single state. During the Han and succeeding dynasties, the Hsiung Nu were held in check mostly by force of arms; but the weaker emperors were accustomed to sending their sisters and daughters across the frontiers, instead of generals, flattering the vanity of the barbarians and replacing armaments with the sentimentalities of family alliance. These marriage transactions helped the amalgamation of races, and at the same time supplied rich materials for poetry and romance.

During this period there was another important event— a mass migration—which helped the amalgamation of races in China. On the one hand, many Chinese migrated northward, into the territories of the frontier peoples, especially that of the Huns. On the other hand, the alien peoples were allowed to move freely into China proper. In consequence of this great migration, as well as the marriage transactions, the frontier tribes joined the main stream of the Chinese people and created a newer and greater Chinese race, constituting the Chinese people of the Sui (581–618) and the T'ang (619–907). The greatness of these two dynasties lay in the successful amalgamation of races.

The third period began with the end of the T'ang dynasty and included the Yüan (Mongol) dynasty (ending in 1368), when many new races, such as the Chitans and the Mongols, joined the Chinese people. Of the 631 years from 1280 to 1911, China was under national rulers for 276 years and under alien rulers for 355 years. The alien rulers were first the Mongols, and later the Manchus. It is interesting to note that the alien rulers in the earlier period came mainly from the northwest, and not until the thirteenth century did people from the northeast rule over China. This is due to the fact that only people who have attained a certain level of civilization are capable of dominance. In the early days, eastern Mongolia and Manchuria were at a relatively low level of civilization, from which they emerged only gradually through permanent contact with other nomadic peoples, and extended their power by alliance and conquest over surrounding regions.

Although the Mongols tried hard not to let themselves become Chinese, yet when they conquered China they had already to a considerable degree adopted the Chinese culture. Their prolonged and extensive occupation of Chinese territory must have been followed by their intermixing with the Chinese people; consequently, they must have made a more or less permanent contribution to the population of China.

Thus was formed the Chinese race of the Ming dynasty (1368–1644), coming at the end of the third period; the greatness of the Ming dynasty was also due to the successful amalgamation of races.

During the fourth period, which extends from the coming of the Manchus (1644) to the present day, many new races again joined the Chinese people, including the Manchus and Tibetans. The Manchus were descendants of the Juchen, another barbarian group in southern and central Manchuria. The Mongols at first subjugated the Juchen, but the latter became virtually independent after the collapse of the Mongol rule. Then the Manchus conquered China and established their own empire, known as the Ching dynasty, succeeding the Ming dynasty. The Manchus readily took to the Chinese culture and were absorbed by the Chinese. They also persuaded all the other racial groups within the nation, especially the Tibetans, to adopt Chinese way of life. These racial groups were not, of course, originally of one mold; the lines of distinction between them were effaced gradually. The process of amalgamation is by no means complete even today.

Enough has been said to show that the Chinese race has been constantly absorbing foreign elements and has never ceased its expansion and modification; but at the same time the main stream always remains dominant and manifest, neither engulfed nor dispersed. The Chinese people are remarkably homogeneous in their physique and tenacious in their mentality, owing largely to the unity and continuity of the culture under which they have lived. The political structure of the imperial government, manned by a bureaucracy recruited on the basis of worth as determined by the civil-service examination, helped to produce a more or less fluid society in which wide intermarriage of the various races was comparatively easy. The political unity of China during a large part of her history and the consequent absence of internal political barriers to migration also made for physical and cultural uniformity.

Part One: Social and Political Institutions

CHAPTER III. THE FUNDAMENTAL CONCEPTIONS

Let us start with some of the fundamental conceptions
—national or racial, religious, political, and humanistic—that
have contributed as important factors in the development of
Chinese social and political institutions.

1. The National or Racial Conception

The extent to which the feeling of national or racial consciousness is developed is of vital importance in the history of any country; but as far as we can judge from the
recorded history, the ancient Chinese seem to have had no
marked national or racial feeling. It is true that from the
early days the Chinese had made a sharp distinction between
the Hua Hsia (Chinese) and the Yi Ti (barbarians), but the
emphasis of this distinction was more cultural than racial.
Thus it has well been said: "When the Chinese adopted the
ways of barbarians, they were considered as barbarian; and
when the barbarians absorbed the Chinese culture, they
were considered as Chinese." Chinese culture was the only
criterion of difference between the Chinese and barbarians.
For instance, in the Chou dynasty, those who lived in Central
China at the confluence of the Hwang Ho and its tributaries
and developed an agrarian civilization, were called Chinese;
while the nomadic tribes living in the mountainous regions
or on the banks of the Hwang Ho and doing little or no

farming were regarded as barbarians, even though they were of the same stock as the other Chinese races.

Analysis of the racial elements of the Chinese in the Ch'in and Han dynasties reveals the following peoples: the Hua Hsia, who started the Hsia and Chou dynasties; the Yi of the east sea coast, to which the Shangs belonged and later the Tungus tribes as well; the Man of the south, who were of mixed origin; the Yueh of the farther south, including the various tribes in South China; and finally, the San Miao of the west, some of whom were traditionally reported to be ancestors of the Tibetan tribes.

Vast as the territory of China is, in the early days the different elements of the Chinese people had already scattered to different parts of the country. They were separated from one another through long periods, and they came to possess different customs and traditions. If the ancient Chinese, by whom we mean the Hua-Hsia, were racially prejudiced, it would have been difficult for them to achieve national unity, and there would have been many independent states in China; as a result, the course of Chinese history would have been changed.

Let us again turn to another important historical fact. For two extended periods China was ruled by aliens, i.e., the Mongols and the Manchus. It is interesting to note that although the Mongols and the Manchus were originally of different races, the Chinese traditionally have considered the Yüan (Mongol) and the Ching (Manchu) dynasties as simply two of the many dynasties that have followed one another in the history of China.

Because the Chinese did not stress racial distinction, they absorbed many alien elements, but at the same time the main stream of the Han-Chinese remained unchanged and manifest. Indeed, the Chinese, the Mongols, the Manchus, and the Tibetans, as we see them today, are not distinguishable except by some peculiarity of costume.

At present China has fifty or so "minority nationalities," [1] with 35 million people in all and occupying more than half of China's territory. In the northern part of China is the huge Inner Mongolian Autonomous Region, with about one and half million Mongolians who are largely

[1] This is the term which the Chinese Communists use to designate ethnic minorities in China.

pastoral. In the far west of China is the Sinkiang Uighur Autonomous Region, with about three and half million Uighurs who are agricultural. South of Sinkiang lies the Tibetan plateau, the roof of the world. In the mountainous region along the Szechuan-Yunnan border are the Yis, numbering some three million, while the Miao, the Yao, and the Tung peoples are scattered through the five southern provinces—Hunan, Kwangsi, Kwangtung, Kweichow, and Yunnan. Taiwan and Hainan are China's two biggest islands, where minority peoples are also found. The Kaoshans of Taiwan number about 160,000 and the Li people of Hainan about 360,000. These minority groups have been encouraged to become assimilated into the national norm, but they also have been allowed to keep on their own traditions and to wear their own native costumes.

2. The Religious Conception

The Chinese people in the early days seemed to have a conception of a Supreme Being, which they called Ti or Shang Ti. Shang Ti dominated over the human lives below by either sending down rain to the earth or holding it in check and sending down famine instead. Hence Shang Ti became the supreme ruler of human affairs, for an agricultural society depends for its food on the timely rain more than anything else. The Supreme Being did not come into direct contact with the people below, but made His wishes known through the Royal House which acted as His medium. The early Chinese religion was tinctured with political considerations. This religious idea was clearly expressed in the ancient historical records and in the *Shih Ching,* or *Book of Odes.*

It would be wrong, however, to think of the ancient religion of the Chinese people as simply a political tool of the ruling class. Shang Ti was a god of humanity, who did not come into direct contact with any individual person, not even the king himself. As soon as the king ceased to represent the people, he became a private individual and lost the right to communicate with Shang Ti. Moreover, Shang Ti did not belong to one particular clan or race, and He had no fixed will but that of the people. Was it not said in the *Shu Ching,* or *Book of History,* that "Heaven sees with the people's eyes, and hears with the people's ears"? Here the word "Heaven" is another term for Shang Ti, the great deity whose dictates were manifested in the will of the people. Take, for instance, Shun, the sage-king of antiquity. Though of humble origin, he was made king because the people wished him to be a ruler. And when Shun was accepted by the people, he was also accepted by Heaven. This is likewise exemplified by the manner in which one dynasty succeeded another, as sanctioned by the approval of the people, which was indeed the tangible expression of Heaven's mandate on earth.

This emphasis on the value of the people later came to be the basis of democracy. Chinese political theory based on the religious conception of Heaven was at variance with the doctrine of divine right. The emperor was the Son of Heaven, and the first servant of the state. He ruled by the mandate of Heaven, and if he should prove unacceptable to Heaven because of his wickedness and cruelty, Heaven would transfer Its mandate to another house, noted for great virtue, to form a new dynasty. This theory of Heaven's mandate has been called the "right of revolution." The Chinese term for "revolution" is *keh ming,* which comes from the *Yi Ching,* or *Book of Change.*

Though the early Chinese political thinkers seldom questioned the validity of the royal authority, basic democratic ideas had long been dominant in Chinese thought. Long before John Locke (1632–1704) formulated the concept for Western political thought, the Chinese believed in government by the consent of the governed, and the right of revolution. Majority rule, the technique of balloting, and legislative assemblies were, however, unknown to them. Boycott and rebellion were their only means of expressing lack of consent, and only by a successful rebellion could they bring about a change of government.

The Chinese government worked upward from the people rather than downward from the emperor. The religious ideas of the Chinese people were dominated by their political ideas, which were in turn dominated by their humanistic ideas. Heaven placed the people below and prepared for them the sovereign, who ruled with the mandate of Heaven, but

Heaven's mandate was discernible only in the will of the people. The people were not only the root but also the final judge of the government. The mandate of Heaven was not based upon constitutional concepts; it was founded upon a sentiment that had been handed down through the ages. Mencius perhaps expressed it best: "The people rank highest in a state, the spirits of the land and grain come next, and the sovereign is of the least account" (*Mencius*, VII-14).

3. The Political Conception

From the age of Confucius (sixth century B.C.) onward, the Chinese people in general and their political thinkers in particular attempted to work for an ideal world. For instance, Confucius and his followers always tended to place the world before the state, and ignored national barriers to consider the welfare of the world and the peace of humanity at large. The opening section of the *Ta Hsueh*, or *Great Learning*,[2] offers a good illustration:

> The teaching of the Great Learning is to manifest one's illustrious virtue, to love the people, and to rest in the highest good. . . . The ancients who wished to manifest illustrious virtue throughout the world, first ordered well their own states. Wishing to order well their own states, they first regulated their families. Wishing to regulate their families, they first cultivated their persons. . . .

And conversely, this section continues:

> . . . Their persons being cultivated, only then did their families become regulated. Their families being regulated, only then did their states become well ordered. Their states being well ordered, only then did the world at peace.

[2] The *Ta Hsueh*, attributed to K'ung Chi, the grandson of Confucius, was originally a chapter of the *Li Chi*, or *Book of Rites*, and later was grouped with Confucius' *Analects, the Mencius,* and the *Chung Yung*, or *Doctrine of the Mean*, to form the Four Sacred Books.

The author of the *Ta Hsueh* was thinking about the ideal state in terms of world politics and world peace. He was not the first to think in this way, but it is significant that he did it remarkably and systematically. This section is in fact a synthesis of Chinese political philosophy and a program of practical politics, leading from the cultivation of one's personal life, through the regulation of one's family and ordering of one's state, to the accomplishment of world peace for the welfare of humanity at large. Being an all-inclusive and self-consistent program, it tells us not only how to cultivate ourselves but also how to govern other men. Therein are to be found all the fundamental principles of government. But for the author of the book, the good order of one's own state is not the final goal. The highest ideal of a state is "to manifest illustrious virtue throughout the world," that is, to achieve peace in the world.

The ideal of *Ta-tung* (the Great Commonwealth or Great Unity), as advocated by Confucius and his followers, was esteemed by the two great reform leaders K'ang Yu-wei (1858–1927) and Sun Yat-sen (1866–1925), although, one being a conservative and the other a revolutionary, they differed in their interpretations. The profound ideal of *Ta-tung* is described in the chapter "Li-yun" of the *Li Chi* (*Book of Rites*) as follows:

> When the Great *Tao* prevails, the world becomes a commonwealth; men of talents and virtue are elected, and mutual confidence and harmony prevail. Then people not only love their own parents and care for their own children, but also those of others. The old people are able to enjoy their old age; the young men are able to employ their talents; the juniors respect their elders; widows, orphans, and cripples are all well cared for. The men have their proper occupations, and the women their homes. If the people do not want to see the wealth being discarded under the ground, they do not have to keep it for their own use. If they labor with their strength, they do not have to labor for their own profit. In this way, selfish schemings are repressed and cannot develop; bandits and burglars do not show themselves; and as a result, the outer doors remain open and need not be shut at night. This is the age of *Ta-tung,* or the Great Commonwealth.

Since the ancient Chinese had no racial prejudice and believed in a Supreme Being that governed all humanity without preference for any particular tribe or race, it was only natural that they should be free from national sentiment and cherish the desire for a world organization which would operate for the security and welfare of mankind. In the above passage, Confucian scholars had tried to demonstrate how through the cultivation of virtues, the utilization of natural resources, and the improvement of people's livelihood, there can be built a world organization for the promotion of peace and human welfare.

4. The Humanistic Conception

We have studied the conceptions of the Chinese people concerning race, religion, and the state. These three interrelated conceptions form one consistent philosophy that has been the main source of Chinese culture and the basis of the great unity of imperial China, which lasted from the third century B.C. until the abdication of the Manchu emperor in 1911, when the Chinese republic was established—a period of over 2,000 years. Now we come to another aspect of Chinese thought: humanism. By humanism, we do not mean the negative feelings of tolerance and forgiveness so much as the more positive quality described by Confucius as *chung shu* (loyalty and altruism) and by Mencius as *ching ai* (reverence and love). To treat others with loyalty and altruism, with love and reverence, unreservedly and sincerely, is true humanism.[3]

Chinese humanism emphasizes human relationship, and teaches men how to live in harmony with one another. A sense of justice and fairness, a spirit of tolerance, a readiness to compromise, coupled with a determination to enforce the observance of these virtues against the teachings of extremists—these are the true foundations of human relations. In the course of centuries, the Chinese have developed many institutions and customs to conserve and perpetuate society, to give joint protection to individuals,

[3] See Ch'u Chai, "Chinese Humanism: A Study of Chinese Mentality and Temperament," *Social Research,* Vol. XXVI, No. 1, 1959, pp. 31-46.

and to strengthen proper relationships among the people. The basic and most characteristic Chinese institution has been the family. In human relationships, mutual affection first arises out of the family and then extends to the community. This is to say, affection manifests itself in different degrees of intensity. What is called filial piety and brotherly love in the family is known as loyalty and altruism in the wider sphere of human relations. Thence humanism is extended beyond the family circle, but the center of humanism is the family and not the individual. On the basis of the family system, institutions have been developed whereby the humanistic ideal worked down to the common people, institutions that reflected the application of that ideal to the political, economic, judicial, educational, and social fields.

Chinese political and social thought germinated from this humanistic ideal and developed into the ethico-political system of a paternal government. Chinese political and social thinkers, under the influence of humanism, looked at all political and social problems from a human perspective and based all their judgments on a human standard. They demanded in turn that government should be conducted for the sake of humanity. Their greatest contribution to the science of government lies in their effort to bring about harmonious relations between the ruler and the ruled. We see, therefore, that humanism is the social philosophy behind the family system and that it is the doctrine that worked for social order in China.

CHAPTER IV. THE CHINESE GOVERNMENT

1. The Structure of the Imperial Government

One of the most noteworthy achievements of the Chinese people has been in the realm of government. To those who know only modern China, with her prolonged political chaos, this statement may seem strange and unwarranted. Yet it can be justified. As judged by the area and population over which it governed, the length of time it endured, as well as its record in promoting the unity of the country and maintaining order and ensuring justice, the political structure of the Chinese imperial government, which disappeared in the twentieth century, can be compared favorably with that of any other government ever known to us.

The imperial government can be traced back to the Chou dynasty, but its essential features, as they were to be seen toward the close of the nineteenth century, were basically formulated during the Ch'in and the Han dynasties, especially at the time of Emperor Wu of the Han dynasty, in the second century B.C.

The Moral Leadership of the Emperor. The imperial government of China was very different from modern Western government. In comparison with the feudalism of the Chou dynasty, it was centralized; but when compared to Occidental machinery of state, it appears ineffective and incompetent. However, the essence of China's success in the art of government was that the community was held together not by power of law as much as by ethics and customs. To the Chinese political thinkers, ethics and politics were one and the same; the state and the individual were regarded as one entity under the control of the same principles, that is, a code of ethics. Hence they maintained that good government depended not upon legal and institutional principles, but upon good administration, underscoring the need of moral cultivation on the part of the ruling class. As a result, ethics became the cornerstone of Chinese political thought.

It was to Confucius and his followers that imperial China was indebted for an ethico-political system under which the emperor was responsible for setting a perfect moral example for his officials and for his people so that all would be ruled by the power of his goodness and imbued with his virtue and moral influence. The most important duty of a sovereign, in the view of Confucius, was to gain the people's confidence. Of the three essentials of good government, Confucius considered the confidence of the people as the most important; the remaining two are sufficient food and sufficient arms. He said: "From time immemorial, death has been the lot of all men; but a people that no longer trusts its ruler is lost indeed" (*Analects*, XII, 7). Then the question is how to gain the people's confidence. Confucius' answer is that the ruler should so inspire the people by his model behavior that they would come to him of their own accord. "He who rules by the example of his virtue is like the polar-star, which abides in its place while all the stars revolve around it" (*ibid.*, II, 1).

The Legalists discredited these Confucian principles and attempted, instead, to set up a complex and inflexible set of laws to govern the nation. Confucian scholars of the Han dynasty tried to substitute education and moral suasion for laws and regulations. Upon the emperor they placed responsibility for "the cultivation of virtues, the utilization of natural resources, and the improvement of people's livelihood," with the object of educating and transforming the people.

Tung Chung-shu (*c.* 179—*c.* 104 B.C.), the leading Confucian of his time, said:

> . . . Heaven, earth, and man are the basis of all creatures. Heaven gives them birth, earth nourishes them, and man brings them to completion. Heaven provides them at birth with a sense of filial and brotherly love, earth nourishes them with clothing and food, and man completes them with rites and music. The three act together as hands and feet join to complete the body and none can be dispensed with. . . . But the enlightened and worthy ruler, being of good faith, is strictly attentive to the three bases. His sacrifices are conducted with utmost reverence; he makes

offerings to and serves his ancestors; he advances brotherly affection and encourages filial conduct. In this way he serves the basis of Heaven. He personally grasps the plow handle and plows a furrow, plucks the mulberry himself and feeds the silkworms, breaks new ground to increase the grain supply, and opens the way for a sufficiency of clothing and food. In this way he serves the basis of earth. He sets up schools for the nobles and in the towns and villages to teach filial piety and brotherly affection, reverence and humility. He enlightens the people with education and moves them with rites and music. Thus he serves the basis of man. If he rightly serves these three, then the people will be like sons and brothers, not daring to be unsubmissive. . . .[4]

The Delegation of Power.   The key of the imperial government, as we have seen above, was the emperor. He held the kingdom as the "Son of Heaven" and a kind of father of his people. He exercised his parental authority through a vast bureaucracy of "superior men." In theory, the emperor was supreme over all the people in the empire, and he was the sole source of authority. He was the administrative director of the state, and officials derived their authority and titles from him. In the emperor resided the power of legislation, and at the same time he was the supreme judge. Therefore, the whole power of the government—legislative, executive, and judicial—was vested in his person. The imperial government was characterized throughout by the paternalistic biases of Chinese family life, in which no restraint was put on the authority of the father.

In practice, most of the imperial power had to be delegated. In ancient times, imperial China was an entire world to herself; her territory was vast and communications were inconvenient; moreover, the body of officialdom, particularly that of the local authorities, was large and the population was huge. Under these circumstances, the emperor had to leave the administration of government to the care of his ministers, whose offices, not hereditary, were filled on the basis of virtue and ability. These ministers, when in con-

---

[4] *Ch'un-ch'iu Fan-lu,* or *Luxuriant Dew from the Spring and Autumn Annals,* Sec. 19. See *Sources of Chinese Tradition,* compiled by W. T. de Bary and others, eds., New York, Columbia Univ. Press, 1960, Chap. VIII, p. 178.

ference, constituted a privy council that assisted the emperor in making important political decisions, appointments, dismissals, and promotions or demotions of high officials. They also assisted in planning military operations.

The administrative divisions varied in different dynasties. As early as the Han period, there had been a dual administration—the civil and, independent of it, the military administration. Each area belonged to two separate prefectures, one administrative and one military. This organization persisted until the T'ang dynasty, when the central administration consisted of three divisions, or boards: the Division of Ministers (*Shang-shu-sheng*), the executive branch of the government controlling six administrative departments; the Division of Secretariat (*Chung-shu-sheng*), an agency that drafted laws and orders and recorded the merits and punishments of officials; and the Division of Palace (*Men-hsia-sheng*), responsible for editing the imperial history and conducting ceremonial rites. During the Manchu dynasty, in addition to the Six Ministries, which had been inherited from the Tang dynasty as the central administrative departments, there were the Grand Secretariat (*Nei-ko*), the leading organization of the Manchu government, and the Grand Council (*Chün-chi Chu*, literally "Place for Military Strategy"), handling military and important state affairs.

The structure of the imperial government, in which the emperor delegated a great deal of his power to the ministers, was inaugurated by the political thinkers of the Han dynasty. After the fall of the Ch'in dynasty, Legalism had fallen into disgrace because of its absolutism, and the old-fashioned Confucianism, clinging to the institutions and traditions of the past, was not adaptable to the new age. Hence it was necessary to work out a new philosophy that would justify the imperial system and at the same time impose a check on its absolute power. Han political thinkers maintained that the ideal state was a combination of "democracy" and "aristocracy," and that the best ruler was one who ruled the least. On the basis of these ideas, they naturally favored a government based on the Taoist doctrine of *wu-wei* (nonaction, or *laissez faire*) and the delegation of authority.

The Han scholars went a step further than their predecessors in an effort to find a divine basis for their political theories, and made the ingenious discovery of a formula "subjecting the people to the ruler, and the ruler to Heaven," which they hoped might be a useful and practical weapon with which to combat misgovernment on the part of the emperor. We must admit that politically there was no limitation on the power of the emperor. Yet the emperor was at least subject to the judgments of Heaven, the Supreme Divine Being, whose reaction was shown by the manifestation of abnormal phenomena in the world of nature. Natural phenomena were interpreted by the scholars as divine disapproval of the emperor's misdeeds, and by such means they were able to effect certain reforms.

Two Innovations. In early times China was blessed with a "constitution" which was threefold in its distribution of powers. While only the emperor could rightfully exercise the legislative, executive, and judicial powers, the power of examination and the power of impeachment were exercised by his ministers, independent of him, to ensure an efficient and honest government.

The examination of applicants as a means of securing administrative personnel for government service may date back to the period of the legendary rulers Yao and Shun, at about 2500 B.C. During the Chou dynasty, the Duke of Chou instituted *li* (rites) and *yueh* (music) to educate and transform the people. The examination system became, then, closely integrated and coordinated with education. History records that when the government was badly in need of capable officials to administer the great empire, Emperor Wu of the Han dynasty introduced an examination system based upon the Five Classics. The Sui (581–618) and the T'ang (619–907) dynasties devised a new system of examination under which successful candidates were entitled to the degree of *chin shih,* or "doctor of letters," which paved the way for them to a political career. A successful candidate might be assigned to the Imperial College, or Han-ling Yuan, to study the operation of the various ministries. Not infrequently they were appointed to positions as ministerial officials and district magistrates. The Imperial College was practically a reservoir from which government officials were recruited. Throughout Chinese history, the emperors counted heavily upon the assistance of loyal, capable ministers, who employed the system of examination to ensure that elites were selected for government service. This time-honored system was inherited continuously, dynasty after dynasty, and served to guard against the inequitable distribution of political power.

The term "examination" in Chinese is composed of two words—*kao* and *shih*. *Kao*, as explained in the *Li Chi* or *Book of Rites*, means testing the learning of candidates. *Shih* means appointment; the *Shu Ching*, or *Book of History*, says: "*Shih* serves to test the ability of the appointee." Thus by means of *kao* the candidate is given an opportunity to show his learning, while by means of *shih*, he is given an opportunity to demonstrate his ability. It follows that the combination of *kao* and *shih* virtually represents not only examination, but also appointment. Whenever a candidate passed a government examination, he was justified in expecting to be appointed to government office.

The examination system also made for a kind of popular representation in the imperial government. For instance, the members (*chin shih*) of the Imperial College were chosen not only in accordance with their individual academic achievements, but also in proportion to the population of the localities from which they came. Ssu-ma Kuang, prime minister of the Sung dynasty (960–1279), complained of the disparity in representation between the central regions and those of the border, and proposed to equalize the regional distribution by instituting a system of circuit quotas. His scheme failed, however, to meet the approval of the emperor. When the Mongol rulers controlled China, they decided to revive the examinations according to the quota principle by region and by national groups. The Ming rulers at first discarded the Mongol quota system, but they later adopted a threefold division, allowing a middle quota region in addition to the northern and southern areas. Under the Manchu dynasty the system was further elaborated by the assignment of numerical *chin shih* quotas for each province, according to the regional percentages, and by the addition of quotas for Chinese, Mongol, and Manchu bannermen who chose the examinations as a path of promotion.

Another important innovation in the imperial government was the system of impeachment and censorship, which dates from the Han dynasty, or perhaps goes even farther back to the Chou dynasty. The censors, called *yü shih*, were appointed by the emperor. The functions of the *yü shih* were to admonish the rulers for misconduct and misgovernment, misconstruction of laws and injustice of legal trials, and to investigate corruption and maintain legal discipline in government. The censorate system was improved gradually, and reached its apex of efficiency in the Ming dynasty, when the *Tu-ch'a Yüan*, or the Board of Censors, was established with substantial powers of impeachment and censorship. The Manchu dynasty employed the censorate as the general supervisory organ, consisting of the president, senior and junior vice-presidents, twenty supervising censors, and forty-four inspecting censors. The supervising censors were responsible for supervising the central administrative organs of the Ch'ing government, while the inspecting censors were responsible for inspecting the local governments in the provinces.

In the early days, the *yü shih* were as stern and inflexible as the Roman *censor morum*. Though it is true that the censors of the old days did not function entirely independent of the emperor, yet there was no lack of instances where the *yü shih* acted promptly and uncompromisingly, in the face of all obstacles, to defend law and justice. They pointed out administrative errors and mistakes committed by the emperor and his ministers, and impeached those who were guilty of misconduct, no matter how high their ranks. They also criticized the emperor for improper conduct, and redressed the grievances of the common people. The entire empire was subject to the supervision of the censors.

We read in Chinese history of many remarkable censors who were esteemed for their straightforwardness and moral courage. They often even laid down their lives for a just cause. And on occasion even the emperor had to bow to their authority. Of course, it is true that the emperor always had the last say; yet he was usually wise enough to know better than to weaken the authority of the censors.

Without question, such a form of government fell short of what we may call modern democracy; still, we have to admit that the separation of the power of examination and the power of impeachment and censorship did much to mitigate the force of despotism.

The Local Government. China in the time of the Ch'in and Han dynasties was organized on the provincial system. When the first emperor of the Ch'in dynasty united the empire, it was divided into 36 provinces; by the end of the Han dynasty, the number of provinces had increased to 103, comprising more than 1,400 districts, including the 32 districts inhabited by the mountain tribes. These provinces were equal. They all paid taxes and conscripted men for military service. They were all governed by the same law, and chose their own scholars to compete in the examination for admission to the Imperial College. The members of the Imperial College, as we have noted above, were chosen in proportion to the size of local populations. In the later part of the Han dynasty, one scholar was chosen in each province for every 200,000 men. Thus in theory and in practice, China in those early days had a "written constitution" based on equality and the "principle of self-determination." In reality, every province and district was a free unit of the state and not a subject area. And most of the districts were self-governing. Although the district magistrate was appointed by the emperor, the actual management of the district, that is, in the villages and towns, was in the hands of a group of "headmen" selected by the people. The hierarchy intervened only when the districts failed to function or fell out with one another. The central government received from every district annual reports regarding the local administration, in which were listed statistics on births and deaths, taxes, conscription, lawsuits, education, and other public affairs.

The central government sent inspectors to the various districts annually, and the whole of China was divided into thirteen areas for inspection. The central government would take into consideration the reports of the local governments in decreeing the promotion and punishment of the local officials. When the magistrate of a district distinguished himself, he would be promoted to the position of governor of a province. If the governor of a province was outstandingly good, he might be promoted to a higher post in the imperial court. Most of the prime ministers of the Han dynasty rose from the rank of provincial or district officials.

The main features of the imperial government may be summarized as follows:

1. While only the emperor, as the source of authority, could rightfully exercise the legislative, executive, and judicial powers, the power of examination and the power of impeachment and censorship were exercised by his ministers, independent of him.

2. The emperor, while absolute in theory, in practice delegated a great deal of his imperial power to his ministers.

3. Admission to the Imperial College, from which ministerial and district officials were recruited, was granted only to successful candidates in the civil examinations, and these candidates were chosen on the basis of their academic achievements, and in proportion to the relative size of the population of their home districts.

4. Powers of government were distributed fairly between the central and the local governments. While the central government had over-all authority, the local government enjoyed a large degree of local autonomy.

This, then, was the system of government under the ancient dynasties. Like all human institutions, it had its weaknesses. It was men but not laws that ruled; to make government dependent upon the good example of the emperor was to take a considerable risk. While the delegated powers were handled by the ministers, no legal means had been devised to differentiate between the political power as represented by the emperor and the administrative power as vested in the ministers. And again, though the theory of the Heavenly mandate in the early days acted as a check on the emperor, it was not enough to restrain him from breaking the power of the ministers, if he wished, and encroaching on the rights of the people. But these failings must not be allowed to obscure the achievements of the imperial system. Whatever its defects, the imperial government of old China, which was to disappear early in the twentieth century, was among the most remarkable and successful ever devised by man.

2. The Structure of the Nationalist Government

Constitutional rule was a symbol, in the historical sense, of the goal for which the Chinese nation long struggled. The early nationalist revolutionaries who opposed the Manchu regime regarded Western constitutionalism as one of their principal political aims and a necessary condition for the establishment of China as a modern nation. China's constitutional movement dates back to the first Sino-Japanese

War of 1894–1895. Since that time, various constitutions have been drafted and adopted. Among these may be mentioned the "Outline" of 1905, the "Nineteen Articles" of 1911, the "Provisional Compact" of 1912, the "Tien-Tan [Temple of Heaven] Draft" of 1913, and the so-called "Tsao Kun Constitution" of 1923.[5]

Dr. Sun Yat-sen himself declared that the country must pass through three stages to arrive at a constitutional form of government. The first stage was the unification of the country by military force. Then there should be a period of political tutelage under the Kuomintang (the Nationalist Party). Finally, at the end of Kuomintang tutelage, the country should adopt a constitutional form of government.

The Nationalist government came into power in 1928, and adopted a Provisional Constitution in 1931. By the end of 1932, the central executive committee of the Kuomintang decided that a national assembly should be convened and a draft constitution drawn up by the Legislative Yüan. Accordingly, the first draft constitution was completed and promulgated on May 5, 1936.

When the Sino-Japanese hostilities began in August 1937, more than half of the 1,200 delegates to the National Congress had been chosen. This body was scheduled to meet in November 1937, but was postponed indefinitely as a result of the outbreak of war. During the first two years there was little discussion of early constitutional action. In fact, the extraordinary session of the Kuomintang in April 1938 declared in its manifesto: "Following the day when war is won we should wind up military affairs and expedite the carrying out of constitutionalism. . . ." Meanwhile the People's Political Council, which had served during the war as a bridge to constitutional government, was established in March 1938.

Toward the end of the war, the government agreed to hold a "political consultation conference" at Chungking, the wartime capital, to settle all the outstanding problems that allegedly caused friction among the major political parties. The conference was attended by leaders of all political parties, as well as by prominent social and civic leaders. Six

[5] See *Political Science Quarterly*, June 1924, for the text of the various constitutions.

principles [6] were adopted as the basis for the revision of the Draft Constitution, also known as "the Double-Five Draft Constitution" of 1936. Wang Chung-hui (1881–1959), the noted jurist of China, was entrusted with the task of embodying these six principles in the document, and when this was done, it was once more passed by the Legislative Yüan.

On November 15, 1946, the National Assembly was convened at Nanking for the purpose of adopting a permanent constitution for the Republic of China. The Communists did not participate in the Assembly. After a prolonged discussion lasting forty-two days, the draft finally passed the three readings and was formally adopted as the permanent Constitution of China. It was promulgated on January 1, 1947, and scheduled to be enforced on December 25, 1947.

The Constitution consists of 175 articles, classified in 14 chapters, and covers all the major points of Dr. Sun Yat-sen's constitutional theories as well as the six principles adopted at the Political Consultation Conference. The essential points of the New Constitution are discussed below.

Five-Power Constitution Versus Three-Power Constitution. Like the constitutions of other democratic countries, the Nationalist Constitution provides for an executive, a legislative,[7] and a judicial department that function generally in the same manner as they do in any three-power government (Articles 53—89). What is characteristic of the Nationalist Constitution is this: the power of administering the civil-service examination has been transferred from the executive branch to an independent examination department; the powers of impeachment and censorship, from the executive to an independent control department (Articles 83–89, 90–100). The addition of these two independent departments is a device, based on the doctrine of Dr. Sun Yat-sen,[8]

[6] The six principles may be summarized as follows: (1) amendment of provisions for laws restricting the people's freedom; (2) establishment of a representative and parliamentary government; (3) establishment of a cabinet system; (4) election by the people of the members of the Legislative Yuan; (5) responsibility of the Executive Yüan to the Legislative Yüan; and (6) their own constitutions for the provinces.

[7] Members of the Legislative Yüan shall be elected directly by the people (Article 64).

[8] See Sun Yat-sen's *Fundamentals of National Reconstruction,* p. 38. Dr. Sun Yat-sen compared the constitutions of the western democracies with that of old China, and summarized them as follows:

intended to ensure an efficient and honest government.

Under the three-power constitution, the legislature is concerned with the enactment of law; the executive, with the enforcement of law; and the judiciary, with the application and interpretation of law. These three powers are exercised by three distinct departments independent of one another. In other words, the legislature represents the popular will which is to be translated into law; the executive is to carry out such laws as are enacted by the legislature; and the judiciary sees to it that in carrying out the law no fundamental principles of the government are violated, and no individual rights encroached upon. Not infrequently, however, have we seen instances of deadlock between the legislature and the executive, and failure on the part of the judiciary to cooperate with one or the other.

The deficiency of the three-power constitution is that it makes no provision for human weakness. Law alone is not enough to ensure good government; much depends on the man who administers the law.

The Nationalist five-power constitution acknowledges the human element in its provision for independent examination and control departments,[9] to be concerned respectively with the supply and control of government personnel.

Presidential System Versus Cabinet System. The Nationalist government formed under the Constitution of 1947

---

[9] Members of the Control Yüan are to be elected by provincial and municipal councils (Article 91).

Chinese Imperial Government:
1. Powers of the Emperor—legislative, executive, and judicial
2. Power of Examination
3. Power of Impeachment and Censorship

Modern Democratic Government:
1. Legislative Power—concurrently the power of impeachment and censorship
2. Executive Power—concurrently power of examination
3. Judicial Power

Five-Power-Constitution Government:
1. Legislative Power—vested in the Legislative Yuan
2. Executive Yuan—vested in the Executive Yuan
3. Judicial Power—vested in the Judicial Yuan
4. Power of Impeachment and Censorship—vested in the Control Yuan
5. Power of Examination—vested in the Examination Yuan

NOTE: "Yuan is a governmental department on the highest level.

does not follow exactly either the presidential system or the cabinet system, as these are known in Western countries, but it borrows something of both. Article 57 of the Constitution reads:

> The Executive Yüan shall be responsible to the Legislative Yüan in accordance with the following provisions:
> 1. The Executive Yüan has the obligation to present to the Legislative Yüan its administrative policies and its administrative reports. . . .
> 2. If the Legislative Yüan does not concur in any important policy of the Executive Yüan, it may, by resolution, ask the Executive Yüan to alter such a policy. With respect to such resolution, the Executive Yüan may, with the approval of the President of the Republic, request the Legislative Yüan to reconsider it. . . .
> 3. If the Executive Yüan deems a statutory, budgetary, or treaty bill passed by the Legislative Yüan difficult to carry out, it may, with the approval of the President of the Republic, request within ten days after the delivery of said resolution to the Executive Yüan, that the Legislative Yüan reconsider the same. If, after reconsideration, two-thirds of the attending members of the Legislative Yüan uphold the original resolution, the President of the Executive Yüan shall either abide by the same or resign.

From the above provisions it would appear that the relation between the executive and the legislature is similar to that under the cabinet system as practiced in Great Britain, inasmuch as the president of the Executive (prime minister) is made responsible to the Legislative Yüan. But since the president of the Executive Yüan and the other officials of the ministerial rank are not necessarily the leader and members of the party enjoying a majority in parliament, it is not exactly of that nature. On the contrary, Article 75 expressly prohibits members of the Legislative Yüan from holding governmental posts concurrently. What is more, though the president of the Executive Yüan is given a veto power on the decisions of the Legislative Yüan, he cannot exercise it without the approval of the president of the state, nor is he given the power to dissolve the legislature.

In a way, the system provided for in the Nationalist Constitution also resembles the American presidential system.

The president of the state is given the power to nominate and appoint the president of the Executive Yüan with the consent of the Legislative Yüan (Article 55). However, the president of the state is concerned with the choice of the president of the Executive Yüan only. As to the heads of the various ministries, it is for the president of the Executive Yüan to make the choice and then recommend the candidates to the president of the state (Article 56). Furthermore, all important policies are to be passed by the Executive Yüan Conference, which includes the president and vice-president of the Executive Yüan and all of its members (Article 58). In case of disputes or conflicts in regard to such policies or measures, arising between the executive and the legislative departments, it is the president of the Executive Yüan, not the president of the state, who shall bear the responsibility. This is different from the American system, where the president alone makes the ultimate decision in regard to important policies and measures, and bears the sole responsibility.

Central Government versus Local Government. The Constitution of 1947, which is inclined neither to centralization nor to decentralization, is aimed at striking a due balance between the central and local governments. The framers of the Constitution strictly followed Dr. Sun Yat-sen's doctrine of the distribution of powers: matters which by nature require uniform action on the part of the nation are assigned to the central government; matters which by nature should be dealt with locally are assigned to the local governments. In the Constitution, the powers that are to be exercised by the central government and by the local governments, respectively, are specifically enumerated (Articles 107–110). For matters not so specified, the same shall fall either within the jurisdiction of the central government, if it is national in nature, or within the jurisdiction of the province, if it is provincial in nature; and in case of dispute, the matter shall be referred to the legislative Yüan (Article 111).

There are four levels of local government: namely, the provincial and special municipality level, the district (*hsien*) and municipality level, and the rural district (*hsiang*) and township (*cheng*) level. All the local governments are self-government units, within the scope of authority constitutionally distributed, although they are subordinate to their superior agencies. Local units have their legislature and make their own laws for matters enumerated in Articles 109–110. But local laws are not valid if they are in contravention of the laws and ordinances of their superior authorities. To put it positively, in the case of a district or municipal government its laws and regulations must be consistent with those of the provincial government to which it is subordinate; in the case of a province, its laws and regulations must also be consistent with those of the central government to which it is, in turn, subordinate (Articles 116 and 125).

Another interesting point that may be brought up here is that the district, being the political unit in the entire framework, is designed to be run directly by the people. Though the people elect delegates to form a district legislature, the power of such a legislature is limited to the making of laws and regulations. The people still reserve themselves the direct exercise of all political powers (Article 123). This is designed to set the stage for the introduction of an efficient and genuine democratic government under the direct control of the people.

Local government has existed in China for over two thousand years. But many thorny problems remain to be tackled. The main weaknesses of local government, for instance, lie in its limited revenues and the low quality of its officials. "What is good for the people's livelihood is not done; what hurts the people is left untouched." This refers to local government as it was hundreds of years ago.[10]

3. The Structure of the Communist Government

When the Chinese Communists established their new government at Peking in September 1949, they called a People's Political Consultative Conference to which they invited some 662 delegates from 45 representative units, including political parties, regional areas, field armies, public bodies, and "democratic personalities" specially invited by the Communist government. The first session of the People's Political

[10] This is quoted from Fan Chung-yen's memorandum of 1027 on the reform of local government of the Sung dynasty. See *Chinese Thought and Institutions*, ed. by John K. Fairbank, Chicago, Univ. of Chicago Press, 1957, p. 118.

Consultative Conference began on September 21 and ended on October 30. Its main work lay in the adoption of three important documents—the Organic Law of the People's Political Consultative Conference, the Organic Law of the Central People's Government, and the Common Program of the People's Political Consultative Conference—which represented a detailed statement of the theory and structure of the Chinese Communist government. Other tasks included the election of the chairman, the six vice-chairmen, the 54 members of the state council, and the 180 members of the National Standing Committee of the People's Political Consultative Conference. There is, however, no mention in the records of the conference of any discussion of the three documents. As a matter of fact, the documents, which were passed by the conference, were written by committee behind the closed doors. For instance, the Common Program simply restated the Communist principles and policies as expressed in Mao Tse-tung's classic treatise *On New Democracy*, which were claimed to represent the joint resolution of the four classes—proletariat, peasantry, petty bourgeoisie, and national bourgeoisie.

The People's Political Consultative Conference continued to function until 1954, when it was turned into a National People's Congress. This congress consists of 1,226 deputies from the provincial congresses, the large cities, the national minorities, the armed forces, and the overseas Chinese. The congress met in Peking on September 15, 1954, and adjourned on September 28. It duly adopted the draft constitution which had been drawn up by the Central Committee of the Communist Party and issued by the draft committee headed by Mao Tse-tung.

The Communist Constitution of 1954, which consists of a preamble and 106 articles in 4 chapters, is in fact the combination of the Organic Law and the Common Program of 1949. Much of the constitution was copied directly from the Soviet Constitution of 1936, using a different terminology. For instance, the People's Republic of China is described as "a people's democratic state led by the working class and based on the alliance of workers and peasants" (Article 1), whereas according to the Soviet Constitution, the "Union of Soviet Socialist Republics is a socialist state of workers and peasants" (Article 1). And again, the so-called "people's democratic dictatorship" in the preamble of the Chinese Communist Constitution is just another version of the Soviet Russian "proletarian dictatorship."

However, there are differences in government structure. First, the Supreme Soviet of the USSR is bicameral, whereas the Chinese National People's Congress is unicameral; second, in the USSR the Council of Ministers, including its chairman or premier, is appointed by the Presidium of the Supreme Soviet, whereas in Communist China the premier, the head of the State Council, is nominated and appointed by the chairman of the People's Republic with the consent of the National People's Congress; and third, the National People's Congress, like the Supreme Soviet of the USSR, is the supreme organ of the state power, but it differs from the latter in that the chairman of its Standing Committee is not titular head of the government, but is subordinate to the chairman of the People's Republic. We see, therefore, that the Chinese Communist Constitution grants greater power to the chairman of the Republic than that enjoyed by the president of the Presidium of the Supreme Soviet of the USSR.

Now let us further examine the state structure as provided in the Communist Constitution. While the National People's Congress is "the highest organ of the state authority" (Article 21), the State Council is the "executive organ of the highest state authority" (Article 47). Similarly, "People's congresses and people's councils are established in provinces, municipalities directly under the central authority, counties, municipalities, municipal districts, *hsiang*, nationality *hsiang*, and towns" (Article 54). This parallel system of people's congresses and people's councils is built upon the distinction between the sovereign power of the people as represented by the people's congresses, and the ruling power of the government as represented by the people's councils.

Having made clear the distinction between the sovereign power of the people and the ruling power of the government, there remains the question of how this parallel system actually works in the Chinese Communist government. The underlying spirit of the Communist government is the principle of democratic centralism. "The principle of democratic centralism," the Communists assert, "is contrary to the theory of separation of powers under the old type of democracy," by which they mean "the politics of exploitation and maneuvering, division of spoils and playing tricks." The Communists "prefer a political system which combines discussion and execution in one hand. This is the system of the People's Congress in which all power is centralized." [11] If a political system combines "discussion and execution in one hand," it will naturally deny the separation of power.

In this connection we shall say a few words about the Communist local government. According to the Communist Constitution, there are three levels of local government: first, the provinces, autonomous regions, and municipalities directly under the central authority; second, the autonomous *chou*, counties, autonomous counties, and municipalities; and third, the villages (*hsiang*), nationality villages, and towns (Article 53). Since 1958 the basic administrative unit of the country has been the people's commune, which in fact assumes the role of what the village government had played in the community. The people's commune will be discussed in detail in Chapter VII of this book.

Local people's congresses and local people's councils at all levels have been established in Communist China (Article 54), but the "people's congresses at county level and above have power to revise or annul inappropriate decisions issued by people's congresses at the next lower level as well as inappropriate decisions and orders issued by people's councils at the next lower level" (Article 60). Moreover, the "people's councils at county level and above direct the work of all their subordinate departments and of people's councils at lower levels, as well as appoint or remove personnel of organs of state according to provisions of law. The people's councils at county level and above have the power to suspend the carrying out of inappropriate decisions by people's congresses at the next lower level; and to revise or annul inappropriate orders and directives issued by their subordinate departments, and inappropriate decisions and orders issued by people's councils at lower levels" (Article 65). All these provisions are of course contrary to the fundamental principle of self-government, because it is recognized in all democracies that a local government should have the power to run its own business, including the election of its own officers and the making of its own laws and regulations, if

[11] Quoted from Tung Pih-wu's speech. See Carson Chang's *The Third Force in China*, New York, Bookman Associates, 1952, p. 272.

such laws and regulations are not in contravention of national laws.

In short, this kind of constitution is not only opposed to the democratic form of government, but has struck at the moral basis of the imperial government of China. The important thing to remember is that democratic ideas are integral to the traditional political thought of the Chinese people. It has been their conviction that the fundamental principle of a constitution is to make the people play their role in government. In the *Shu Ching* (*Book of History*) we read:

> It was the lesson of our great ancestor:
> The people should be cherished;
> They should not be downtrodden;
> The people are the root of the country;
> The root firm, the country is tranquil;
> When I look throughout the empire
> Of simple men and simple women,
> Any one may surpass me.[12]

[12] "The Song of Five Sons."

CHAPTER V.   THE CHINESE SOCIETY

1. Agrarian Society and Economy

The course of Chinese history, like that of any other country, is determined by the powerful economic and social forces that affect the fortunes of the people as a whole. Despite the vicissitudes of forty centuries, the evolution of Chinese society and economy forms a continuous thread of change, which alone can explain the events of today.

The traditional society of China was composed of two strata: the lower stratum consisting of the vast peasantry, and the upper stratum made up of a small minority of privileged groups.[1] It was the peasantry that tilled the land and fed the nation. For centuries China had been dependent upon agriculture; the government derived its revenue from land taxation; officials and scholars were supported by taxes and rent paid by farmers. Thus agriculture and the status of farmers have been and will be determining factors not only in the economic life of the country, but in the social and political development as well.

It would be wrong, however, to think that ancient China was already completely agrarian. In the early ages, two modes of living—agriculture and nomadic life—existed together. According to tradition, the clan of Shen Nung was agrarian, and the clan of Huang Ti nomadic. (See Chapter II.) The clan of Shen Nung lived in the west on the loessland suitable for agriculture, while that of Huang Ti stayed in the east on the marshland which was good for hunting and herding. Thus the clan of Huang Ti was at first a nomadic people and later settled down to become a population of agriculturists, because agrarian culture in ancient China spread from the northwest to the northeast.

---

[1] Even today, the portion of Chinese population engaged in farming is estimated at 75 to 80 per cent. About 10 per cent are city dwellers, and the remainder live in market towns and are closely supplementary to the farm population.

Agrarian areas in ancient China were like islands in an
ocean or oases in a desert, all separated each other by a wide
area. Later they increased in size and joined each other, but
by the middle of the Chou dynasty (about the seventh century B.C.) agrarian lands were still scattered, and the reason
for this was chiefly due to the feudalism of the Chou dynasty.

The feudalism of the Chou dynasty was a kind of large-
scale migration of armed settlers. Members of the royal
family and ministers and generals of merit were appointed
as vassals to the conquered territories of Shang. The new
feudal lords built walls to fortify these fiefs. Outside the
city wall there were arable lands, beyond which they built
another wall to mark the boundaries of their fiefs; but outside the boundaries, the lands were uncultivated. The new
fiefs, although scattered over the country, communicated with
each other and with the capital by means of newly built
highways. Relying on these fiefs as military bases, the imperial house of the Chou governed the empire.

The fiefs were distributed on a scale proportionate to the
ranks of the recipients in the feudal hierarchy—baronies,
viscountcies, earldoms, marquisates, and duchies—and
ranged in size from fifty to a hundred square *li* (the Chinese *li* is about one-third of a mile). The land outside the
city was divided into arable land and land not used for
farming. The arable land was parceled out by the feudal lord
to the lesser nobles. As subvassals, the lesser nobles distributed the land equally to their own tenants. According to
the traditional *chien tien* (literally, "well field," meaning
equal plots) system, lands in the fiefs were divided into
nine squares of a hundred *mou* each (the size of the ancient *mou* is not known; the modern *mou* is about one-sixth
of an acre); the eight outer squares were given to eight
peasant families for farming, so that each family would
have one hundred *mou* and enough extra land for a house
on the public square, and each family would have to farm
the ten *mou* of the public square for taxes. It was quite in
accord with the later practice of taxing the farmer a tithe
of his crops.[3]

The *chien tien* system was indeed a form of cooperative
agriculture. Inherited from earlier times, it prevailed during

[3] The *chien tien* system of agriculture was mentioned in the
works of Mencius, *Ku Liang* (*Commentary on the Annals of
Spring-Autumn*), and *Chou Li* (*Book of Chou Ritual*).

the early part of the Chou dynasty. *Chien* means "well" and it is written thus: 井 , and *tien* means "field" and it is written thus: 田 . If the *chien* character is put within a square, 田 , it is seen that we will have a field divided into nine equal squares. This is the *chien tien* system of dividing lands. Under the *chien tien* system there was no private ownership of lands; the title remained with the feudal lord. Nor was the land for sale, and so its ownership could not be in private lands. As a result, there was no landlord class.

With the collapse of the Chou feudalism came also the destruction of the *chien tien* system, and in its place came a personal landownership system, which lasted for more than two thousand years until the conquest of the Chinese Communists on the mainland. This change in the status of land marked the end of feudalism and the beginning of private ownership and wealth. Land was then freely bought and sold. As China had no large industries, wealth was not to be found in industrial investment, but was concentrated most frequently in land. This led inevitably to the concentration of land in the hands of the privileged groups, and the rise of large landowners.[4] What was worse, the small privileged groups, which were closely tied with officialdom, in collaboration with the large landowners, manipulated taxation, renting, and recruiting to the disadvantage of the landless and poor peasants, who continued to till the fields with their sweat and blood for generations without any prospect of improving their servile condition. This was the basic picture of traditional society, in which the fundamental causes of social disturbances are to be found.[5]

[4] The Chinese Communists, on rather flimsy grounds, classified the rural population into five categories: landlords, rich peasants, middle peasants, poor peasants, and farm laborers, but we cannot doubt that there were many absent landowners, who exploited the labor of the vast peasantry.

[5] The general conditions of the farming population before the conquest of the Communists over the mainland may be summarized as follows: "(1) 93 per cent of cultivated land was privately owned; (2) more than 53 per cent of the country's good arable land was owned by 'landlords'; (3) high rent, insecurity of tenure, usury, and exploitation by the middle men were prevalent throughout the country; (4) the unjust distribution of rural wealth and poverty led to some degree of 'class' conflict. . . ." See *Agrarian Reform in Communist China to 1952,* by Human Research Institute, Maxwell Air Force Base, Alabama, No. 41, July 1955, p. 6.

Farmers are customarily viewed as conservative and easily contented, but history shows that the Chinese peasants, carrying on under tremendous economic and social pressure with little margin of protection against disaster, were easily pushed into revolt and rebellion. Throughout Chinese history there were many popular risings, led by peasants, which were precipitated by official corruption and economic distress. These were the revolts of the Red Eyebrows (18), the Yellow Turbans (200), and the Huang Chao (900); the Fang La Uprising (1120); the rebellion led by Li Tse-cheng and Chang Hsien-chung (1636); the Nien Fei Rising (1855); and the Taiping Rebellion (1848–1864). Peasant revolts occurred in China for more than two thousand years, and they were always centered around economic problems: floods, famines, heavy taxes, or high rentals.[6] This economic plight was undoubtedly aggravated by wars and aggressions. To cure these ills Chinese peasants wanted more land, lower rents, and release from indebtedness. Throughout Chinese history, social and economic thinking and policy have centered around the idea of land reform, involving the nationalization of all land, abolition of private landholding, and prohibition of the sale of land. Acute agrarian crises plagued China down through the centuries, from the Han, through the T'ang and the Sung, down to the Ming and the Ch'ing dynasties. This historical fact might serve to explain why and how the Chinese Communists, in their seizure of power, won the support of the vast agricultural population by sponsoring measures of the sort traditionally popular with the peasants, such as limitation of rents and interest rates, and distribution of land.

The Chinese peasants, as noted above, had to produce not only the food they consumed, but also enough to pay the taxes and rentals as well. There is no question that their lot was a very difficult one. If no effective measures were taken to alleviate their sufferings, they would inevitably rise up and revolt. The cycle of agrarian crisis, climaxed by peasant revolts, repeats itself over and over in Chinese history. This

---

[6] J. L. Buck, in his *Land Utilization in China* (Chicago, University of Chicago Press, 1937, p. 198), pointed out that three forms of rent payment were used: (1) 25 per cent of the tenant farmers paid cash rent; (2) 51 per cent paid crop rent; (3) only 2 per cent were croppers. In addition to high rent, there were various implicit charges connected with renting.

was recognized by Dr. Sun Yat-sen, founder of the Kuomintang, and land reform was made the cornerstone of his program of economic construction. Under the "Principle of the People's Livelihood," he spoke of the necessity of the equalization of land rights and advocated the "land-to-the-tiller" policy. This policy, favored by the Nationalists and the Communists alike, was not carried out with great success before his death in 1925. The death of Dr. Sun brought Chiang Kai-shek into power. But Chiang Kai-shek was and is primarily a military man. He felt it essential to subdue the Chinese warlords and bring the Communists under his control before he could turn to internal reforms. Hence he hardly attempted in the twenty years of his rule to translate Dr. Sun's policy into action. At times, the central government under his direction did pass enlightened laws to alleviate the sufferings of the peasants. But these laws were merely transmitted down through the village headmen and were never actually applied.[7]

By contrast, the Chinese Communists, once they secured the control of the Chinese mainland, started upon a land-reform program and then promulgated the agrarian law of 1950. "The essential content of agrarian reform," as Liu Shao-ch'i tells us, "is the confiscation of the land of the landlord class for distribution to the landless and poor peasants. Thus the landlords as a class in society are abolished and the landownership system of feudal exploitation is transformed into a system of peasant land ownership."[8] In this connection, Mao Tse-tung has claimed that the Communist agrarian reform was no more than an attempt to implement Dr. Sun's

[7] In 1949 when the National Government retreated from the mainland to the island of Taiwan (Formosa), a three-stage land-reform program was introduced. In the first stage, land rent was reduced to 37.5 per cent of the value of the main crop, by the Provincial Government of Taiwan. This "37.5 per cent maximum" rental policy was incorporated in a new law adopted by the Legislative Yüan in 1951. The second stage was the sale of government-owned land to the farmers, in the amount of 230,000 acres formerly held by the Japanese-owned Formosan Development Company. The third stage was the implementation of the land-to-the-tiller policy in 1953; that is, the government buys private farm landholdings from the landlords in excess of the prescribed limit and resells them to the landless tenants or to those farmers who do not own enough land.

[8] See his *Report on the Agrarian Reform: Points for Attention during Agrarian Reform*, June 4, 1950.

"Principle of the People's Livelihood." In other words, the great principle of Dr. Sun had been neglected by the Kuomintang and used by the Communists to enlist the support of the peasants on the mainland.

2. Structure of Chinese Society

In the social structure of China, there has never been a caste system or a permanent demarcation of social classes. During the Chou period there were clearly recognized ranks of nobility, and in the ancient feudal society these distinctions were prominent. Under feudalism, the nobles (*chün tzu* referring to nobles as well as to gentlemen) not only held in fief strips of lands parceled out by their lord, but also possessed real political power. On the other side of the social scale, diametrically opposed to *chün tzu*, were *hsiao jen* (literally "small people"), or the commoners. In the feudal period, as the ranks and manors of the feudal lords and nobles were hereditary, a commoner could never become a nobleman. In ancient China, as in modern China, the great mass of the population, as noted above, was comprised of farmers born to the soil, on which they worked with their sweat and blood. But the nobles, who governed the commoners, enjoyed the produce of their fields as well as their service. The following verse from the *Shih Ching*, or *Book of Odes*, voices the resentment of the peasants against the nobles:

You do not sow, you do not reap,
Yet you get the produce of these three hundred farms!
You do not hunt, you do not chase,
Yet we see badgers hanging up in your courtyards!

In the early days of the Chou period, when land was feudal grant rather than private property, and was equally distributed among the peasants under the *chien tien* system, there was a kind of family relationship and communal life between the nobles and commoners. Though their status was determined at birth, the nobles and commoners maintained harmonious relations. From the third century B.C. onward, when an absolute monarch was established, the situation changed completely. With the collapse of feudalism, the hereditary aristocratic class was abolished. As a result, a power vacuum was left between the people and the monarch. In the feudalism of the Chou period, there existed an aristocracy that held the balance between the king and the people. Now that there was no longer an aristocracy the people had been leveled into one class. Thus the official posts were no longer monopolized by the nobles, and the commoners were given a new opportunity for social mobility. Men of ability either could be recommended as candidates for official appointment or pass a civil service examination. By these means a formal channel for social mobility was set up, and there arose a gentry which is often referred to as *shih ta fu*, the scholar-official class—the men of letters, who were destined to play a vital role in the future administration of the Chinese government.

After the collapse of feudalism, there was another important change. With the abolition of the aristocracy, the emperor constituted the sole political power in the country, and was therefore the administrative director of the state. The official posts, including those of the local administration, were not hereditary, but were appointed by the emperor. However, no officials were appointed by the emperor below the district level. From the district downward extended the self-governing community—the village and township— free from imperial interference so long as it paid its tax allotment and kept the peace. The district magistrate who represented the emperor was the "parent-official" who was supposed to maintain an intimate relationship with the people. The officials and the commoners formed two different status groups, the officials being the superiors and the commoners the inferiors. There was little communication between the two groups. Consequently, the district magistrate, the backbone of the ruling class, was "as high as the sky" and no commoner could reach up to him. Therefore it was necessary to have some sort of representative or medium through which the communication between the magistrate and the people was possible. Only by understanding this communication can we know how the Chinese traditional society worked.

The Chinese people, in accordance with Confucian principles, were traditionally divided into two classes: the "mind-laborers" (chün tzu) and the "body-laborers" (hsiao jen). The "body-laborers," or commoners, who were supposed to devote themselves to manual work, were again divided into three social groups: the peasants, the craftsmen, and the merchants. In the social and economic thinking of Chinese philosophers, there is a distinction between what is known as "the root" and what is known as "the branch." The "root" refers to agriculture and the "branch" to commerce. The reason for this distinction is that agriculture is concerned with food production, while commerce is only concerned with its consumption. In an agrarian society food production is the activity which the state supports; the farmers are the class that it encourages. It is therefore not surprising to learn that throughout Chinese history, social and economic theories and policies have all attempted to "extoll the 'root' and suppress the 'branch.' "

The mind-laborers were supposed to work with their brains. As a group, they were superior to and expected to be served by those who were body-laborers. This was clearly pointed out by Mencius in the following passage:

> . . . Some labor with their minds, and some labor with their strength. Those who labor with their minds govern; those who labor with their strength are governed. Those who are governed serve; those who govern are served. This is the principle universally recognized.[9]

Thus the mind-laborers, as a group, were taken as the reservoir of Chinese officialdom, and therefore were looked upon as the backbone of the traditional society in China. Because of their distinguished status, they enjoyed certain political and social privileges. While they were at court, they were civil officials; when they retired, they styled themselves gentry, or shen shih, and became local leaders in village communities. In their capacity as village leaders, they served as a useful link between the government authorities and the local self-governing community.

The unit of local administration, as we noted above, was the village, which had been invested with the right of local self-government. It was from the self-governing unit thus formed that a headman was chosen, or rather nominated, by the inhabitants as the administrator of public affairs and

[9] Mencius, III-A, 3.

arbitrator of personal affairs. It is important to note that while the imperial government in China might be despotic in its outlook, it placed no restriction on the right of free assemblies by the people for the discussion of their own affairs. However, the headman of a village was not entirely beyond official influence. After he was chosen by the people, he had to be confirmed in the appointment by the district magistrate, before entering upon his duties.

The gentry, though the responsible leaders of community, had no direct connection with politics. In fact, they strove to keep clear of any official dealings with the government. It was the headman who represented the community in his dealings with the government. The orders of the government were issued not to the responsible leaders of the community, but to the headman. The headman, after he had received an order from the government, reported to the village leaders. The leaders then talked the matter over with one another, and if they decided that the order was unacceptable, they rejected it and turned it back to the headman. This rejection would be in turn communicated to the district government. As the refusal of the order was not direct but was made in a roundabout way, the dignity of the government would not have been hurt. Meanwhile the leaders of the local community would make a friendly call on the district official to discuss the matter. If no agreement resulted from this discussion, the local gentry would be inclined to take the matter up with the higher levels of the bureaucracy. Eventually, an agreement of some sort would be reached.

There are two important aspects to the traditional structure of Chinese society. First, the Chinese village was a local self-governing unit, and the village headman together with local leaders constituted the executive board through which actions were taken. Second, the leaders of the village were the gentry class, and the local gentry tended to have influence in government, though they had no real political power. This was the traditional Chinese system of representation, which might not meet the standards of modern Western democratic institutions, but it safeguarded the welfare and interests of the local population.

Local self-government was finally challenged by the *pao chia* system of mutual guaranty and responsibility, as introduced by the Nationalist government in 1931. This was an old system of social control, according to which ten households, the members of which were mutually responsible for each other and were obliged to denounce one another's crimes, were grouped into a *chia*, ten *chia* forming a *pao*. This system was in fact first instituted in 1069 by the famous statesman Wang An-shih, to organize the peasants for military purposes and supplant the mercenaries. The Nationalists used it again so as to register and organize the people more effectively against the Communists. Under this system, each family must post on the top of the front door a card bearing the name, age, sex, kinship, status, and occupation of each member of the family. But such a system had never been successfully carried out in the villages, because "the villagers would not report that a son of their neighbor was involved in anything wrong. This reluctance is largely due to the traditional relations between neighbors, which make it very hard for one villager to report another villager's bad behavior to a government authority or an outsider." [10]

With the introduction of the *pao chia* system, the highly developed local self-government was demolished. The *pao chia*, as we know, was an administrative system which executed orders from above and at the same time managed local affairs. Under the traditional system, this double function was shared by three different groups, namely, the district official, the village headman, and the local leaders. Now it became the responsibility of the *pao tsun*, the chief of the *pao chia* administration, who was supposed to execute the orders of the central authorities. Such being the case, the government orders were absolute and no compromise could be made. The impractical and reckless *pao chia* system served to antagonize all classes of society and cost the Nationalist government the backing of the intellectuals—students in particular—who had earlier supported it, rousing them to stage protests, strikes, and demonstrations. Their discontent and agitation was one of the factors in the success of the Communist revolution in China.

[10] Martin Yang, *A Chinese Village*. New York, Columbia Univ. Press, 1945, p. 150.

3. Secret Societies

The secret societies are not in the strict sense an occupational group, but they have held an important position in Chinese society. The capacity of the Chinese for organization along these lines has been often noted, but no one has ever succeeded in getting to the bottom of their activity and organization. Generally speaking, in the beginning these societies were merely organized for social and financial reasons, but eventually they developed into political and religious machines. For instance, in the Han dynasty poor peasants, because of heavy taxation and landlords' exploitation, fled from their homes and became outlaws, under the protection of some powerful patrons. Then the patrons and outlawed peasants formed a syndicate to carry out certain financial or industrial projects. Such a syndicate was a secret organization, and its projects were largely illegal, such as illicit mintage, illicit mining, illicit woodcutting, and robbery. The patrons had, on the one hand, desperate outlaws as their followers and, on the other, enough money to bribe officials; thus they became very powerful members of society. The secret of their strength lay in the general impoverishment that displaced the people from their fields and turned them to outlawry. They were held responsible for all the social evils, regardless of the fact that the fundamental causes lay in maladministration. The secret organizations had at first nothing to do with politics, but when no proper measures were taken to alleviate the sufferings of the people, they precipitated antidynastic revolts. It is in the character of antidynastic organizations that secret societies became formidable in the imperial government.

These secret organizations, as they developed in the course of time, might be divided into two groups. One group predominated in North China and was called *Chiao* or *Chiao-tang,* literally the "Religious Sect," and another group predominated in South, West, and Central China and was called *Hui* or *Hui-tang,* literally the "Society." The *Chiao-tang* of North China was headed by the White Lotus or *Pai-lien Chiao,* which had a number of loosely organized branches. The White Lotus, which had its origin in Amitabha pietism, was chiefly religious, but in the first years of the Mongol dynasty it became a secret organization and participated in the antidynastic revolts. The *Hui-tang* was under the general leadership of the Hung Society (*Hung Men*), which was probably organized in the middle of the seventeenth century by the supporters of the Ming dynasty with the purpose of overthrowing the Manchus. Like most secret societies, the *Hung Men* had developed into many branches, two of which stood out prominently. One was called the *San-ho Hui*, or the Triple Harmonies, referring to the harmony of Heaven, earth, and man; it was also called the *San-tien Hui*, or the Triad Society, and was very strong in South China, taking an active part in Sun Yat-sen's revolution of 1911 and in the resistance against the Japanese invasion in the Second World War. The other branch, the *Ko-lao Hui*, or the Elder Society, flourished late in the Manchu period and was particularly strong in Central and West China. In recent times it was the most extensive and influential of China's secret societies. A majority of the overseas Chinese were affiliated with one or more of the southern societies.

Whatever their nature—political, religious, or social— these secret societies, built around the leadership of a grand master, were based on several factors. As in any other fraternities, loyalty constituted an important one. The members observed a code of "group ethics," including oaths and disciplines, which aimed at cherishing the knightly spirit—a sort of chivalry. For the good of their master and "brothers," they were ready to engage in any activity whatever; unless they practiced the *tao* of chivalry they were judged as unworthy to be the members of the society. Their first loyalty was to their fellow members rather than to the community or state.

Religious cults and ceremonies were another factor. In their nocturnal sessions, and complicated ceremonies of initiation the secret societies employed many Buddhist and Taoist emblems to deepen and strengthen a sense of solidarity, and their members were united under the common oath: "equally to share fortune and misfortune."

Of much greater significance was the factor of strict discipline. The societies employed passwords, hand signals, and mystic symbols concerning which members were pledged to keep absolute secrecy on pain of death. Thus they concealed their conspiratorial activities from the notice of authorities.

The secret societies, as we have noted above, were regarded as the source of resistance to and conspiracy against the existing administration. Against these organizations the Manchu government proceeded with the greatest possible severity, without achieving much success. However, under the Communist regime members of the secret societies, composed mainly of the peasantry and local tradesmen, have been liquidated as "reactionary elements."

1. The Function of the Family in Chinese Civilization

One of the outstanding features of Chinese civilization has been its emphasis upon social relations. The main objective of Chinese philosophy has been to achieve and maintain an orderly society. For instance, Confucianism, so long dominant in the intellectual and moral life of the nation, lays great stress upon right relations among human beings. In the course of centuries, the Chinese have developed many institutions and customs to conserve and perpetuate society, to give joint protection to individuals, and to strengthen proper relationships among the people. The basic and most characteristic Chinese institution has been the family. Moral conduct and ethical ideas arise primarily in the family; so do the fundamental functions of social organization.

The family, of course, constitutes an outstanding feature of the life of every nation. Among the Chinese, however, it has been emphasized more than among most other peoples. It has played a leading part in economic life, in social control, in moral education, and in government. In China there are five traditional social relationships—governmental, parental, conjugal, fraternal, and that of friendship. Out of these five relationships, three concern the family; the remaining two, though not familial relationships, can be conceived in terms of family. But these are only the major family relationships, and there were many more in ancient times. In the *Erh Yah*, the oldest dictionary of the Chinese language, dating from about the second century before Christ, there are more than one hundred terms for various family relationships, most of which have no equivalent in the English language.

The family concept in Chinese thought is very deep-rooted. All the past Chinese dynasties were hereditary and lasted for hundreds of years. This long period of heriditary monarchy inevitably strengthened the idea of family. Furthermore, in China most families have a history of several hundred years, so that we can trace descent by means of names. For instance, Confucius' ancestry can be traced to the beginning of the Shang dynasty in about 1700 B.C. The genealogy of the direct descendants of Confucius is known to the present day.[1] It is therefore no wonder that Confucius upheld family ethics and stressed family continuity. In fact, much of Confucianism is the rational justification of this social institution.

Under the term "family" may be included various types of organizations. There is what may be called the "small family," made up of a man, his wife, and their children. In China it has been common for several "small families" to dwell together under one roof and have a common life. The head of such a large family, by virtue of his wisdom, power, and position, commands the love and obedience of all its members. The leadership normally passes to the eldest son, but by common consent it may be entrusted to the son adjudged most worthy. Elders, including widowed mothers or grandmothers, may exert marked influence. This family system is especially adapted to an agrarian country, whose affiliations to the soil are very close. As China is predominantly agricultural by occupation, it is not surprising to learn that most Chinese people live where their fathers or grandfathers lived, and where their children will continue to live. The families are units of production; it is economically necessary for the members of the family to live and work together. As a result, the family was so well-defined and organized as to make it impossible for the Chinese people to forget their lineage. This form of social immortality has something of a religious appeal, which is enhanced by the virtue of filial piety and the ritual of ancestor worship.

The Chinese family system was originally the effective basis of government in the days of ancient feudalism, so that the family assumed many functions otherwise assigned to government, such as education, poor relief, support of the aged, and settlement of disputes among its members. It would be wrong, however, to imagine that feudalism was the cause of the family concept. As China was an agrarian coun-

---

[1] Confucius' descendant of the 72nd generation, K'ung Teh-chen, now living in Formosa, is devoted to learning and the study of ancient classics, as a custodian of Confucian teachings.

try, the Chinese family had land as its economic basis. It would be far from true, however, to say that the family appeared with the birth of private ownership. The family, based on blood relationship, is a natural growth. Moreover, in the feudalism of the Chou period there was no private ownership of land, but the Chinese family system was well developed as an important social institution. Throughout Chinese history the family, strengthened by a code of ethics sanctioned by ancestor worship, has influenced the molding of individual personality and ensured the perpetuation of the Chinese cultural pattern.

2. The Ethical Basis of the Chinese Family

Confucianism, as the philosophy of social structure, provides the ethical basis for the Chinese family system. In regard to society, Confucius stressed human relationships—every man in his proper place and with his proper responsibilities and duties. This is what Confucius called *ming fen*, the "rectification of names". *Ming* means "name," and *fen* means "duty". Every name in the social relationship implies certain responsibilities and duties. The Confucian doctrine is that if every man knows his duty and acts according to his duty, social order will be secured. This is the implication of Confucius' statement: "Let the ruler be ruler, the minister minister, the father father, and the son son" (*Analects,* XII, 11).

Mutual affection first arises out of the family, and then extends to the community. In other words, affection manifests itself in different degrees of intensity. From affection arises an appropriate attitude in a given moral situation, which one person assumes as reciprocal duty to the other. Thus for the parents, the appropriate attitude is kindness; for the children, filial piety; for the brothers, fraternity; and for the married couples, fidelity. Ethical relationship is indeed a relationship of affection and the appropriate attitudes that go with it. It is through the genuine fulfillment of the ethical relationships that exist in the family that the fulfillment of other relationships in the entire community is brought about. In other words, it is family affection that binds together all social relations, and hence is the basic unit of all social institutions.

This is what we know as the Confucian ethical principle, or what may be called the Chinese social norm. This concept of the social norm is indeed the significant contribution made by Confucius and his followers to Chinese civilization. They certainly believed that when every man was encouraged to practice filial piety and fraternal love his resulting right conduct, when extended to the larger social groups of which he became a member as his relationships expanded, would mean not only the regulation of the family but also the good government of the state, and eventually bring about the peace of the world. What is called filial piety and fraternal love in the family is known as loyalty and reciprocity in the wider sphere of social relations. The great virtues embraced in the ideal of the social norm comprehend the whole duty of man toward Heaven, toward himself, and toward his relations; and they are fostered in the family.

In this connection, a passage from the *Hsun Tzu* is worth quoting:

Li [rites] rest on three bases: Heaven and earth, which are the source of life; ancestors, who are the source of the human race; sovereigns and teachers, who are the source of government. Without Heaven and earth, where would life come from? Without ancestors, where would the offspring come from? Without sovereigns and teachers, where would government come from? If any of the three had been lacking, there would be no men or no peace. Therefore, according to the rites, man must pay homage to Heaven above and earth below, worship ancestors, and honor sovereigns and teachers. Herein lies the threefold basis of ritualism.[2]

This threefold basis of ritualism was probably symbolized in the five characters—"Heaven, Earth, Emperor, Ancestors, and Tutors"—glitteringly inscribed on the tablet which was once installed in the shrine of almost every household.

[2] Chap. 19.

3. The Cult of Ancestor Worship

Ethical concepts as expressed in the ideal of the social norm have contributed to the strength of the family. We have already noted that the social relationships—particularly the "five cardinal relationships"—are central in Chinese ethical teaching. Of these five relationships three concern the family; the ethical teaching in the family is the basis for general ethical teaching in the society. This explains why filial piety has been regarded as "the basis of virtue and the source of instruction." The Chinese word for "culture" or "religion," *chiao*, is composed of *hsiao*, filial piety, and *chih*, meaning "to support [filial piety]". So filial piety, according to Confucius, is not merely a domestic virtue, but diffuses its influence through all actions of life; it originates with the bonds of a common parentage and extends to other relationships until it reaches the stage of *jen*, or humanity —love due to men. As to the development of humanity, Confucius said: "A youth should be filial at home and brotherly abroad; then he should be earnest and sincere, and have kindly feelings toward all, but feel a disposition toward humanity" (*Analects*, 1, 6). With a keen sense of reality and practicality, Confucius made the virtue of filial piety the chief cornerstone of social structure. This is beautifully elaborated in the *Hsiao Ching*, or *Book of Filial Piety*: "Confucius said: 'The Superior Man teaches filial piety in order that man may respect all those who are fathers in the world; he teaches brotherly love in the younger brother, in order that man may respect all those who are elder brothers in the world.' "

Intimately connected with the practice of filial piety is the cult of ancestor worship. It is in fact on filial piety that ancestor worship is dependent for its existence. For the same reason that family system developed, ancestor worship developed. In a family living in a particular place, the ancestor worshiped was usually the first of the family who had established his descendants there on the land. He thus became the symbol of the unity of the family, and such a symbol is indispensable for a large and complex organization.

Ancestor worship, which binds one to all the preceding generations, has been used by Confucianism as one of the means to integrate the kinship group. The secular function of ancestor worship, as we know, is to cultivate kinship values, such as filial piety, family loyalty, and continuity of the family lineage.

For the common people, ancestor worship is the leading element in Chinese relation. Death in no sense breaks the bond between the members of a family. According to the Chinese people, the family consists of its dead as well as its living members. Every household has somewhere within its doors a small shrine in which are deposited the tablets of ancestors. Each clan has its ancestor temple, in which, as in the smaller shrines of the household, the objects of worship are not images, but tablets—strips of wood inscribed with the names of the deceased together with the dates of birth and death. In these tablets, according to popular belief, dwell the spirits of the dead. Incense is burned daily and twice in the month offerings of food are presented in honor of the dead; Outdoor worship, on the hills or at the tombs, takes place in spring and autumn.

It is to Confucius and Confucian scholars that China is indebted for the strictness with which the ceremonial rules and rites of ancestor worship are universally observed. These ceremonies contain much of superstition and mythology. In justifying them, Confucius and his followers gave them new interpretations and read into them new ideas. In so doing, they enabled the Confucian doctrine, as an ethical system, to work with religious elements in traditional Chinese society. In Confucianism the family, with its ancestral tablets in every household and its ancestral temple in every village or town, performs the function assumed by the church in Christianity. However, there is an important difference between Christianity and Confucianism as religions —religions in the broad and universal sense of the word, systems of teachings with rules of conduct which are accepted by the mass of population. In this broad and universal sense Confucianism, like Christianity, has become a religion; its teachings have been acknowledged to be true and its rules of conduct to be binding by the Chinese people. The difference is this: Christianity is a personal or church religion, whereas Confucianism is a social or family religion. The church religion of Christianity says: "Glorify

God and obey him," whereas the family religion of Confucianism says: "Honor your forefather and worship him." The church religion of Christianity says: "If you want to glorify God and obey him, you must first love Jesus Christ," whereas the family religion of Confucianism says: "If you want to honor your forefather and worship him, you must first love your parents." The essence of Christianity, the love of Jesus Christ, makes a man good in his individual life. The essence of Confucianism, the love of parents, makes a man good in his relations with his fellow men.

The cult of ancestor worship ensures the stability of the family. The stability of the family ensures the perpetuity of the society, which in turn ensures the immortality of the race. Hence the cult of ancestor worship in China depends not so much on the belief in the immortality of the soul as on the belief in the immortality of the race. A Chinese, when he dies, is consoled not by the hope of a future life, but rather by the underlying sentiment for the welfare of the coming generation, who will remember him, think of him, and love him to the end of time. The cult of ancestor worship is not a dead form, but a living faith; and it is this living faith that gives to the Chinese people the same sense of security while they live, and the same sense of consolation when they die, that the belief in the immorality of the soul gives to other peoples.

In the *Chung Yung,* or *Doctrine of the Mean,* we read: "The Master [Confucius] said: 'Filial piety is the force that continues the purposes and completes the affairs of our forefathers. . . . To gather in the same place where they before us have gathered; to perform the same ceremonies which they before us have performed; to play the same music which they before us have played; to pay respect to those whom they honored; to love those who were dear to them; in fact, to serve those now dead as if they were living, and those now departed as if they still were with us. This is the highest achievement of filial piety" (Chap. XIX). This passage makes explicit the influence of filial piety as a religious force in awakening and kindling in men the sentiment necessary to make them continue the purposes and activities of ancestors. The sentiment of filial piety so permeated the ceremonies of ancestor worship that the two were really one, and operated together in the transmission of accumulated culture from one generation to another.

4. The Institution of Marriage

In a society based on the family, the institution of marriage is of great importance. The purpose of the Confucian moral code was to transform the chaos of sexual relations into an orderly institution for the rearing of children. In the traditional society, sons were indispensable in carrying on the family line and in maintaining the honors to ancestors, and accordingly failure to have sons was regarded as a major offense against filial piety.[3] Marriage was a means of perpetuating the family line and ancestor worship. It is therefore not surprising to learn that the mating of couples was regarded as a concern of the elders and of the family.

In order that the institution of traditional Chinese marriage be understood, we must say something about its ceremonies. There were in every traditional marriage six ceremonies: (1) asking for the name (*wen ming*), i.e., formal proposal; (2) receiving silk presents, (*nei tsai*), i.e., betrothal; (3) fixing the wedding day (*ting ch'i*); (4) fetching the bride (*tsing ying*): (5) pouring libation before the wild goose (*tien yeng*), i.e., plighting the troth, so called because wild geese fly in pairs; and (6) temple presentation (*miao chien*).

Of these six ceremonies, the first three were the principal formalities necessary in the celebration of a marriage: The preliminary arrangements made by parents, with or without the help of go-betweens (*mei jen*), such as the exchange between the betrothed of the eight horoscopic characters pertaining to the year, month, day, and hour of their births, for purpose of comparison; the exchange of presents; and signing of the betrothal in public. Generally the prospective bride and groom had no voice in the arrangement and had not even seen each other until the wedding day. Betrothals were often made when the children were very small and could not easily be broken. They were, indeed, almost as binding as marriage. The fourth ceremony, fetching the bride, was generally dispensed with, as it entailed too

---

[3] "There are three things which are unfilial," said Mencius, "and the greatest of them is to have no posterity" (*Mencius*, IV-A, 27).

much trouble and expense to the bride's family. The bride, instead of being fetched, was sent to the bridegroom's house. When the bride arrived there, the bridegroom received her at the gate and led her to the hall of the house. There, in front of a table, spread with two red burning candles, dried fruits, and symbolic articles, the bride and bridegroom worshiped Heaven and earth and poured the libation on the ground in the presence of a pair of wild geese, thus plighting their troth. During the ceremony they vowed to be true to each other, like the pair of wild geese they saw before them. Then they did obeisance to each other. From this moment they became husband and wife, bound only by the moral code—the word of honor which they had given to each other—but not yet by the "civil law."

The ceremony of plighting troth might be called the moral or religious marriage as distinguished from the "civil marriage," which took place three days later. In the moral or religious marriage, the man and woman became husband and wife in the moral code—before Heaven and earth. The bride was not yet formally introduced to the members of the bridegroom's family. On the third day came the last ceremony, the temple presentation, which might be called the civil marriage. It took place on the third day in accordance with the rule laid down in the *Li Chi*, or *Book of Rites*. But to save trouble and expense, it was generally performed on the day after, either in the ancestral temple or before the miniature ancestral shrine of the household. The ancestral temple or shrine of the household, as we have noted, was the church of the Chinese family religion.

The temple presentation was extremely impressive. Incense was burned and ceremonial offerings of food and drink were presented. The father of the bridegroom or the nearest senior member of the family, on his knees before the ancestral tablets, reverentially announced that a young member of the family had brought a wife home into the family. The bridegroom and the bride, one after the other, went to their knees before the ancestral tablets. From this moment they became husband and wife before the "civil law," or the state.

A passage from the *Li Chi* presents the Chinese view of marriage: "Marriage is to make a union between two persons of different families, the object of which is to serve, on one hand, the ancestors in the temple, and to perpetuate, on the other hand, the coming generation." It was for this reason that the Chinese people were concerned about the assurance of having children, who would keep the fires burning on the family altar and make periodical oblations. Producing children might involve continuous sacrifices of many kinds, especially on the part of the mothers, but it served as the basis for a stable family life. Conjugal love, no matter how it started, was something that must be constantly created and nourished. A passage from the *Chung Yung* offers a good illustration of a happy home:

> When wife and children dwell in union,
> 'Tis like to harp and lute—well played in tune;
> When brothers lived in concord and in peace,
> The enduring harmony shall never cease.
> May you make your home always gay and bright;
> Your wife and dear ones shall be your delight.[4]

5. The Family Reform

The first challenge to the supremacy of the family came early in the beginning of the present century, when more and more Chinese began to hold the traditional family system responsible for "social evils" such as nepotism, clannishness, authoritarianism, conservatism, and so on. These critics, oriented toward the culture of the West as represented by the families of Western merchants and missionaries in China, sought to reform the system of parent-arranged marriage and emancipate women.

However, no effective measures were taken for family reform until 1931, when the Nationalist government promulgated the new Civil Code. The Law of Family and the Law of Succession, which were embodied respectively in Part IV and Part V of the Civil Code, aimed at introducing family reform and correcting the "evils" of traditional Chinese family life. These two statutes contain 258 articles divided into 10 chapters. The important measures for family reform may be summarized as follows:

1. Article 872 provides that "an agreement to marry shall

[4] Chap. XV.

be made by the male and female parties of their own accord." This opposes the system of parent-arranged marriage.

2. Article 982 provides that "a marriage must be celebrated by open ceremony and in the presence of two or more witnesses." This is to simplify the traditional wedding ceremony and to reduce its expense.

3. Article 985 provides that "a person who has a spouse may not contract another marriage," and Article 986 prohibits the marriage of adulterer and adulteress. This is to maintain monogamy and hence to eliminate concubinage.

4. Provisions are made for the dissolution of engagement (Article 976), annulment of marriage (Article 1052), and even divorce by mutual consent (Article 1049).

4. The new law also recognizes the property rights of women including the wife's right to hold separate and independent property, protected from infringement by the husband (Article 1044), as well as the right of inheritance (Article 1138).

In spite of these radical innovations, the family still remained a powerful institution among the Chinese people. This was due to the fact that only in the larger towns and cities and among the educated strata of the population was there understanding of the new provisions. Only in the cities did marriage by free choice tend to prevail; the majority of marriages were still arranged by the parents. Those values which spring from the traditional family were still cherished in the hearts of the people.

The most striking change made by the Communists, since their seizure of power in China has been the destruction of the old family system. A social revolution was set off when Communist agitators encouraged the poor farmers to struggle against the "landlord" classes and employees to struggle against employers. In a similar manner, a family revolution was started when the youngsters were encouraged to repudiate their parents and elders, and wives were set against husbands. The old family virtues, such as filial piety, respect for the aged, brotherly love, and conjugal devotion, which had been considered the ideological foundation of Chinese family solidarity, now come in conflict with loyalty to the Communist regime. Therefore the Communists have worked to uproot these "feudalistic virtues" and discard the "feudalistic relations" or the "patriarchal system." This is their first step to "revolutionalize" the Chinese family.

The second stage of the family revolution was signaled by the introduction of the Marriage Law of 1950. This was the first civil code introduced by the Communists after they took over the Chinese mainland. The complete statute is divided into eight chapters, with twenty seven articles. By the new marriage law, the Communists want to build up a "new democratic marriage, which is based on free choice of partners, on monogamy, on equal rights for both sexes, and on protection of the lawful interests of women and children" (Article 1). For this purpose, provisions are made for the prohibition of "polygamy, concubinage, child betrothal, interference with the remarriage of widows, and the exaction of money or gifts in connection with marriage" (Article 2). These provisions are not revolutionary in Western terms, nor are they radically different from the civil code of the Nationalist government. As it is enforced, however, the new marriage law is much more revolutionary and destructive than its provisions indicate. Marriage shall be the voluntary union of individuals, but to engage in economic production and to build up a new society are among the duties of husband and wife (Article 3). In other words, personal sentiments of love and mutual attachment must be subordinated to loyalty to the Communist Party and through it to the state. Armed with the ideology of Engels and Lenin, the Chinese Communists believe that love is not a personal but a social affair, and hence cannot be separated from politics. Only in this sense can one understand the tremendous emphasis placed on the registration of marriage and divorce as required in Articles 16 and 17. The primary objective at which the new marriage law has been aimed is weakening the marriage tie, as evidenced by the fact that divorce rates have increased and that hatred and suspicion have been stirred up among the members of the family. The Communists have been trying to introduce a new concept of husband-and-wife relationship, as well as a new pattern of courting behavior.

The deathblow dealt to the structure of family and society has been, however, the institution of the people's communes. According to the Communist theory, collectivism and the family cannot exist side by side, and therefore the major effort of the regime has been to destroy the time-honored solidarity of the family. By establishing community canteens, nurseries, kindergartens, and homes for the aged, they have worked to transfer to the communes most of the economic functions which previously belonged to the family. Worst of all, the family has been scattered: children are delivered to community nurseries; aged parents live in "homes of respect for the aged"; families move into barracks; in some localities, even wife and husband live in different dormitories. As has been noted previously, in the traditional society the members of the family had a great desire to be near one another. In the large family, members of several generations lived under the same roof. This has not been the case in Communist communities; Communist law has encouraged different domiciles for husband and wife. Under the communes, the people are ready to go wherever they are needed by the regime. "Family privacy" and "family affection" as things of the past have no place in the Communist cultural pattern.

The recent years of war dislocated the economic and social bases of the family and imposed broader problems than the family could solve. Thus the Communists have met with some success in their deliberate efforts to break up the family. Basic values of family life that have been called "feudal" and "reactionary" disappear with the disintegration of the family system. This change might have liberated the Chinese people, especially the Chinese women, from "the fetters of traditions," but it has not brought them happiness. The Chinese people have already paid a very high price for the family revolution.

CHAPTER VII. THE PEOPLE'S COMMUNES

1. The Communist Agrarian Policy

A cursory examination of the agricultural picture preceding the Communist period reveals that about five-sixths of China's huge population engaged in farming, but only about 10 per cent of the total land area including Manchuria was arable, averaging 3.5 acres per farm household or 0.7 acre for each member of a five-member household. Because of the small size of the typical farm, agricultural production was low and the peasants were poverty-stricken. However, the basic aim of Communist agrarian policy has been not to relieve the impoverished peasants, but to develop the collectivization of farming. Every step in the agrarian programs has been closely co-ordinated with the development of collectivization. It might seem that the Communists were taking an indirect way to promote collective farms by first dispersing land ownership among millions of tenants and farm laborers. But it would be difficult to carry out a program of immediate collectivization without going through the intermediate stages of agrarian reform and cooperative farming.

As promulgated in the Agrarian Reform Law of 1950, agrarian reform was designed for the abolition of landlordism and the distribution of lands to the poor peasants and farm laborers, providing a majority pressure group which could be relied upon for steady support of further collectivization. The Communists worked out different timetables for land reform to fit different areas in China. The general line and tactics were that "reliance should be placed on the poor peasants and farm laborers, while uniting with the middle peasants and neutralizing the rich peasants in order to eliminate the feudal exploitation system step by step and with discrimination, and to develop agricultural production." [1] One of the chief agencies in the implementation

[1] Liu Shao-ch'i, *Report on the Agrarian Reform Problem: Points for Attention during Agrarian Reform,* June 14, 1950.

of the land-reform program was the Peasants' Association, whose membership totaled more than 88 million, of whom about 30 per cent were women. It was one of the many mass organizations, like the Youth League, Women's Association, Children's Corps, and so on, set up by the Communists in the rural areas. These organizations not only were instrumental in strengthening the influence and control of the Communist regime, but also served as auxiliary agencies for the carrying out of agrarian reform programs. The Peasants' Association was often the sponsor of the "mass trials" against landlords, serving a variety of political, social, and psychological functions.

The land-reform movement continued on a massive scale for the years from 1949 to 1952. By the end of 1952, the movement was reported to have been basically completed on the Chinese mainland (except in Tibet and Sinkiang). According to official reports, in the whole course of reform some 700 million *mou* (one *mou* equals approximately one-sixth of an acre) of land [2] had been confiscated from the landlord class, to be distributed to some 300 million peasants who had previously held little or no land. Thus the average amount of land distributed to the peasants varied from 7 *mou* in North Manchuria to 1.5 *mou* in East China.[3] The division of land was too small to be conducive to agricultural development. As a result, the peasants were not so enthusiastic as expected, and productivity had not increased so markedly as "to provide more capital for industrialization."

The Agrarian Reform Law of 1950 had eliminated the landlord class, but still preserved the institution of private ownership of land. But the Communist policy was "to lead the peasants through several distinct, appropriate transitional stages to channel their enthusiasm for individual economy into mutual aid and cooperation; this will overcome any spontaneous tendency toward capitalism (a tendency springing from individual economy) and will put them on the

[2] Much of the data is controversial, with various authorities differing on the figures.

[3] See Chao Kuo-Chün, *Agrarian Policies of Mainland China: A Documentary Study (1949–1956)*, Cambridge, Harvard Univ. Press, 1957, p. 37.

road to socialism." [4] The Central Committee of the Communist Party issued two policy documents on this matter—*Decisions on Mutual Aid and Cooperation in Agricultural Production of 1951* and *Decisions of the Development of Agricultural Producers' Cooperatives of 1953*.

The stages in the development of collective farms are described in the following passage:

> To carry out the cooperative farming, the actual path to be followed begins with mutual-aid teams, voluntarily organized for the mutual benefit of the peasants, using collective labor, but on a basis of private ownership of property. Next come semi-socialist agricultural producers' cooperatives, with collective labor, common use of land, and single management. The last stage of the road is the higher form of cooperatives, the fully socialist agricultural producers' cooperatives—collective farms. [5]

The Communists reasoned that mutual-aid teams and cooperatives would "easily be accepted by the peasants and would also gradually reform the system of peasant private ownership." Just as the mutual-aid teams form the basis on which the agricultural producers' cooperatives develop, so the operation of the cooperatives prepares for collectivization.

Mutual-aid teams constituted the lowest form of collectivization and were in most cases organized on a seasonal basis for limited sharing of manpower, draft animals, and farm implements, but in the case of permanent mutual-aid teams, there would be some arrangement for unrestricted sharing of these assets. The peasants accepted this form of cooperation insofar as mutual aid means "collective labor, but on a basis of private ownership of property." In the early part of 1952 a large majority of peasant households joined mutual-aid or cooperative organizations, but since 1953 mutual-aid teams have been gradually transformed into agricultural producers' cooperatives. The land was pooled and worked as a unit; each member was credited with a number of shares which entitled him to a land dividend according to the size

[4] *Decisions of the Development of Agricultural Producers' Cooperatives,* Section II. See *Agrarian Reform Laws.* Peking: Foreign Languages Press, 1953.

[5] Teng Tze-hui, *The Outstanding Success of the Agrarian Reform Movement in China.* Peking: Foreign Languages Press, 1954, p. 18.

of the land which he originally invested. This was the intermediate stage of collectivization, which was often referred to as the lower-stage cooperative. The third and higher stage which preceded the establishment of the people's communes called for the common ownership of all the land and farm tools; that is, the collective farms. The principle of land dividends was abolished; payments were given out of the profits of the cooperative in proportion to the working hours which each member contributed. This is known as the socialist principle of distribution—"from each according to his ability, to each according to his work."

As a result of agrarian reform, the movement for cooperatives and collectives developed in varying degrees in different parts of the country. By the end of 1956 practically all the rural households had joined collective farms. In spite of this process of collectivization, there was some indication that China was still going through a severe economic crisis. The stepped-up production was unable to keep up with the population increase. Promised deliveries of goods to Moscow in repayment of loans were not met in their entirety. Further collectivization was deemed necessary to meet the demands on China's rural economy, which must feed the whole nation and also provide "surplus" agricultural products that help to pay for critically needed imports. Henceforth, all farm collectives, rural industries, and local militias would be consolidated into communes, which may be considered as the final stage of the collectivization movement.

The experiment began in April 1958 when the Weihsing (Sputnik) People's Commune in Suiping County, Honan Province, as a result of the "Great Leap Forward" movement that began in the winter of 1957, was established by the merger of 27 agricultural producers' cooperatives of four townships. The commune has 9,300 households comprising 43,000 people. This new experiment has been by far the most radical and ruthless yet; J. C. Harsch, writing in the *Christian Science Monitor*, termed it "the greatest mass sacrifice of human heritage, human comfort, and human effort in all time." [6] While it was undoubtedly an attempt to solve the pressing problems that confronted the Communist regime— China's rapidly increasing population, her inadequate food supply, and her lack of industrialization—it was also a means

[6] See *Christian Science Monitor*, December 24, 1958.

to put an end to the traditional society so as "to accelerate socialist construction and the transition to Communism." [7] On August 29, 1958, the resolution on the establishment of people's communes in the rural areas was adopted by the Central Committee of the Chinese Communist Party. By the end of 1958, there were 26,500 communes, which averaged 5,000 households each. There was another nation-wide mobilization of the masses, especially in the countryside, to produce pig iron and steel in back-yard furnaces. [8] For 1958, the Communist regime claimed a great leap in both agricultural and industrial output. But the commune movement was not the success claimed by the regime. The downward revision of the official figures for 1958 and the slowdown of the program for 1959 indicated that the Communist governnent had run into difficulty. However, this did not mean that there would be a reversal in the program itself; on the contrary, the goals of the commune program have been sturdily re-emphasized. In 1959 almost 500 million villagers were mobilized into a massive human work force, and the family was utterly destroyed as a social unit. Moreoever, urban communes came into existence in the beginning of 1960, and the Peking regime is now committed to their maintenance as inflexibly as to that of the rural communes. [9]

To recapitulate, the Communist agrarian policy after 1949 started with the program of agrarian reform, emphasizing land redistribution; went over in a few years to collectivization, making the shift from individual landownership through cooperatives to collective farming; and finally went on to the communes in 1958, uprooting the traditional family pattern and instituting collective institutions such as public messhalls, nurseries, "happiness homes," and so on. The basic aim of this policy is not so much the development of rural production as "the building of Socialism."

The problem of poverty among the peasants can be finally solved only if agricultural production can be

[7] See *Hong-gi* (*Red Flag*), No. 7, Sept. 1, 1958.

[8] The project was finally abandoned in the spring of 1959.

[9] The first urban people's commune was founded in the district of Chunshu, near Peking, in the autumn of 1958. See "Chunshu's Progress Report," in *Peking Review,* May 31, 1960, pp. 23-25.

greatly developed, if the industrialization of New China can be realized, if the living standards of the people throughout the country can be raised and if China finally embarks upon the road to Socialism.[10]

In the actual operation of the agrarian reform campaign, "socialism" as conceived by the Communists is a more important objective than productivity or raising the living standard. Only in this sense can one understand why the agrarian reform has moved toward collectivization, and finally toward the commune program, in which the individual loses land, equipment, wealth, and the freedom to act alternatively.

2. What Is a People's Commune?

Let us first proceed to a comparison between the commune and the collective. The commune is much bigger than the collective. The average commune as of the end of the year 1958 held 5,000 farm households, while the collectives contained only a few dozen, at most a few hundred families. A commune generally corresponds to a township. If a township is too small, then several townships may be combined to form a commune. And again, being large, the commune can undertake more fields of operation and extend its activities to a wider sphere than the collective. "It is no longer an organization dealing with agriculture alone . . . but a basic social unit which has as its task the over-all development of agriculture, forestry, animal husbandry, side occupations, and fisheries, and which integrates industry, agriculture, trade, culture and education, and military affairs into a single whole." [11] The commune represents a much higher degree of socialist development and collectivization than the collective. The Communists assert that it is the best form of organization for accelerating socialist construction and the transition to communism. Unlike the collective, where members were allowed to own their own plots of lands and

[10] See Liu Shao-ch'i, *Report on the Agrarian Reform Law: Points for Attention during Agrarian Reform*, June 14, 1950.

[11] See Wu Chih-pu's "From Agricultural Producers' Co-operatives to People's Communes," *Hong-gi*, No. 8, Sept. 16, 1958.

private property, the commune is the owner of all lands and other assets. In the method of payment, some of the communes were making experiments in both the wage and supply systems. This suggests that they are at the beginning of the transition to the stage of "from each according to his ability, to each according to his needs." [12] The commune is thus considerably more socialistic than the collective.

From this comparison, we may discern some significant features of the people's commune, such as (1) large membership; (2) the all-around management of agriculture, forestry, animal husbandry, side occupations, and fisheries; (3) the merger of industry, agriculture, trade, culture and education, and military affairs within the commune; and (4) the disappearance of private ownership and personal possessions. The commune, the Communist regime says, "will develop into the basic social unit in Communist society." [13]

As there is still not yet any universal blueprint concerning the commune, we may take the tentative regulations of the Weihsing (Sputnik) People's Commune as an illustration of its nature, organization, management, distribution, and welfare features. The Weihsing People's Commune, according to its tentative regulations, is "a basic unit of society in which the working people unite their own will under the leadership of the Communist Party and the People's Government"; "its task is to manage all industrial and agricultural production, trade, cultural and educational work and political affairs within its own sphere" (Article 1). As to the membership of the commune, the tentative regulations provide that "citizens who are over 16 years old are admitted as full members," but "former landlords, rich peasants, counter-revolutionaries and other people deprived of political rights may be accepted as unofficial members" (Article 3). "Unofficial members have not the right to elect, to be elected, or to vote in the commune, but they may enjoy the same economic treatment as full members" (Article 3).

Common ownership extends to certain means of production that were privately owned in the former cooperatives. The

[12] At present ownership in the commune is still collective, and the system of distribution is "to each according to his work" and not "to each according to his needs."

[13] Resolution on the Establishment of People's Communes in the Rural Areas, adopted by the Central Committee of the Chinese Communist Party on August 29, 1958.

tentative regulations provide that "when the agricultural producers' cooperatives merge into the people's commune, they must, regardless of excess or deficiency, turn over all their collectively owned property to the commune in the communist spirit of wide-scale coordination" (Article 4). Moreover, "the members of the cooperatives must turn over to the common ownership of the commune all privately owned plots of farmland and house sites and other means of production such as livestock, tree holdings, etc." (Article 5). As the commune is all-inclusive and supervises all agricultural, economic, cultural, political, social, educational, and military activities within its boundaries, the first things to be done in the Weihsing People's Commune are "to set up mines, iron and steel plants and factories for manufacturing ball bearings, farm tools, fertilizer and building materials and for processing farm produce, repairing machinery, building hydroelectric power projects, installations for utilizing methane, and other enterprises" (Article 6). As its massive-scale production requires organization with a higher efficiency and greater maneuverability of labor as well as the participation of all the women in production, community canteens, nurseries, sewing groups, old folks' homes, and other kinds of establishments are being set up (Articles 17-21). Since peasants working in large groups need discipline to ensure punctuality and a good work pace, its organization is along military lines; work squads, platoons, companies, and battalions can be transformed overnight into military cadres (Article 10). The commune, no longer solely an economic organization, combines economic, cultural, political, and military affairs into one entity. All this, the Communist regime says, will help gradually to eliminate the differences between town and country, between industry and agriculture, and between mental and physical labor.

The "congress of the commune," includes "representatives of all production brigades and all sections of the people" and elects the management committee to take care of the commune's affairs (Article 12). However, the commune must be under a "system of centralized leadership, with management organs at various levels, in order to operate a responsibility system in production" (Article 13). Members of the commune are grouped into several "production contingents" which are in turn divided into production brigades, basic units for organizing labor (Article 13). The production contingent has a representative conference, which is composed of the contingent's deputies to the commune congress and elects members to form its management committee and supervisory committee (Article 13).

According to the tentative regulations, the yearly income of the Weihsing People's Commune is divided under the following headings (Article 22):

1. Production cost incurred for the current year
2. Depreciation of public property
3. State taxes
4. Grain supply for members of the commune
5. Basic wages and awards for members of the commune
6. Public welfare funds, in general not exceeding 5 per cent of the total income, to be spent on education, health facilities, culture, and other welfare services
7. Reserve funds, comprising the remainder of the income, to be used for stockpiling and expanded reproduction (including the construction of transport facilities)

The tentative regulations further provide a wage system and a grain supply system on the basis of the principle "from each according to his ability, to each according to his work" (Articles 14-16). Those who work "energetically and do well" will be rewarded, while those who work in a "slovenly way and fail to carry out their assignment will be penalized through deduction from their wages" (Article 14).

What are the Chinese Communist' motivations for the establishment of the people's communes? A leading Chinese agricultural economist pointed out two possible reasons for the inauguration of the communes on a nation-wide basis in September 1958: (1) to suppress all revolutionary movements and consolidate the Red rule in China, and (2) increase agricultural production and step up industrial reconstruction.[14] This view has been challenged by many scholars. For instance, R. H. S. Crossman, a British Laborite journalist, has pointed out: "I am inclined to . . . conclude that the movement for the People's Communes did indeed come not from a remote official stratosphere but from that hard puritan

[14] Ch'iang Mon-lin's "Communist China's Commune Movement," *Central Daily News,* Taipei, Taiwan, December 7, 1958.

elite of peasant Communists who have emerged in their tens of thousands through the countryside." [15] Whatever their arguments, we are inclined to believe that the Communist choice of policy cannot be explained merely by economic motives.

The Communists had based their revolution on a promise to the peasants: "Land to the tillers." This promise had secured economic results, but if the regime had gone through with its "reformist agrarian policy" to appease the peasants, it would have been forced to abandon its political objectives. So when the time was ripe, the Communists did not hesitate to repudiate this promise and regiment the peasants into a system that had no place for private landownership and personal-asset possession. A program of rural collectivization was announced in 1954, and by 1957 practically all rural families had been organized into collectives. But the collectives had not been as successful as claimed; there arose in the villages numerous and almost insurmountable difficulties. Even more alarming was a general decline in agricultural production on the mainland as a result of collectivization. Meanwhile, there had been growing unrest in many parts of China, as evidenced by the nation-wide movement for the "liquidation of counterrevolutionaries." The "let a hundred flowers bloom, let a hundred schools of thought contend" campaign initiated by Mao Tse-tung in 1957 was originally intended to let off a part of the steam that had built up. The Communists, however, never expected that the movement would lead to nation-wide agitation. They not only failed to appease anti-Communist sentiment, but also tended to create an anti-party and anti-socialist movement. When the situation became worse, the regime resorted to another wave of liquidation, which concluded with huge numbers of people either executed or put into labor camps. The chain of events that led up to the development of the people's communes seemed to the Communists justification for taking a bold step which would not only suppress the popular revolt but offer a new and rational solution to the baffling agricultural difficulties. It was felt that if these difficulties were not promptly and effectively overcome, economic growth and political stability would be jeopardized.

[15] "The People's communes," *New Statesman*, January 10, 1959.

3. The Prospects

In the preceding chapters, we have attempted to show the general features of the Chinese traditional society, which was built on the family-and-village system, which the Confucian scholars strengthened with ethical concepts to foster a mass concern for human relationships. As a result, the Chinese people became absorbed in the affairs of family and village and took no active interest in government. Under this family-and-village system, it was assumed that if social conditions would change, or be brought to change, according to the normal courses as anticipated by the Confucian scholars, then a state of "good government" and "world peace" would be attained. However, the social conditions did not seem to follow the normal courses as anticipated, nor were the other factors kept intact. Hence there were social disturbances, which the classical economists called "frictions" in social phenomena. The Chinese Communists attribute all social disturbances to "deviation" (*pien chai*) caused by "brains not yet washed." Obviously, the causes for social disturbances are in the main such "originating forces" as civil wars, foreign aggressions, natural calamities, overpopulation, and maladministration. The traditional social system responded to these forces by effecting a series of changes in the social institutions such as family, government, and education. In this process of change, there are two salient points which deserve our attention. First, the social and economic bases of the Chinese society have been dislocated, and second, the traditional concept of social norm has been collapsing. Thus the Communists, although they cannot promptly brainwash the traditional social philosophy and codes of behavior with Marxian ideology, have been meeting with some success in their efforts to destroy the time-honored solidarity of the family-and-village system. If the Communists succeed in this, what is the likelihood of the success or failure of the people's communes?

It is evident that the Chinese Communists have reaped certain political and economic gains from the commune movement. First, the social structure has been greatly simplified by the amalgamation of farm collectives into communes. Management is centralized and therefore it is much easier for the Communist Party to carry on its political, economic, cultural, and social activities. Secondly, through the commune movement an immense army of people's militia has been organized; in peacetime the militia serves as the labor force, and in time of war it can be transformed overnight into an army. Thirdly, through the communes the Communists have strengthened their programs of local reconstruction in agriculture and industry, and by directing farm labor to non-agricultural uses, also averted large-scale rural unemployment. And finally, the commune system, by uprooting the traditional family and replacing it with collective institutions for dining, housekeeping, and so on, has made an enormous womanpower available for agricultural and industrial labor.

On the other hand, the commune system has also created many serious crises and difficulties for the Chinese Communists. In spite of the reports on "the happy life" of the peasants in the communes, traces of unrest and outright rebellion are still discerned. As early as September 1958 the peasants began to show discontent. The causes of the unrest were not confined to economic factors. In October 1958 purges took place in Liaoning and Shantung provinces with the result that the provincial governors were removed, and some 40,000 members of lesser party cadres were ousted from their posts.[15] Thousands of people were executed, imprisoned, or placed in labor camps. The threat against personal safety was ever-present, and a sense of insecurity was oppressive. This was enough to generate unrest. A further major blow was the disintegration of the family system in the communes. The Communists stated in December 1958 that husbands and wives had not been separated in different barracks,[16] but when people feed in common messhalls, children are brought up in common nurseries, and every hour of each individual's day is rigidly supervised, there is no private life, not to say family life.

Thus widespread discontent had been growing, particularly among the peasants. The December announcement of a slowdown in the organization of the program indicated

[15] See Stanley Rich, "Mao's Big Family," *New Republic*, January 5, 1959, p. 14.

[16] The announcement was issued by the Communist Party at the Wuhan Conference to slow down the program.

formidable opposition among the people. Henceforth many of the radical features of the commune system were modified. Greater allowances were made for the possession of personal effects, such as clothing, furniture, and savings; participation in communal messhalls became voluntary; parents were allowed to take their children home occasionally; except at times of harvest, every worker was assured eight hours' sleep, with four hours' freedom for meals and recreation, leaving twelve hours for "work and study." Thus at the end of 1959, the people's communes still remained in the transitional stage of socialism.

Although this suggests that the Communist regime has run into difficulty, there is no indication that a change of direction is in the making. The goals of the commune program have been sturdily re-emphasized. Toward the end of 1959 99 per cent of the country's peasant families had been incorporated into communes.[17] We have reasons to believe that for some time to come the communes will continue as basic social units and basic organs of state power. There are two important reasons why Communist China has been motivated to establish the people's communes in the rural areas. One is her ideology, which glorifies the venture into pure communism. The people's communes, which represent an advance from the Russian form of collectivization, will accelerate the speed of socialist construction and shorten the road to communism. If the Chinese Communists meet with success, they will have taken the lead in the race toward the eventual realization of the pure Marxist doctrine. Only in this sense can one understand the priority given to the "building of Socialism" in the Communist choice of policy. The second reason is related to the agricultural problem, which still awaits urgent solution. The 650 million people on the Chinese mainland, as well as the 13 million newly born babies every year depend upon agricultural products for their livelihood. The raw materials of many industries come from agriculture, and capital investment for industry is obtained through the sale of "surplus" agricultural products. For all efforts to increase agricultural productivity, massive labor forces are required, forces that can only be mobilized if the government maintains absolute control over the peasantry. The traditional family-and-village system must first

17 *Jenmin Jihpao* (*The People's Daily*), August 29, 1959.

be destroyed, then reconstituted into the massive production units of the people's communes. Every able-bodied worker, man and woman, is assigned to the fields, to irrigation projects, to factories and blast furnaces, so as to meet the needs of "Socialist reconstruction and industrialization." Whereas it is a moot question how far Communist China can realize her over-all aim—"the great leap forward"— it is certain that in the coming years the Chinese peasants will continue to expend their sweat and blood without hope of improving their servile lot.

Russia's collectivization resulted in an Age of Iron, which cost the USSR about ten million lives. It remains to be seen how many millions of human beings will be liquidated as the Communist leaders try "to fetch the Age of Gold" to the People's Government of the Republic of China. In this connection, the following passage from *Mencius* is worth quoting:

> Chieh and Chou [the wickedest rulers] lost their empires because they lost the people; they lost the people because they lost their hearts. There is only one way to hold their hearts—that is to get for them what they like, and not to impose on them what they dislike.[18]

History offers many examples that confirm this statement. Historical precedents do not doom the Chinese communist regime, but they cannot be dismissed as irrelevant.

[18] *Mencius,* IV-A, 9.

CHAPTER VIII

CHINESE LAW

1. The Conception of Law: *Li* versus *Fa*

There have often been discussions about the conflict between individual freedom and public welfare. In the ancient Chinese feudalistic society there were two kinds of codes. One was the code of honor, known as *li*,[1] which governed the conduct of *chün tzu*, or the aristocrats. The other was the code of punishments, known as *fa* (laws) or *hsing* (punishments), which governed the conduct of *hsiao jen*, or the common people. The *Li Chi*, or *Book of Rites*, says: "The *li* do not go down to the common people; the *hsing* do not go up to the ministers" (Chap. 10).

In the feudal period there was a great dividing line between aristocracy and commonalty. Kings, princes, and feudal lords were all related to each other either by blood or by marriage; being relatives, their personal conduct and social contacts were regulated by the code of *li*. Thus the *li* were social rules or "gentlemen's agreements." The kings and princes at the top had no direct dealings with the common people. They left such matters to the lesser feudal lords and nobles, who ruled the commoners under them on a personal and patriarchal basis. Hence laws and punishments were applied to secure the subordination of the ruled to the ruler. They therefore stood unquestioned as to their justice. It was probably for this reason that *fa* and *hsing* were supposed to denote

---

[1] The English language and Occidental thought seem incapable of supplying a term which can express the full meaning of *li*. To consider it as referring to propriety, or to the rules of etiquette, is to take a view too superficial. Although we use the term "code of honor," it really means more than that. In many connections, it might mean "social order," "social institutions," or "all regulations that arise from the relations between man and man."

a decay in government. And it was also probably for this reason that the people's rights found their protection in the virtue of the ruler. In the *Tso Chuan*, or *Tso's Commentary*, written about 400 B.C., it was said: "In our country what need is there for any code? When once the people know the grounds for contention, they will cast *li* [rules of propriety] away. . . . Disorderly litigations will multiply, and bribery will walk abroad. . . . There is a saying: 'When a state is about to perish, there will be many new codes.' " [2] In this passage, the belief is that more laws would produce more litigations and crimes. Too many lawsuits were considered to be a bad sign for the government. Hence Confucius said: "I can try a lawsuit as well as other men; the important thing, however, is to achieve that there be no suit" (*Analects*, XII, 13).

This Confucian attitude has been a part of the general Chinese tradition of dealing with litigations in a personal rather than an impersonal manner, stressing the administration of justice by good and virtuous men rather than relying on codes of law. Confucius had a low opinion of law conceived as a set of rules designed to prohibit people from doing wrong, and he said: "If the people are governed by laws and their conduct is regulated by a system of punishments [*hsing*], they will only try to avoid punishment, and will lose the sense of shame. On the other hand, if the people are governed by morality, and their conduct is regulated by rules of *li*, they will have the sense of shame and will also become good" (*Analects*, II, 3). Confucius thus ranked *li* above *fa* for the regulation of public and private behavior, applying the rules of *li* to the common people as well as to the nobles.

On the other hand, the Legalists, as typified by Han Fei Tzu, a scholar and acute thinker of the third century B.C., placed emphasis on the administrative system of *fa* and *hsing*. To make government depend upon the virtue of the rulers, said the Legalists, was to take a considerable risk. Not the rules of *li* but the codes of *fa* should rule, they argued. Moreover, they reasoned that as the states became larger and human activities became increasingly complex, public or civil offenses inevitably multiplied and the existence of codes

---

[2] Lao Tzu says: ". . . The more laws and edicts are imposed, the more thieves and bandits there will be" (*Tao-te Ching*, LVII, 126).

of law became a necessity. The Legalist conception of *fa* was in some respects similar to the Western conception of law, but its objective was very different from what is commonly thought of in the West as the objective of law. To Westerners, "the safeguards of the law" mean protection for the individual against arbitrary exactions by the government. The Legalists, however, regarded *fa* as an instrument for the control of the people by the government. In effect, *fa* constituted a set of rewards and punishments, which, they emphasized, should be administered fairly and impartially. "Rewards," Han Fei Tzu wrote, "should be generous and certain, so that the people will value them; punishments should be severe and inevitable, so that the people will fear them; laws should be uniform and definite, so that the people will understand them. Therefore, the ruler should reward without stint, and punish without mercy" (*Han Fei Tzu*, Chap. 19).

Here we have what Aristotle called "the vexed question whether the best law or the best man should rule." Hsun Tzu, the great Confucian thinker of third century B.C. and teacher of Han Fei Tzu, had tried to reconcile these two opposite views, maintaining that *fa* is documentary and *li* is its essential practice. According to his teachings, laws cannot be well enforced if the people do not behave in conformity with *li*. Hence *li* and *fa* are mutually supplementary in keeping social order and cultivating personal virtues. Hsun Tzu insisted that men cannot live without some kind of social organization, but in order to have a social organization, they need "rules of decorum," that is, the *li*, to govern their individual and social conduct.

Chinese tradition, under the influence of Confucianism, had been in a sense anti-legal, but it had never been lawless. It insisted that law should never be separated from the concept of virtue or morality and always placed equity and social justice above the letter of the law. This is especially emphasized in the Confucianist conception of *li* as "the code of honor" or "natural law" which is inherent in human nature. According to the teaching of Confucius, human nature is essentially good, and therefore the sanction of virtue is its being admirable and desirable. Thus Mencius said: "Men's mouths, as regards flavor, have the same taste; their ears, as regards music, enjoy the same sound; their eyes, as regards colors, appreciate the same beauty. Is there nothing in common among the minds of men? It is, I say, reason and justice. The sage only apprehended before us what is common to our mind. Therefore, reason and justice delight our mind, just as good food delights our mouths" (*Mencius*, VI-A, 7).

Human nature is originally good, but that does not mean that man is born perfect. His perfection consists in the full development of the four cardinal virtues: love, justice, propriety, and wisdom. But these four virtues have their "beginnings" rooted in human nature. Mencius said: "The mind that sympathizes is the beginning of love; the mind that detests evil as a shame is the beginning of justice; the mind that defers to others is the beginning of propriety; the mind that distinguishes right and wrong is the beginning of wisdom. These four beginnings are to the mind what the four limbs are to the body" (*Mencius*, II-A, 6).

Since the four cardinal virtues are rooted in nature, laws must be consonant with the essential nature of man. It is for this reason that law was not separated from the concept of virtue or morality. It is also for this reason that the rules of *li* were made not only the basis of law but also the beginning of it. According to the teaching of Confucianism, it is through these rules that man becomes a social being and it is through the highest development of these rules that he is guided through the complexities of social institutions—the family, the community, and the state.

2. The Codification of Law

The codification of law began very early in China, although traditional ethical custom, to which the adjustment of relations and ordering of conduct had been shaped, was opposed to such codification in the belief that the primary aim of Chinese law was to promote virtue or morality. Long before Confucius' time there existed already in China an unwritten and undefined code of *li*. These ancient *li* were at first sacrificial and religious in content, and later came to include all kinds of nonreligious observances on the occasions of life such as capping, (i.e., the giving of the cap worn by aristocrats to the young man coming of age), marriage, and mourning, as well as ceremonies observed in feasts, archery contests, and meetings of the feudal princes. In the twelfth century B.C. a great statesman—the man known as the great lawgiver of China, generally spoken as the Duke of Chou [3]—first defined, fixed, and made a written code of *li*, which touched all those activities that a state or community has at different periods found it necessary to regulate. Thus the written code of *li* to some extent replaced the laws by which the Western nations, following the Roman example, were able to maintain the social order.

During the Chou dynasty, there were many books on the code of *li*, and Confucius was keenly interested in the study of ancient *li*. There must have been many discrepancies between the written *li* of the Chou dynasty and the unwritten *li* of past ages; there must also have been many discrepancies between the traditional *li* of different feudal states. During the course of time, some reports were lost and some were incomplete. For this reason, not only did the feudal princes fail to understand the ancient *li*, but they even introduced new practices which were contrary to the spirit of the ancient *li*. As a teacher, Confucius was versed in the *li* not only of the Chou dynasty, but also of the two earlier dynasties of Shang and Hsia. However, it was the more complete and elegant *li* of Chou that especially captivated him. Confucius emphasized the origin and significance of given *li*, upholding the spirit of the ancient *li* against the ill practices of the time. Moreover, he popularized the code of *li* and insisted that not only the nobles, but the mass of the people as well, should be governed by them.

There were three prominent treatises on the subject of *li* in ancient times: the *Chou Li*, supposed to have been written by the great Duke of Chou, but most certainly a product of the Warring States period, if not later; the *Li Chi* (*The Records of Li*), a compilation of the Han dynasty, which may retain much of the original material of the Chou

[3] The Duke of Chou, whom Confucius highly praised as a model statesman, helped his father, King Wen, and his brother, King Wu, to found the Chou dynasty and to institute the feudal system.

period; and the *Yi Li* (*The Book of Ancient Li*), written after the time of Confucius and dealing with the proper observances of everyday life. These three books extend like a golden thread through all the ages, as the core of the Chinese legal system.

However, Chinese codes began to be inscribed in metal and placed on bronze tripods about 500 B.C. and thus in spite of the traditional prejudice against written law and the opposition of Confucian scholars, who saw in it a step toward litigation rather than a step toward justice, the written code system became well established and persisted throughout the following dynasties. We find, therefore, that from the Han dynasty down to the Manchu dynasty, there were always some codes of law in force, although the earlier codes did not persist. Of the various dynastic codes of law, the most important one is the Code of the Great T'ang in the seventh century A.D., which not merely simplified the administration of the law, but also gave the people some idea of the laws under which they lived. Indeed, this code has been found in the following periods as the basis of the modern codes. It is only by approaching the study of the *li* books and the dynastic codes, especially the Code of the Great T'ang, that we can understand the shape which the Chinese legal system has taken, its achievements in the past, and its influence upon the modern codes.

As the imperial government both in theory and practice remained personal, there was no opportunity for the development of the laws which the West calls legislative or municipal. China clung to the ancient legal institutions and ideas for the administration of justice. But when the need for a modern system of law arose after the revolution of 1911, efforts were taken for the revision of the imperial codes and penal reforms on Western lines. These judicial reforms were not pursued strenuously until the Nationalist government was established at Nanking in 1927. Then the Legislative Yüan began to draft a series of codes on the most important branches of law, such as the Civil Code, the Code of Civil Procedure, the Commercial Code, the Criminal Code, the Code of Criminal Procedure, and so on. While many of their provisions doubtless are indigenous in origin and distinctive in historical development, these codes no doubt borrow much from the laws of Continental countries. There is also much borrowing from Anglo-American law, particularly in the field of commercial transactions.

In their attempt to purge the country of everything "feudalistic" and "imperialistic," the Communist regime has rejected the Nationalist system of codes and made a new start on the basis of "Socialist principles." When we remember that the Communist law is not the product of adequate organs of lawmaking, has not yet developed an "ethical" tradition, and cannot serve as a basis for the development of a workable body of law for a modern society, it can be understood why the Communist code is merely a set of rules designed for the control of the people by the government.

3. The Administration of Law

In the traditional society, law was weak and unpopular. The people preferred to be governed by custom and tradition, and to settle their disputes peacefully among themselves, in a practical and simple way, through the medium of the headman. "Win your lawsuit, lose your money" was their motto. When there was a dispute, they would often request the headman to arbitrate. The headman would bring the litigants together and offer a compromise. If not successful, he would call up a committee, the members of which were selected by him, with the consent of the party litigants, for the settlement of the dispute. In the process of reaching a settlement, justice would be observed, custom and tradition would be considered, and the dispute would be arbitrated according to what was morally right. If no satisfactory settlement was reached, the dispute might be referred to the magistrate's court. But if the complainant had recourse to the magistrate's court without first referring the dispute to the headman, he would be subjected to public reprimand. In practice, this rarely happened, for this type of arbitration, known as the "headman adjustment," had grown out of the need of the people for a speedy and equitable administration of justice.

The magistrate's court, up to the end of the Manchu dynasty, functioned in a manner quite different from the modern court. Trials were simple and arbitrary; no lawyers were allowed to argue a case in court, though licensed notaries might prepare, and present to the magistrate, a statement in behalf of a client. Suspects were often arrested and detained; tortures were often used to elicit confessions; and punishments were severe. It has often been charged that the traditional magistrate's courts were incompetent and corrupt. Since the revolution of 1911 the Chinese people have been endeavoring to reconstruct the legal system along the pattern of the European Continental legal system. Because of the civil wars and foreign aggression, the new legal system has not met with success. However, the adoption of the new legal system has laid the foundation for limiting the administration of justice by codes of law. Legal procedure in the Republic of China recognizes three trials in three grades of courts, i.e., the supreme court, the high court, and the district court. The supreme court, as the court of final appeal, has jurisdiction over appeals against judgments in both civil and criminal cases rendered by high courts. The high court has jurisdiction over (1) cases of the first instance of insurrection, treason, and conspiracy against the government, and (2) appeals against the judgments in civil and criminal cases rendered by district courts. The district court handles all civil and criminal cases of the first instance. In addition to these, there is the administrative court, which is charged with the adjudication of all administrative suits. The people's courts of the Communist government have adopted the so-called three-level and two-trial system; as a result, a single appeal may ordinarily be allowed from the judgment of a lower-level court. The district people's courts are the basic courts of first trial, and the provincial people's courts are the basic courts of second trial. Generally, the provincial people's court trial is the final one, but in more important cases the provincial people's courts may conduct the first trial, with the appeal to the supreme people's court for a second trial.

However, we hold that the proper administration of justice depends not merely on a modern system of law but quite as much on a strong, well-trained judiciary and a strong, well-trained bar. Back of the development of an adequate bench and bar must be an adequate general education and particularly an adequate legal training. These are necessary to the due administration of justice anywhere. The Chinese have not had time, in a generation of revolution and war, to develop an independent judicial system.

Part Two: Chinese Thought and Learning

CHAPTER IX. THE SPIRIT OF CHINESE CULTURE

Modern science gives us the freedom to study the specific, but it deprives us of the ability to see life in its entirety. Human life is not compartmentalized. In dividing it into units we miss much that is significant. In Chinese culture we can discern a unity of spirit to which we find no parallel in Western culture. Chinese art, literature, philosophy, and religion are not confined each to its own circle of ideas, but are closely associated with one another. This is the fundamental spirit of Chinese culture, which may be considered from two points of view: that of cosmic conception and that of attitude toward life. In the former the spirit of Chinese culture is manifested as a continuous whole; in the latter it is manifested in the union of the individual with the whole.

1. Cosmic Conception

The Chinese cosmic conception is based on the assumption that all that happens in the universe, natural and human, is a continuous whole, like a chain of natural sequences. This is illustrated in the *Yi Ching,* or the *Book of Change*: "Following the existence of heaven and earth, there is the existence of all things. Following the existence of all things, there is the distinction of sex. Following the distinction of sex, there is the relation between husband and wife. Following the relation between husband and wife, there is the relation between the sovereign and the minister. Following the relation between the sovereign and the minister, there is the distinction of superiority and inferiority. Following the distinction of superiority and inferiority, there are the arrangements of propriety and righteousness" ("Orderly Sequence of Hexagrams," Sec. II).[1] This basic assumption, which conceives of the universe as a continuous whole, leads inevitably to the following characteristics of the Chinese cosmic conception.

First, the universe is regarded as a current, or "the great void": all in the universe is but a transitional process, with no fixed substance for its substratum. The universe is thus supposed to have no reality of its own, outside and independent of its phenomena. In Chinese writings the universe is often identified with the *Yi* (Change)—thus emphasizing that all things in the universe are ever in a process of change—or with the *Tao* (the Way, by which all things come to be). To quote again from the *Yi Ching*: "In the *Yi* there is the Grand Terminus, which generates the Primeval Pair. The Primeval Pair produce the Four Forms, from which are derived the Eight Trigrams. The Eight Trigrams determine the good and the evil, and from this determination is produced the great achievement" ("The Great Appendix," Sec. I, Chap. 11). "In the *Yi* there is no thought, no action. It is in itself still and calm; but, when acted on, it penetrates forthwith to all phenomena and events in the universe. If it were not the great mystery, how could it be found doing this?" (*ibid.*, Chap. 10).

In the works of Lao Tzu we read: "From the *Tao* there

---

[1] Though the commentaries on the *Yi Ching* were written after the time of Confucius, the text itself existed before his time. From this text, originally a book of divination, evolved the later Chinese philosophy. The system of the book has as its basis the eight trigrams (symbols composed of three lines each), which were supposed to be the symbolic representation of the eight worldly natural objects or phenomena. Then each of the eight trigrams was combined with all the others, resulting in sixty-four hexagrams (symbols composed of six lines each). Each hexagram was supposed to be the symbolic representation of one or more phenomena of the universe, either human or natural. All the hexagrams put together were supposed to represent symbolically all that had happened in the universe, from heaven and earth to the complexity of human affairs. The book is indeed a remarkable treatise in the history of philosophy.

comes One; from One comes Two; from Two comes Three; from Three comes all things" (*Tao-te Ching,* Chap. 42, Sec. 93). And: "There is something evolved from chaos, which existed before the creation of heaven and earth. It is inaudible and invisible; it remains eternal and immutable; it pervades and never ceases. It may be conceived as the Mother of heaven and earth. I do not know its name, and call it *Tao.* Arbitrarily, I may say that it is great; great means outgoing; outgoing, far-reaching; far-reaching, reversion" (*ibid.,* Chap. 25, Secs. 54-55).

These passages make two points clear. First, in the universe there is a cosmic force that is the source of life. The cosmic force is the *Yi* or the *Tao,* which generates One, or the Grand Terminus; and One, or the Grand Terminus, produces in turn the *Yin* (the passive element, the matter) and the *Yang* (the active element, the form)—a kind of dualism, as designated by Two, or the Primeval Pair. Through the interaction of the *Yin* and the *Yang* springs life, as designated by the Four Forms, out of which arise all things. And second, the *Yi* or the *Tao* is life, spontaneity, evolution, or a transitional process. The comment on the third line of the eleventh hexagram states: "there is no level place without a bank, and no departure without a return." This statement is regarded as the invariable law of nature, according to which all things undergo change. This is the *Yi* or the *Tao* of the transformation of all things.

This conception of the universe as a transitional process originates in the fundamental spirit of Chinese culture. The whole is not to be severed into units. From the standpoints of the *Yi* or the *Tao,* there is no separation of things; there are only phases of the same thing, such as the distinction between positive and negative, between subjective and objective. Thus in this state of experience there is nothing but the One, by which all things come to be. Apropos of this, Chuang Tzu said: "When there is life, there is death, and when there is death, there is life. When there is possibility, there is impossibility, and when there is impossibility, there is possibility. Because there is right, there is wrong. Because there is wrong, there is right" (*Chuang-tsu,* Chap. 2).

Things are subject to change and have many aspects, for "all these by means of the *Tao* are united and become One." By ignoring the distinction of contraries, such as life and death, possibility and impossibility, right and wrong, "we all are embraced in the unity of the One," by which all things come into being, naturally and spontaneously. The *Yi* or the *Tao* is the totality of the spontaneity of all things in the universe. Hence when we say that the *Yi* or the *Tao* produces all things we mean nothing more than the plain fact that all things produce themselves, naturally and spontaneously. Thus Confucius, looking at a running stream, exclaimed: "Alas! That which is passing is just like this, never ceasing day and night" (*Analects,* IX, 16).

The second basic characteristic of the Chinese cosmic conception is the principle that the universe does not proceed onward, but revolves, without beginning and without end. All phenomena in the universe move not toward a bourne whence nothing returns, but in a circular process. The entire universe is one continuous chain in which nothing is absolutely completed or finished. This may be illustrated by quoting a passage from the *Yi Ching*: "One who surpasses others is sure to remedy [evils that exist], and therefore the hexagram *Hsiao Kwo* [a little better] is followed by the hexagram *Chi Chi* [something accomplished]. But the succession of things can never come to an end, and therefore the hexagram *Chi Chi* is followed by the hexagram *Wei Chi* [something not yet accomplished]. With this hexagram [the *Yi*] comes to a close" ("Orderly Sequence of Hexagrams," Sec. II).

One hexagram is usually followed by another that is opposite in character—a conception that is prominent in the writings of many of the ancient philosophers. Here is a statement from the works of Lao Tzu on the evolution of the universe: "The way of heaven is like stretching a bow. When the upper part is leveled, the lower part is raised up. When the excess is diminished, the deficiency is replenished" (*Tao-te Ching,* Chap. 77, Sec. 170). This is the normal rhythm of nature. Were the universe to reverse the normal rhythm, it would cease to function. In the *Yi Ching* it is said: "When the sun goes, the moon comes; when the moon goes, the sun comes—the sun and the moon thus take the place each of the other, and their shining is the result. When the cold goes, the warmth comes; when the warmth goes, the cold comes—it is by this mutual succession of the cold and the warmth that the year is completed" ("The Great Appendix," Sec. II, Chap. 5). This is the invariable law of nature, that anything develops to its extreme, invariably reverts to its opposite; that is, to borrow an expression from Hegel, everything involves its own negation—though, according to Hegel, when a thing is negated a new thing commences on a higher level; whereas according to the Chinese philosophers, when a thing is negated the new thing simply repeats the old.

The earliest of the Neo-Confucianists of the Sung period (960–1279) were chiefly interested in cosmology.[2] Using deductions based on principles found in the *Yi Ching,* they were authorities on natural phenomena that presented examples of the circular process in the succession of day and night, the periodic ebb and flow of the tide, the disappearance and return of planets, and the other sequential phenomena.

Chou Tung-yi (1017–1073), for instance, known as the great cosmological philosopher, studied and developed the ideas found in the *Yi Ching* and used diagrams to illustrate the process of cosmic evolution. In his famous *Diagram of the Grand Terminus* (*T'ai Chi Tu*) he begins with a ring or circle of uniform whiteness, representing the *T'ai Chi,* or the Grand Terminus. Then follows a circle partly dark, which shows the primordial essence, differentiated into static and dynamic forces, called the *Yin* (the passive element) and the *Yang* (the active element). In his explanation of the diagram he said: "The Grand Terminus through movement produces the *Yang.* This movement, having reached its limit, is followed by quiescence, and by this quiescence it produces the *Yin.* When quiescence reaches its limit, there is a return to movement. Thus movement and quiescence, in alternation, become each the source of the other. The distinction between the *Yin* and the *Yang* is determined. . . . by their interaction [they] operate to produce all things, and these in their turn produce and reproduce, so that transformation and change continue without end" (*Collected Works of Chou Tung-yi,* Book I). This passage presents at least two ideas: that in the process of evolution everything involves its negation; and that in the process of evolution "transformation and change continue without end."

Another cosmological philosopher was Shao Yung

---

[2] See Ch'u Chai, "Neo-Confucianism of the Sung-Ming Periods," in *Social Research,* Vol. XVIII, No. 3, September 1951.

(1011–1077), who also deduced his system from the ideas found in the *Yi Ching*, and, like Chou Tung-yi, made use of diagrams to illustrate his cosmological theory. According to Shao Yung, the *Yin* can be interpreted as merely negation of the *Yang*. Hence if the *Yang* is the constructive force of the universe, the *Yin* is its destructive force. On the basis of the interaction of the *Yin* and the *Yang*, he illustrated the universal law that everything involves its own negation, a principle that was stressed in the *Yi Ching* as well as in the works of Lao Tzu. This law applies not only to the alternation of seasons throughout the year, but also to the alternation of day and night every twenty-four hours. Even the world as a whole is no exception to this universal law. Thus Shao Yung maintained that the world, when it has reached the golden age of civilization, is sure to degenerate; when it has reached the age of decay, is sure to be renovated.³ The world is thus created and destroyed.

The third cosmological philosopher was Chang Tsai (1020-1077) who, like his predecessors, based his cosmological theory on the *Yi Ching*. His theory especially emphasized the idea of *Ch'i* (Matter), a concept that became more and more important in the cosmological and metaphysical theories of the later Neo-Confucianists.⁴ In his *Cheng Meng*, or *Correct Discipline for Beginners*, Chang Tsai said: "The Great Harmony is known as the *Tao*. Because in it there are interacting qualities of floating and sinking, rising and falling, movement and quiescence, there appear in it the beginning of the emanating forces which agitate one another, overcome one another, and contract or expand, one with regard to the other" (*Collected Works*, Book 2). The Great Harmony is a name for the *Ch'i*, or

³ In the *San Kuo Yin Yi*, or *Romance of the Three Kingdoms*, it is laid down as a law of the national life, confirmed by history, that the world, when it has been long united, is sure to be divided; when it has been long divided, is sure to be reunited.

⁴ "In the universe," said Chu Hsi (1130–1200), "there are *Li* and *Ch'i*. The *Li* is the *Tao* that pertains to 'what is above shapes,' and is the source from which all things are produced. The *Ch'i* is the material that pertains to 'what is within shapes,' and is the means whereby things are produced. Hence men or things, at the moment of their production, must receive this *Li* in order to have a nature of their own. They must receive this *Ch'i* in order to have their bodily form" ("Reply to Huang Tao-fu," *Collected Works*, Book 58).

Matter in its entirety, which Chang Tsai described as "wandering air." The qualities of floating, rising, and movement are those of the *Yang,* while those of sinking, falling, and quiescence are those of the *Yin.* Thus the *Ch'i,* influenced by the *Yang* qualities, floats and rises, while, influenced by the *Yin* qualities, it falls and sinks. Hence the *Ch'i* is constantly either condensing or dispersing. Its condensation results in the creation of things; its dispersal results in the dissolution of these things.

This conception of the universe as a circular process, like the conception of the universe as a transitional process, originates in the fundamental Chinese conception that the whole is not to be severed into units. The universe is composed of pairs of opposites, such as good and evil, right and wrong, subjective and objective, positive and negative. In the process of evolution every phenomenon involves its own negation. We cannot have, for instance, a positive without a negative, or vice versa. They are correlatives. Thus the universe proceeds in cyclic recurrence, without beginning, without end.

And finally, the third basic characteristic of the Chinese cosmic conception is that it envisages no divine power that controls the motion of the universe. Lao Tzu said that within the universe there are four great ones—*Tao,* heaven, earth, and king—but God is not one of them (*Tao-te Ching,* Chap. 25, Sec. 56). Confucius considered man to be the center of heaven and earth, and spoke of heaven as being on the side of righteousness. Mencius, who lived in the fourth century B.C. and represented the idealistic wing of Confucianism, identified human nature with heaven (in Chinese, *tien,* which is sometimes translated as heaven, or divinity, and sometimes as nature). Hsun Tzu, who lived in the third century B.C. and represented the realistic wing of Confucianism, even ventured to argue that heaven could be controlled for human purposes.

An exception was Mo Tzu, who lived in the fifth century B.C. and founded the Mohist school, opposing the traditional institutions and practices and theories of Confucius and the Confucianists. He preached the principle of all-embracing love and embodied the principle in a personified God: "Those who desire wealth and honor must obey the will of God," but also "I do what God wills, while God endows me with what I deserve" (*Works,* Chap. 26). Thus the relationship between God and man is one of reciprocity, and indeed, God helps only those who help themselves. Moreover, Mo Tzu had only an inconclusive argument to prove the existence of God and His power: "All people are the subjects of God. Why does He not love them? Besides, I said that one who kills the innocent must have bad fortune. Who kills the innocent? Man. Who imposes the bad fortune? God" (*Works*, Chap. 26). This inconclusive argument was refuted by later philosophers. But Mo Tzu, like most practical philosophers, had no interest in pure metaphysical truth. His doctrine of the will of God was intended only to induce people to believe that they will be rewarded if they practice all-embracing love, and punished if they do not. In other words, Mo Tzu simply used the divine power as a motivating force for his principle of all-embracing love, which, like that of Confucius, is essentially human and this-worldly.

Then, in the Han school of thought, which aimed to make Confucianism the orthodox belief of the Han dynasty, we are told that heaven punishes the unjust with bad fortune and rewards the just with good fortune. But the concept of heaven as conceived here is personified; thus it is no longer the center of power, but simply a way in which the good or the evil of man is given reward or punishment. It is so because of the design of man, not the will of God. Consequently, reward and punishment by heaven are the results of man's own efforts. During the Sung-Ming periods, Neo-Confucianism identified *tien li*, or heavenly reason, with the conscience of man. There can be little doubt that this philosophy must have helped to confirm and perpetuate the fusion and intermixture of the authority of God with the power of man, and the decree of heaven with the laws of government.

The absence of a conception of a controlling divine power may be illustrated by reference to Chinese mythical legends and fables. In the mythical and legendary period of Chinese history we encountered the figure of Queen Nu Kua, who repaired heaven with colored stones; that of King Hou Yi, who shot at the sun with an arrow; and that of K'ua Fu, who chased after the sun—but we have never found any legendary figure who created heaven and earth. The Chinese lack a poetic mythology to advance a practical conception of the creation of the universe. Even P'an Ku, the "Chaos Man," who seems to have come into being endowed with perfect knowledge, had the function of setting the economy of the universe in order, not of creating it. He is often depicted as wielding a huge adz and engaged in constructing the world. With his death, the details of creation began. His tears became rivers and seas; his breath, wind; his voice, thunder; his pupils, lightning; and the parasites infesting his body were progenitors of the human race. Thus P'an Ku did not create the universe; the universe came into existence after his death.

Here again, in the lack of a conception of divine supremacy in the universe, we find a reflection of the fundamental conviction of Chinese culture that the whole is not to be severed into units. Divine power or a Creator owes its existence to a unit that is subtracted from the whole. But the Chinese cosmos is a united whole, undivided and indivisible. Anything divisible must be divided by something other than itself. Since there is nothing other than the whole, there cannot be units apart from the whole. Consequently, the idea of supreme power or a Creator cannot be conceived.

2. Life Attitude

Now let us turn to a consideration of the characteristics of the Chinese attitude toward life. Chinese philosophy posits not antagonism but continuity in the world, as is illustrated by the following characteristics.

First, the Chinese see life as good. Buddha said that life itself is the root and fountainhead of its misery. To the Hindus the present world is "a sea of bitterness" and life is like a dream. And according to Christianity, endless evils emerged from life after the fall of man. But the Chinese, so far as their literature is concerned, are not pessimistic in their outlook on life. In Chinese philosophy the expression of a distinctively pessimistic type of thought is wanting.

Even Yang Chu, who probably lived between the times of Mo Tzu and Mencius (a chapter representing his philosophy is contained in the *Lieh Tzu*, a Taoist work of the third century), held a view of life only slightly tinged with pessimism. According to his view, life is short, and a great part of it, strictly speaking, is not life. Therefore, "we ought to hasten to enjoy life and pay no attention to death." In his basic outlook Yang Chu was a hedonist rather than a pessimist, "despising things and valuing life." His hedonist ideas are reflected in the ancient classics: "There is a man whose policy is not to enter a city which is in danger, not to remain in the army. Even for the great benefit of the whole world, he would not exchange one hair of his shank. . . . He is one who despises things and values life" (*Han-fei-tzu*, Chap. 50). "Preserving life and maintaining what is genuine in it, not allowing things to entangle one's person: this is what Yang Chu established" (*ibid.*, Chap. 13).

Reflection of this hedonist idea can also be found in the works of the great Taoist philosophers. In the *Tao-te Ching* of Lao Tzu we read: "Therefore, if a man esteems the world as much as he esteems himself, he will find safety therein. If a man loves the world as much as he loves himself, he will find security therein" (Chap. 13, Sec. 25); and "fame or life—which is more precious? Life or property—which is worth more?" (Chap. 44, Sec. 97). These passages again express the idea of despising things and valuing life. And also in the works of Chuang Tzu we read: "When you do something good, beware of reputation; when you do something evil, beware of punishment. Follow the middle way and take this to be your constant principle. Then you can guard your person, nourish your parents, and complete your natural term of years" (Chap. 3). According to the early Taoists, this is the best way to preserve life against the harms that come from the human world.

Nearly all the philosophers of the Confucian school appreciated the good of life. Thus we read in the *Yi Ching*: "For the universe, the most essential is life. For the sage, the most precious is the state. That which maintains the state is man. That which maintains the people is wealth. The administration of wealth, the education of people, and the prohibition of wrongdoing are his righteousness" ("The Great Appendix," Sec. II, Chap. 1). Nature is life; state, wealth, education, and prohibition are all to make life better. Confucius' own life is certainly a good example of this aspect of his teaching. Disapproving of the degeneracy of his own times, he turned at an early age to the vocation of reformer. He traveled everywhere and talked with everybody. Although his efforts were in vain, he was not disappointed.

Among the Chinese, every man, rich or poor, educated or uneducated, has a passionate love of life. All are imbued with this one great ideal, which touches their common existence in every direction and furnishes an important and steady influence on the nation. The Chinese may lament over their human ills, but they never curse life as such. Whatever may be their innermost thoughts, they bear their crushing burdens and desperate privations with extraordinary fortitude and little complaint. What they insist on is simply the idea that in order to live well, one must live; but in order to live, one must try to get the best out of life. Feeling the continuity of the whole, the Chinese do not seek for the "happy land" outside the world, because one cannot be totally excluded from this world.

The second characteristic of the Chinese attitude toward life is that it cherishes *jen* (human-hearted) love. Love is an emotion common to mankind, but *jen* love is peculiar to the Chinese. If we were asked for a definition of *jen* love, we would confess that we could not give any precise answer. Perhaps the same purpose will be served if we present some of the leading traits that distinguish it from Buddhist love, Christian love, and Platonic love.

Buddhist love is charitable, motivated by charity, as exemplified in the life of Buddha. Usually it takes the form of compassion. Is it not charity to men that the abbot expressed when he said: "My desire is to pluck every creature that is endowed with feeling out of this sea of bitterness"? Thus the lover and the loved live in two different spheres of existence. Christian love, on the other hand, is cosmopolitan. Jesus Christ offered a faultless example of a life dominated by love. "For God so loved the world that He gave His only begotten son, that the world through Him might be saved." It is the will of God that man should love his neighbor as himself. Platonic love, finally, is abstract. The phrase "Platonic love" is on the lips of many, but usually with a meaning quite different from Plato's own conception of love. According to Plato, love is always concerned with beauty. Having learned to love beautiful objects, the soul passes on to love other beautiful objects. Platonic love lays stress on the idea of beauty.

According to the Chinese *jen* love, the lover and the loved live in the same world, for each other and with each other. *Jen* is fundamental in Chinese love, just as compassion is dominant in Buddhist love. "*Jen*," Confucius said, "consists in loving others" (*Analects*, XII, 22), and therefore he held that human relations should be based on the moral sentiment of *jen* leading to positive efforts for the good of others. "*Jen*," said Mencius, "is the love due to man. . . . One who loves men will certainly be loved by them." This is the first point. The second point is that *jen* love is based on fairness. It is not equal and universal love. It manifests itself in different degrees of relative affection, such as filial piety, brotherly feelings, conjugal love. Hence *jen* love plays its part in the relations between different kinds of people; its exaggeration or total absence would upset the social order. This fact serves to distinguish it from Christian love. The third point is that Platonic love is too subtle an idea for popular comprehension. Ancient Chinese thinkers considered beauty one of the virtues, and virtues are cultivated by man. Hence *jen* love is based not on the idea of beauty but humanity.

We may conclude that *jen* love is love of humanity. The Chinese do not follow God or Buddha in loving others; nor do they conform to any abstract ideal of loving others. Their love is mainly humanistic, and has been displayed in Chinese cultural achievements for thousands of years. The Chinese do not divide the universe into two different spheres of existence; they live all in the same world, occupy themselves with human relations, and pass on to the love of others —again a merging of the unit in the whole.

The third characteristic of the Chinese attitude toward life is its rational approach to happiness. The Chinese are well known as a cheerful and easily contented people; they have always been jealous of their right to happiness, which no poverty or disgrace can take away from them. In the *Analects*, we read: "The master said: 'The wise are free from doubts; the virtuous, from concern; the courageous, from fear'" (IX, 28); and "The master said: 'The superior man is completely at ease; the petty man is always on edge'" (VII, 36). Thus Confucius made happiness the chief requisite of the way of the "superior man."

The Chinese have always been interested in the problem of happiness, and their approach to it is very rational. A Chinese depends for his happiness not on external circumstances, but on his own virtue. He wants only what leads to happiness, and at the same time does not insist on having what is beyond his reach. The Chinese have much to offer to counteract our modern ills, particularly by showing the folly of self-seeking and the value of contentment. "One who is contented is always happy" is a saying that contains much of human wisdom. As for himself, Confucius said: "To eat only vegetables and drink only water, with bent arms for pillow, I am still happy in such a life. But ill-gotten wealth and honors are to me as wandering clouds" (*Analects,* VII, 15). This spirit of happiness is found in both the educated and uneducated classes, for such is the penetration of the Chinese racial tradition.

The Chinese attempt no separation of happiness and virtue. Happiness and virtue are correlatives which are complementary to each other. "One who has not tasted the bitterness of life can never be expected to appreciate the sweetness of life." This maxim has taken so strong a hold on the mind of the Chinese as to have molded their mentality and temperament. The theory of virtue as its own reward is too abstract for the mass of mankind. The great majority of the people are so utilitarian that virtue has no charm when it is totally dissociated from happiness. Thus happiness must not be divorced from virtue. The fundamental principle underlying the combination of happiness and virtue is the continuity of the universe: happiness and virtue are simply phases of a continuous whole.

Fourthly, the Chinese favor enjoyment of the present life, and are not much concerned with a life in a world to come. Of the four objects on which Confucius would not speak, "spiritual being" was one. When he was once asked by a disciple about the meaning of death, Confucius replied: "Not yet understanding life, how can you understand death?" (*Analects,* XI, 11). This is not to imply that the Chinese deny the existence of a spiritual world; it means that they attach paramount importance to the world of humanity.

Westerners attempt to secure rewards in another world by working and suffering in this world; for instance, the Greek "spiritual world," Plato's "intellectual world," and the Christian "city of God" took shape from the hope for a "paradise." Westerners' attitude toward life looks outward upon the external world; they emphasize the expansion of power in space, and strive for a future world in which all that is bad and ugly in the present world will be metamorphosed into the good and beautiful. Thus their life tends to sever the world into units, and to separate man from heaven. It is this that determines the character of the Greco-Roman-Christian attitude toward life.

The Hindus are impressed by the transitory nature of

things, and lament over the endless ills of life. They profess to draw man away from the world and its vanities, in order to reach the freedom and peace of Nirvana, that is, to attain the extinction of consciousness by ascetic exercises. Thus they need not sever the whole into units, for neither exists; nor do they need to separate man from heaven, for both have passed beyond the sphere of sensory perception.

But the Chinese, unlike the Hindus, believe that in the present world there is enough good for us to enjoy. The Chinese have no "lost paradise" in the past, and hold to no promise of an afterlife. They look inward upon themselves, emphasizing the continuation of life in time and looking for the betterment of life in the present world. Thus a Chinese, when he dies, is consoled not by the hope of a future life but by a sentiment for the welfare of the coming generation.

To the Chinese mind the universe is a united whole. For the universe there is no end of evolution; for man there is no end of activity. The union of the universe and man is called "perfection." In the *Chung Yung,* or *Doctrine of the Mean* (traditionally attributed to K'ung Chi or K'ung Tzu-ssu, the grandson of Confucius), it is said: "Perfection is the beginning and end of things. Without perfection there can be nothing. Therefore the superior man considers the attainment of perfection as the most excellent" (Chap. 25). It is for this reason that the Chinese do not look for another "happy land" on which depends the hope of immortality; nor do they believe in a former state of existence to which the fate of present life is attributable. Their constant endeavor is to maintain the continuity of the present, in which all things are in harmony and in accord: "All things live together without injuring one another; all courses are pursued without collision with one another" (*ibid.,* Chap. 30).

And lastly, the Chinese are possessed of a sense of moderation. Westerners lay emphasis on the hope of entering the "Kingdom of God," which means the creation of a new world. Hindus place stress on the hope of reaching Nirvana, which means renunciation of the world. Being too extreme, both fail to maintain the balance of the universe. But the Chinese hold the position of the mean. In the *Yi Ching,* the sixth line of the first hexagram, *Chien* (the symbol of Firmness, representing heaven), is "the dragon in extreme," about which Confucius said: "When things are carried to extreme, there will be occasion for repentance" (Sec. I, Chap. 1). The *Yi Ching* says: "Therefore the superior man, when resting in safety, does not forget that danger may come; when in a state of security, he does not forget the possibility of ruin; and when all is in a state of order, he does not forget that disorder may come" ("The Great Appendix," Sec. II, Chap. 5). This is also the doctrine of Lao Tzu: "Calamity will promote blessing; blessing, too, underlies calamity. Who knows the end of this cycle? How can there be absolute right? The right may turn out to be wrong; the good may turn out to be evil. Man has thus been so long astray" (*Tao-te Ching*, Chap. 58, Sec. 129).

This passage provides the principal argument for the doctrine of the golden mean, about which the ancient sages and philosophers often talked in their teachings. The doctrine has had a great influence on the Chinese people: they remain cautious even in the time of prosperity, and hopeful even in the time of extreme danger. To attain the mean is not, however, to pursue a middle course; it is to maintain the balance of the universe, a state of harmony and a doctrine of equality. In other words, this is a way of action that avoids going to extremes, a state of mind in which human reasoning and feeling reach perfect harmony. This is why the ancient sages and philosophers taught the Chinese to attempt "never too much"—that is, not to be one-sided and extreme, but to attain the mean in order that the balance of the universe may be maintained.

3. Conclusion

Harmony and orderliness, as they appear to the Chinese people, are omnipresent in both natural phenomena and human relations. Nature presents examples of harmony and orderliness in the succession of day and night, the periodical ebb and flow of the tide, the disappearance and return of planets, and other observable sequential phenomena. The ancient sages and philosophers instituted rites to maintain orderliness, and music to establish harmony. In the *Li Chi*, or *Book of Rites*, one of the three prominent treatises on the subject of rituals in ancient times, Confucian scholars of the Han dynasty gave interpretations of the ancient rites.

Music imitates the harmony of the universe; rites imitate the orderliness of the universe. There are heaven above and earth below, and between them are the various things with different ranks and dignity. This gives man the pattern of rites. There is the unceasing stream of evolution, in which all things are in harmony and in accord. This gives man the model of music. In the spring all things burst forth with life; in the summer all things grow. This is human-heartedness. In the autumn all things mature; in winter all things rest. This is righteousness. Human-heartedness is akin to music; righteousness is akin to rites. [Sec. I, Chap. 18.]

CHAPTER X.   THE DEVELOPMENT OF CHINESE
PHILOSOPHY

1. "A Hundred Schools Contend"

The Chou period (1122–255 B.C.) is known to historians
of Chinese culture as the Classical Age and is compared to
the Golden Age of Greece. Just as the Greek classical culture has been the norm for the West, so the Chou culture is
the model for China. There is no question that the Chous
more than any others had shaped the Chinese cultural inheritance. The Chou period, especially from the sixth through
the third centuries B.C., saw the flowering of ancient Chinese
philosophy and gave rise to the so-called "hundred [i.e.,
sundry or various] schools" of philosophy, among which
Confucianism and Taoism—the two main streams of Chinese thought—were two important ones. The "hundred
schools" have been generally classified into six schools of
thought; namely, the Taoist school: Taoism; the Ju (Literati)
school: Confucianism; the Mohist school: Mohism; the
Legalist school: Legalism; the Yin-Yang school: "Occultism";
and the school of Names: "Sophism." [1] Of the six schools of
thought only the first four have made lasting contributions
to Chinese philosophy, although the Yin-Yang school and
the school of Names provide a rich field for scientific research and discoveries. The Yin-Yang school was in fact an
offshoot of the Taoist school, believing in the existence of
Yin (female) and *Yang* (male) as the two cosmic principles

[1] The six schools of thought were originally mentioned in
Ssu-ma T'an's "On the Essential Ideas of the Six Schools," as
compiled in the *Shih Chi*, or *Historical Records*—the first his-
torical work of the modern type, written in the second century
B.C. For a detailed study, see Ch'u Chai and Winberg Chai, *The
Story of Chinese Philosophy*, New York, Washington Square
Press, 1961.

in whose interaction all changes in the universe were produced. It was also known as the *wu hsing* (five elements) school because of its fantastic theory that each period of history was characterized by one of the five elements—i.e., earth, wood, metal, fire, and water. All its writings perished, and it later became associated with occult matters, magic, and charms, and failed to develop an independent system of thought. The school of Names evolved from the Mohist school, and its members were a group of sophists and dialecticians. They later became politicians versed in the art of speech, but they could not claim to be philosophers.

With respect to its influence on Chinese life, Chinese philosophy can be classified into four main systems: Taoism, Confucianism, Mohism, and Legalism. All the others were merely offshoots that grew from these four main streams of thought. The Chou period, as mentioned above, was an age of intense political, social, and intellectual activity, in which all established conventions and institutions came in for destructive criticism. "Such a criticism of life," said Josiah Royce in the *Spirit of Modern Philosophy,* "made elaborate and thoroughgoing, is philosophy" (p. 2). In fact, men begin to philosophize only when they feel that the world is not so good as they wish. All the great philosophers of the Chou period saw the same problems arising from the current political and social turmoil; they differed in their respective criticisms of these problems. As a result of their criticisms, great schools of thought were produced and great systems of philosophy established.

Men like Lao Tzu (570?–?480 B.C.) and his followers, seeing that the world was not so good as they wished, thought that there must be something radically wrong in the very nature and constitution of society and civilization. They told the Chinese people to throw away all conventions and institutions. They believed that man had had a paradise but had lost it through his own mistakes, through his own efforts to fetter himself with the bonds of civilization. According to them, the right way of life was to retreat from civilization to primitivism—from the state of culture to that of nature, untarnished by world contacts and unfettered by human rules. This is the naturalistic line of thought known as Taoism, which is based on the exaltation of *Tao* and idealization of nature.

The Taoists all regarded nature as their great retreat,

simple living as their ideal life, and *wu wei* (inaction or noninterference) as the essence of their teachings. But because of their different interpretations of the concept of *Tao*, they divided themselves into two different schools, the one represented by Chuang Tzu (350?–?275 B.C.), and the other by Yang Chu, who lived between the fifth and the fourth centuries B.C. Chuang Tzu considered *Tao* as the totality of spontaneity of all things in the universe; it leaves all things to develop themselves, naturally and spontaneously. This view represents the idealistic aspect of Taoism. But Yang Chu considered *Tao* as a blind physical force; it produces the world not by design or will, but by necessity or chance. This view represents the materialistic aspect of Taoism. In the works of Lieh Tzu, a Taoist philosopher who flourished some years before Chuang Tzu, we find both of these views. Certain chapters deal with the teachings of Chuang Tzu, and others with those of Yang Chu. Whatever their differences, their teachings, deducible from the doctrine of *wu wei*, emphasize that man should be in accord with his nature and be content with his destiny.

There was another important group of men, as represented by Confucius and his disciples, who, disgusted by the chaotic state of society and civilization, thought that the evil was not in the nature and constitution of society and civilization, but in the wrong direction that society and civilization had taken. They told the Chinese people to preserve the social and cultural institutions, and pleaded for a return to the ceremony of the early Chou period. As we know, it was Confucius who had first taken the Chou classics from the imperial archives and presented them to the public; it was he who had transformed the feudal ceremonies into a system of ethics; and it was also he who had tried hard all his life to establish and maintain an orderly society by laying stress upon proper relations among men, according to the doctrine of *jen*, or human-heartedness.

Confucianism has dominated Chinese thought for the last twenty-five centuries. It had its beginning in the teachings of Confucius, but in the work of building its foundation, Mencius (371?–?289 B.C.) and Hsun Tzu (298?–?238 B.C.) took the lead. Though both Mencius and Hsun Tzu revered the teachings of Confucius, they differed from each other not only in character, but also in their teachings. As we have seen, the period of the Warring States (403–221

B.C.) was an age of free thinking, in which various schools of philosophy arose to vie for supremacy. Disgusted by the intellectual anarchy, Mencius felt in duty bound to defend the teachings of Confucius against the heterodox teachings of other schools. For his contributions to Confucianism as well as for his defense of the great tradition, Mencius has been publicly honored as the "Second Sage," next only to Confucius. Like Confucius, Mencius based his teachings on the doctrine of *jen*, but he claimed that for the cultivation of virtues *jen* should be coupled with *yi*, or righteousness: "What one upholds in his heart is *jen*; what one upholds in his conduct is *yi*." Thus *jen* is the "sound principle" of warranting internal sentiment, while *yi* is the "proper way" of guiding external conduct. In his effort to find a psychological basis for the principles of *jen* and *yi*, Mencius arrived at the doctrine that human nature is innately good, his main contribution to Chinese thought.

Another great champion of Confucianism was Hsun Tzu. He was an exponent of the principles of Confucius, but a critic of Mencius, especially concerning his doctrine of human nature. If Mencius represented the idealistic wing of Confucianism, then Hsun Tzu might represent the realistic wing. He was realistic in that he emphasized social control and insisted that man's nature is evil. Hsun Tzu, although he had been nurtured in the Confucian tradition, exalted the functions and prerogatives of the state, so warmly advocated by the Legalists. This has much to do with his relatively low position in the Confucian school. However, he was no totalitarian. Hsun Tzu was in fact eclectic in ideas, for he absorbed not only the teachings of Confucius, but also the best thought of the other schools. In so doing, he summarized for the use of posterity the intellectual achievements of the various thinkers in the most creative period. In the *Hsun Tzu* there is a chapter, "On Freedom from Blindness," in which he criticizes the various schools of thought and holds that their views represent only "single aspects of the *Tao*." "The essence of the *Tao* is constant and includes all changes. It cannot be grasped by a single corner. Those with perverted knowledge and seeing only a single aspect of the *Tao* will not be able to comprehend its totality" (Chap. 21). Hence Hsun Tzu, though a follower of Confucius, did not hesitate to take in anything that he considered good and useful for his own system of thought.

A third group of men, as represented by Mo Tzu (470?–?391 B.C.) and his followers, were interested in the same problems as the Taoists and Confucians, but reached other conclusions. Mo Tzu, coming from a low stratum of society, taught a philosophy of life corresponding to the desires of the common people and hence diametrically opposed to the aristocratic leanings of both Lao Tzu and Confucius. He told the Chinese people that their happiness was in the promising future, not the dead past. According to Mo Tzu, the right way of life is not negatively to undo something, as Lao Tzu advocated, but rather positively to do all things; not passively, as Confucius maintained, to sustain the Chou society and culture, but rather actively to build a different and better world. This is the utilitarian line of thought known as Mohism. Mo Tzu gave us not only an abstract principle of utility, but also a complete structure of society, state, and religion, which was built upon that governing principle.

Mo Tzu made utility the root of all the virtues. Benefit and harm were the standards for judging right and wrong, good and evil. In his book he says: "Benefit is what one likes to have. Harm is what one dislikes to have" (Chap. 40). In order to understand his principle of utility, we need to see what he meant by the words "benefit" and "harm." Mo Tzu pointed out that what produces more good than evil is benefit and what produces more evil than good is harm. Hence we must often forgo a benefit if it leads in the end to a greater harm, and likewise we must be ready to undergo harm if it leads in the end to a greater benefit.

In order to take "the greatest of the benefits and the smallest of the harm," there must be external and objective standards for judging benefit and harm, good and evil, right and wrong. "For testing an argument, there are three standards: . . . to trace it, to examine it, and to use it. Where to trace it? Trace it in the authority of the ancient sage-kings. Where to examine it? To examine it in the facts which the common people can see and hear. Where to use it? Put it into practice and see whether it is useful for the benefit of the country and the people. These are the three standards for argument" (Chap. 35). These three standards represent three methods of study—the historical method, the experimental method, and the pragmatic method. The historical method is to look for the authority of the past, the experimental method is to investigate the facts of the present, and the pragmatic method is to foresee the consequence of the future.

The principle of utility explains everything on the basis of its usefulness for the benefit of the country and the people. Mo Tzu taught the doctrine of all-embracing love and urged the people to believe in Heaven as an active power manifesting love for all men, because it seemed to him to be the most "useful for the benefit of the country and the people." He was ready to fight against anything that seemed to him to be incompatible with the benefit of the country and the people. He was against luxuries, extravagant funerals, long periods of mourning, and other feudal rites at the expense of wealth which should be used for the food and clothes of the people (Chapters 20, 22, and 25). The philosophy of Mo Tzu calls for the sacrifice of immediate pleasure for the benefit of the future.

In addition to the three great systems of philosophy, there were the Legalists who made their influence felt from about the middle of the Chou period (seventh century B.C.) to the Ch'in period (third century B.C.). The writings bearing the names of Kuan Tzu and Han Fei Tzu are generally classified as belonging to the Legalist school. Kuan Chung was a well-known minister in the state of Ch'i in the seventh century B.C., but the book *Kuan Tzu*, attributed to him, was certainly a later forgery. Characteristic of the Ch'un-Ch'iu period (722–481 B.C.), his emphasis was on propriety, justice, prudence, and temperance. His teachings in fact represent the transition in thought from Taoist doctrine to Legalist ideas. In the *Han Fei Tzu* we have a complete synthesis of the Legalist ideas of the fourth and third centuries B.C. The Legalist ideas, as propounded by Han Fei in his book, originated in the *shih* (authority) of Shen Tao, the *shu* (statecraft) of Shen Pu-Hai, and the *fa* (law) of Shang Yang. Han Fei took Hsün Tzu's theory of human nature for his contention that law is essential in keeping social order and peace, and Lao Tzu's doctrine of *wu wei* for his political principle that the elaborate legal machinery of government should function of its own accord, obviating the necessity for personal intervention of the ruler. In short, the Legalists, as typified by Han Fei, stood for firm and autocratic government and for laws as the framework of the social order, and hence they came in direct conflict with the Confucian scholars, who stressed the ethical values and personal influence of the administration. This had much to do with the notorious edict of 213 B.C., issued by the Ch'in emperor Shih Huang Ti (First Emperor), at the instigation of his Legalist minister Li Ssu, ordering the destruction of the ancient classics, especially the books of the Confucian school. As a result of this edict, the intellectual activity of the previous period came to an abrupt end.

Such, in outline, are the four great systems of philosophy of the Chou period—Taoism, Confucianism, Mohism, and Legalism—as represented by the great thinkers of this period, whose teachings and ideas have continued to play a dominant role even in our own day. Though these four great schools of thought differ widely, they have influenced and colored one another, and together have shaped the character of Chinese philosophy as a whole.

2. The Revival of Learning

Before the Ch'in dynasty (255–206 B.C.) there was much intellectual freedom and progress, and there were a "hundred schools" of thought. In the new age that followed, there was need of unity both in the intellectual and political spheres. For this purpose, the Ch'in emperor Shih Huang Ti decreed that all writings of the "hundred schools" of thought in public circulation, and all other literature except works on medicine, divination and agriculture, be delivered to the government and burned. This decree ensured that there should be no freedom of thought, and as a result, Chinese philosophy, more particularly Confucianism, suffered a decline and lost much of its vitality and appeal.

The Han dynasty (205 B.C.–A.D. 220) was marked by the resurrection of Confucian classics and the revival of letters. Though they disapproved of the drastic methods of the Ch'in, the Han rulers also attempted to unify the thought of the empire in order to maintain political unity. This new attempt was made by the Han emperor Wu (140–87 B.C.), who, instead of rejecting all schools of philosophy indiscriminately, selected Confucianism and gave it pre-eminence as the state orthodoxy. This innovation was attributed to

Tung Chung-shu (*c.* 179–104 B.C.), the greatest of the early Han scholars. In a memorial presented to the emperor in the year 136 B.C., he advocated a system of education based on Confucianism. Thus it was he who created the institutional basis for Confucian orthodoxy, the famed Chinese examinational system. However, it should be noted that Confucianism as propounded by Tung Chung-shu and adopted in the early Han period developed into something very different from the early Confucianism of the Chou period. What Tung Chung-shu tried to do was to work out a new philosophical interpretation and justification for the Han imperial institution. His work is one of the great achievements of Chinese thought.

Han Confucianism was tinged with the ideas of other rival schools, especially those of Taoism. Mohism had failed to revive as a vital philosophy after the drastic measures taken to suppress the "hundred schools"; and Legalism, which helped to unify the imperial rule by strict regulation and autocratic power, had fallen into disgrace, but its political theory still lingered in the mind of the ruling class. However, Taoism, the chief rival of Confucianism, had in the early Han period become very influential among government officials, who adopted the Taoist doctrine of *wu wei* as their state policy and its occultism as their personal creed. This fact determined the general character of Han Confucianism.

Generally speaking, the Han scholars divided themselves into two groups: one known as the New Script school, so called because its version of the Confucian classics were written in the current script, and the other as the Old Script, so called because it claimed to possess the ancient texts which existed before the time of "the Ch'in fire"—that is, the burning of books. The controversy between these schools was one of the greatest in the history of Chinese scholarship. Their disagreement on the texts of the Confucian classics was accentuated by a difference in their views about Confucius and Confucianism. The New Script school considered Confucius as a "throneless king" and a savior of the world, as claimed in the apocryphal literature. In opposition to this view, the Old Script school maintained that Confucius was essentially a sage and inherited the cultural legacy of the past, which he gave new interpretations and transmitted to posterity. The view of the New Script school would seem absurd, but it became popular in the Han period. All the circumstances of the time were adapted to favor forgery. Pecuniary rewards, imperial favor, and popular esteem, all encouraged zealous scholars to exercise their inventive faculties in the production of plausible substitutes for lost books. Zeal for the Confucian school may be counted as another motive; and scholars were not averse to expressing their own ideas in the name of Confucius. The absurdity of the New Script school, more than anything else, was responsible for its ultimate decline in the second half of the Han dynasty. Meanwhile, the influence of Taoism had spread, together with that of Buddhism, which had been introduced from India in the first century after Christ, or even earlier; and Chinese philosophy blossomed afresh during the ensuing period.

3. Introduction of Buddhism

The period from the third century to the tenth century was the age when Chinese civilization began to be infused with the culture of foreign countries. The philosophical thought of this period might be represented by the Taoist metaphysics of the Wei-Tsin period (220–420) (known as the *hsüan hsüeh* in Chinese—literally, "mysterious learning"—which is in fact a continuation of Taoism) and the Buddhism of the Sui (581–618) and T'ang (619–907) dynasties, which had little connection with politics, but exercised a great influence on Chinese culture. During this period, Buddhism of Indian origin, in collaboration with Chinese Taoism, flourished in China and overshadowed Confucianism: its scriptures, translated into Chinese, grew to vast proportions, and its temples and monks multiplied so rapidly that they had to be checked by imperial decree.[2]

Here it should be noted that there is a distinction be-

---

[2] By the imperial decree of the year 845, 40,000 Buddhist temples were destroyed, 250,000 monks and nuns were secularized, and a tremendous acreage of land belonging to the temples was confiscated.

tween the terms "Chinese Buddhism" and "Buddhism in China." To state it briefly, whereas "Buddhism in China," as represented by the School of Subjective Idealism (known as the *Hsiang tsung* or *Wei-shih tsung* in Chinese, or the Vijnanavada School), is the form of Buddhism that clung to the Indian tradition and played little part in the development of Chinese philosophy, "Chinese Buddhism," as represented by the Middle Path School (known as the *San-lung tsung* in Chinese, or the Madhyamika School), is the form which has been close to Chinese thought and developed in conjunction with Chinese philosophy. As we know, there is some similarity between the Middle Path School of Buddhism and Chinese Taoism, and their interaction with each other resulted in the Ch'an (known as Zen in Japanese, or the Dhyana) School.

The Chinese term *ch'an* or *ch'an-na* is derived from the Sanskrit *dhyana*, which is usually translated in English as "meditation." Originally, *ch'an* meant "directly pointing to the human mind" and "to become a Buddha by seeing one's own Buddha-nature" or "by identifying the individual with the Universal Mind." This is to be achieved through meditation. Ch'anism is a philosophy of silence through its emphasis on "a special transmission outside of the Sacred Teaching." Its Meditation doctrine is based not on classic Buddhist scriptures, but on enlightenment through "the realization of the idividual original identification with the Universal Mind." Interpretations of the Universal Mind among the Ch'an masters are various, but in general it is conceived as the Void, that is, something that cannot be designated by words or perceived by physical senses. Hence to penetrate the Universal Mind, Ch'an masters either urged *wu nien,* absence of thought; or advocated *wang ching,* "ignoring our feelings"; or recommended *jen hsin,* "letting the mind follow its own course."

From the above, it is by no means surprising that the teachings of the Ch'an masters have much in common with Taoism. It was said of Hui-neng (627–713), founder of the Southern School of Ch'an, that "he did not at all understand Buddhism. He understood *Tao* and no other thing." As a matter of fact, the early Buddhist writers used Taoist terminology (such as *yu,* "being"; *wu,* "nonbeing"; *yu wei,* "action"; and *wu wei,* "nonaction") to express Buddhist ideas. Sudden Enlightenment, which leads to Buddhahood, is often referred to by the Ch'an masters as the "vision of *Tao*." Thus Buddhism of Indian origin, synthesized with Chinese Taoism, was transformed into a Chinese form of Buddhism.

The most significant element of Ch'anism is the mind. The mind must be sharpened and sensitized before it can be identified with the Universal Mind. For this purpose, the Ch'an school developed various techniques which are quite different from those of Indian dhyana. As a result, Chinese *ch'an* can be distinguished from Indian dhyana by two major points, and we need only to mention them briefly. First, whereas Indian dhyana is conceived as religious enlightenment and stresses concentration and the ability to ignore outside influence, Chinese *ch'an* is regarded as philosophical wit and emphasizes wisdom and the ability to handle critical situations. Second, whereas in Indian dhyana the mind tries to neglect the external world and aims at intellectual understanding, in Chinese *ch'an* the mind works in this world and aims at self-realization.

In short, one of the chief contributions of Buddhism to Chinese thought is the doctrine of Universal Mind, which assumed an important role in the Neo-Confucianism of the Sung (960–1279) and Ming (1368–1644) dynasties. Before the introduction of Buddhism there was in Chinese philosophy only the mind, but not the Mind. On the other hand, when Buddhism in China became Chinese Buddhism, it lost its spiritual tradition and became colored with Taoist ideas. Its interaction with Taoism resulted in the Ch'an school, which, by the time Neo-Confucianism was being advocated in the Sung period, was the only Buddhist school of any consequence.

4. The Rise of Neo-Confucianism

The period from the tenth century to the seventeenth century was another important age of Chinese philosophy, and noted for the rise of *Li Hsueh Chia,* or the School of Study of *Li,* usually known in the West as Neo-Confucianism.

The word "Neo-Confucianism" is in fact a misnomer. It does not stand for a genuine revival of Confucianism. The Neo-Confucianists were no doubt Confucian scholars, but their intellectual activity was stimulated and determined by the speculations of Ch'an masters. They assumed the tasks of criticism, reviewed the evidence of antiquity, and recorded their conclusions. Thus Neo-Confucianism was a kind of summing up or revision of the ethics, morals, and beliefs of the past, and as such was in keeping with the spirit of the times. It contained the principles of Confucianism in a new form, tinged with Buddhism. Just as Buddhism interacted with Taoism and emerged as Ch'anism, so Confucianism interacted with Buddhism and emerged as Neo-Confucianism, or *Li*-ism.[3]

The close relationship between Buddhism and Neo-Confucianism may be seen in the following illustrations. The state of Nirvana, according to Buddhism, is a state of mind of stillness. To Confucianism, for the universe and the human mind the essential state is permanent activity; thus the *Yi Chiang, or Book of Change,* declares: "The movement of the heavenly bodies is constant, and the Superior Man seeks to improve himself without rest." Neo-Confucianism developed the concept of "stillness which is in constant activity, and activity which is in constant stillness." This conception has been applied and expanded in the doctrine of mind. There are several illustrations which the Neo-Confucianists liked to cite: The mind is like a mirror; all the varied images that fall upon its surface are unceasingly active; the mirror remains still and is not bewildered. The mind is like the sun; the clouds pass and vanish under it, but the sun remains constant and is not affected. The mind is like the vast surface of the sea; the waves rise and fall over it, but the general level remains calm and is not disturbed. For the mind is not outside the activity; it is in fact the mind that is active; but while it is active it remains still. This is the union of stillness and activity. This is the highest and best state of mind.

The Buddhists held that the visible world is an illusion, a fiction; it is unreal, empty, the Great Void. But the Con-

[3] See Ch'u Chai, "Neo-Confucianism of the Sung-Ming Periods," *Social Research,* Vol. XVIII, No. 3, September 1951, pp. 370-392.

fucianists believed that there is an objective world, coexisting with man's own subjective idea of it. The Neo-Confucianists accepted the teaching of Buddhists that the external world is an "emptiness," a void, but insisted that it has a kind of illusory substantiality. Chang Tsai (1020–1077), great philosopher of the Sung period, said: "The immensity of space, though called the Great Void, is not void at all; it is filled with *chi* [primordial essence]. In fact, there is no such thing as a vacuum" (*Collected Works of Chang Tzu*, Book II). The word *chi* is a concept which became very important in the cosmological and metaphysical theories of the later Neo-Confucianists.

And again, Buddha said that life is the root and fountain-head of its misery, and to the Buddhists the present world is "a sea of bitterness" and life is like a dream. Hence Buddhism is generally regarded as an "otherworldly" philosophy. On the other hand, Confucius was "this-worldly" in his outlook, and the Confucianists are essentially humanistic, occupying themselves mainly with human relations and virtues, studiously shunning all questions that enter into ontological subtleties or partake of the supernatural. Hence Confucianism is generally known as a "this-worldly" philosophy. To the Neo-Confucianists, both Buddhism and Confucianism are one-sided; the former is illusory and divine; and the latter too practical and humanistic. Neo-Confucianism, impressed by the continuity of the world, has attempted to reconcile the practical "this worldliness" of Confucianism and the "other worldliness" of Buddhism; that is, to make the divine more human, and the human more divine. It was said of Neo-Confucianism that "it is not divorced from daily ordinary activities, yet it goes straight to what antedated Heaven." [4] This is to show that Neo-Confucianism attempts a synthesis of traditional Confucianism with Indian Buddhism.

However, there was a divergence of thought among the Neo-Confucianists that led ultimately to the formation of two separate schools, the rationalistic and the idealistic. By the Chinese the former is called the Sung school of the twelfth century, and the latter the Ming school of the fif-

[4] Fung Yu-lan, *A Short History of Chinese Philosophy*, trans. D. Bodde. Princeton: Princeton Univ. Press, 1953, Vol I, Chap. I, p. 8.

teenth century. Generally speaking, the Sung school was nearer to the whole rationale of Confucian thought, and the Ming school was more akin to the thought of Indian Buddhism. These two divergent schools differed widely in their attitudes and methods of study. The Ming school accused the Sung Neo-Confucianism of being too formal; the Sung school accused the Ming Neo-Confucianists of being too subjective. Notwithstanding their difference, they all agreed that the "prime doctrine" or "fundamental truth" in the universe is *Li* or Reason—somewhat like the position maintained by the Taoist philosophers, though the latter use *Tao*, not *Li*, to express the idea. The Neo-Confucianists of the Sung school began by looking upon the external world, and this fact determined their conception of *Li* as heaven or nature, for they endeavored to permeate Confucianism with Buddhist thought. The Neo-Confucianists of the Ming school began by looking inward upon themselves, and this fact determined their conception of *Li* as the mind, for they endeavored to modify Buddhism with Confucian teachings. In any event, Neo-Confucianism is one of the greatest philosophies that China has ever seen, or is likely to see. It was seized with a mania for philosophical speculation, and grappled with deepest questions of ontology. The intellectual influences that had acted upon China in the past, the culture and thought that had been brought from lands far beyond the borders of China, permeate this body of thought and are crystallized within it. This is Neo-Confucianism, which rendered the world more intelligible to the Chinese than it had ever been before.

5. The New Culture Movement

The period from the Manchu dynasty (1644–1911) to that of the Republic (1911–present) is an age of great social disturbance, political instability, and intellectual anarchy. The whole tendency of this age is skeptical and destructive. All established institutions, marriage, the family, the society, the state, the law, come in for destructive criticism. The foremost scholar, Liang Ch'i-ch'ao (1873–1929) compared this period to the age of the Renaissance in Europe.[5] Indeed the general character of thought during the period is intimately connected with political, social, and moral events of the time. Christianity had acquired a firm foothold in China, and with it came Western science and philosophy, especially the pragmatic theory of John Dewey and the dynamic doctrine of Karl Marx, which exerted a tremendous influence on the Chinese intellectuals. Meanwhile, translations from the works of eminent Western writers such as Tolstoy, Ibsen, Maupassant, Shelley, Emerson, and Marx and Engels were undertaken extensively.

Philosophy goes hand in hand with political, social, religious, and artistic development. It is but natural, then, that during this period an independent school of critics arose and launched an attack on the Neo-Confucianism of the Sung and Ming periods. These critics distinguished themselves for their skepticism and criticism, and they founded a school of pragmatism which has continued to the present day. They were considered to be the most skeptical, critical, and scientific thinkers that China has produced. But, in fact, they devoted themselves to linguistic studies and textual criticism, and neglected philosophical studies. For to exalt intuition, ecstasy, or rapture, above thought—this is end to philosophy.

The period was not fruitful in philosophic thought until the appearance of the New Culture Movement, which reached out in many directions and touched many aspects of Chinese society. The leaders of the movement [6] looked very much to the West, taking positivism as their great inspiration and science and democracy as their chief objectives. The whole burden of this new movement was the demolition of the Confucian system. Confucianism was identified with the conservatism of the past that, to their minds, had interfered with new ideas and the forces of progress. The new era gave

[5] Liang, Ch'i-ch'ao, *An Outline History of Learning in the Manchu Dynasty*, p. 6.

[6] The New Culture Movement was sponsored chiefly by Hu Shih (born in 1891) and Ch'en Tu-hsiu (1879–1942), founder of the Chinese Communist Party. For details read Part III of this book.

birth to a new philosophical impulse, under the influence of which the Chinese are still living. However, to enjoy that new impulse, the Chinese mind had first to pass through the arid waste of skepticism, criticism, and subjectivism.

CHAPTER XI. CHINESE RELIGION

1. The Three Great Traditions

When we speak of religion in China, we usually refer to the three great traditions of very diverse character and origin: Confucianism, Taoism, and Buddhism. These three modes of belief and worship have for ages existed separately and independently, although they have influenced and colored one another. They are found side by side not only in the same locality, but also often in the same individual.

Confucianism, as we have seen, is not a religion, for it has no religious ritual or sanction. It presents high intellectual ideals, but there is nothing to be dreaded by one who fails to live up to them. In competing with a religion that holds out the assurance of immortality, Confucianism suffers from its silence as to the beyond. When Confucius was questioned on this, he replied evasively: "If you do not know life, how can you know about death?" (*Analects*, XI, 11). And finally, Confucianism attaches great importance to humanity. As Confucius said: "If you are not able to serve men, how can you worship the gods?" Confucianism is not a religion, but a philosophy and a system of ethics. The greatness of Confucianism, however, is that it has taken the place of religion; its teachings have been acknowledged to be true and its rules of moral conduct to be binding by the Chinese people. The teachings of Confucius and his followers are embodied in the "Four Books" and the "Five Classics." The "Four Books" are the *Analects,* the record of the Master's activities and conversations compiled by his disciples; the *Great Learning* (*Ta Hsüeh,*) traditionally attributed to Tseng Ts'an, the Master's disciple; the *Doctrine of the Mean* (*Chung Yung*), traditionally ascribed to Tzu Ssu, the

142

Master's grandson; and the works of Mencius (*Meng Tzu*, or *Book of Mencius*). The "Five Classics" are the *Book of Change* (*Yi Ching*), the *Book of History* (*Shu Ching*), the *Book of Odes* (*Shih Ching*), and the *Spring and Autumn Annals* (*Ch'un-Ch'iu*).

Taoism began as a philosophy, but later developed into a religion. In A.D. 165, Emperor Huan of the Han dynasty ordered that official offerings be made to Lao Tzu and a temple be built in his honor. State patronage was repeated in 574 and 591. In 666, Emperor Kao Tsung of the T'ang dynasty canonized Lao Tzu and honored him as the Great Supreme Emperor of Mystic Origin (*Tai-shang Hsüan-yüan Huang-Ti*). Since then, philosophical Taoism has been mercilessly exploited and transformed into a popular religion with the Old Master as its founder. As a matter of fact, Lao Tzu was an atheist, and his teachings ruled out the idea of forming a religion, which would be contrary to his great doctrine of *wu wei*. According to Lao Tzu, life followed by death is the course of nature, and man should follow this course calmly. But the Taoist religion teaches how to avoid death.

In appealing to the masses, Taoism borrowed much from Buddhist theology and rituals in an attempt to produce a popular religion in competition with Buddhism. The head of the Taoist priesthood was called *Tien Shih*, or Heavenly Teacher, and used to live on the Dragon-Tiger Mountain in Kiangsu along the valley of the Yangtze River. Taoist priests, known as *Tao Shih*, were elected and ordained in much the same way as Buddhist priests. Like Buddhist monks, they had to practice fasting, recite liturgies, and perform ceremonies. Unlike Buddhist monks, they were allowed to marry and remain with their families while observing the religious rule.

As a religion of the masses Taoism has a large pantheon, with all the folk deities, such as kitchen gods, door gods, and many others. It has also a host of immortals and spirits, such as the eight immortals (*pa hsien*) each representing a different condition in life, i.e., poverty, wealth, aristocracy, plebeianism, age, youth, masculinity, and femininity. Moreover, the Taoist cult embraced a rich reservoir of superstitions, including an extensive system of divination, witchcraft, fortune-telling, astrology, etc., and also developed an elaborate alchemy for the manufacture of the drug of immortality and the transmutation of cinnabar and mercury into gold. The writings of the Taoist alchemists contributed much to the material culture and scientific development in medieval China. However, because of its search for the "elixir of immortality" and its concern with the exorcism of demons, religious Taoism has degenerated into a hodgepodge of the crudest and tawdriest superstitions, and become little more than charlatanism.

Buddhism is a metaphysical religion of infinite depth, with its "Ten Commandments," enforced by the doctrine of retribution, acting upon the soul in passage through numberless stages of existence. Buddhism contributes imposing ceremonial observances, monastic institutions, and a grand array of images for worship. The principles of Buddhism, originated in the teachings of Gautama Shakya Muni, the Buddha—an Indian prince who lived in the sixth century B.C.—are based on the "Four Noble Truths"; (1) that life itself is the root of all sufferings; (2) that sufferings are due to desires; (3) that desires can be eliminated by negating life; and (4) that this can be achieved by accumulating *karma* ("deeds"), culminating in the emancipation of the individual. These four truths are the common belief of all schools of Buddhism.

The introduction of Buddhism into China was one of the greatest events in Chinese history, and it has been a major factor in Chinese civilization, exercising particular influence on religion, philosophy, art, and literature. By the middle of the second century after Christ, Buddhism seems to have well been established in China, and reached the height of its development during the period from the fifth century to the seventh century. Many Buddhist missionaries from India and central Asia made the pilgrimage to China. Buddhist sutras were translated into Chinese. Many sects flourished at this time. The Buddhist religion, with additions from Chinese tradition, formed the chief spiritual refuge for the people. But it must not be thought that Buddhism was free to expand unchecked. The suspicions of Confucian scholars and the jealousy of the Taoists resulted in a number of minor and a few serious major prosecutions of the Buddhist faith. Buddhism, however, went on to become the greatest religion in the East in respect to the number of adherents. In eastern and southeastern Asia, including China, Japan, Korea, Burma, and Thailand (Siam), the established church is Buddhist.

Such are, in outline, the three great traditions of very diverse character: the philosophical Confucianism, the charlatanic Taoism, and the metaphysical Buddhism. It is worth notice that the three masters who founded the traditions appear to have lived about the same time, in or about the sixth century B.C. The Chinese people venerate all three masters and worship them together, as the Trinity of Sages, without regard to their inconsistencies. The following story of Mr. Tsing Ping will suffice to illustrate the conciliation of these three principal traditions:

> Mr. Tsing Ping, who took the highest degree in the year 1661, had the misfortune to lose his soul, which escaped one day and was unable to find its way back to its body. The lost soul found a Taoist priest sitting by the roadside, who recommended him, as a man of letters, to apply to Confucius, who, as the God of Literature, presided over the intellectual and moral needs of the people, and by whom the case was referred to Buddha, who at last gave him a guide to show where his body still lay.

There can be no greater mistake than to attribute this tolerance in religion to indifference. It is essentially a tolerance which springs from comprehension. The Chinese outlook on life has always been fundamentally a moral, and in a broad sense, a religious one. The Chinese have never been a proselytizing nation; they have never deliberately set out to extend their rule in order to convert others, either by force or by persuasion, to their own point of view in religion. All kinds of creeds and worships seem to have prevailed and flourished simultaneously among the Chinese, who have an instinctive suspicion of dogmatic ideas and doctrines, a preference for avoiding extremity, and a love of compromising differences and ameliorating divergences, in their lives as well as in their creeds and worships.

2. The Popular Beliefs

Now let us turn to the consideration of certain popular beliefs which have shaped the religion of the masses in China. Basic to the structure of popular religion was a belief in an intimate and mutual relationship between various gods and spirits and human beings. According to the popular belief, gods and spirits are not only analogous to men in form and shape, but also are sometimes transformed into human beings. This belief is illustrated in the popular legends and fables. In the popular fiction *All Men Are Brothers* by Pearl S. Buck —an adapted translation of the *Shui Hu Chüan,* or *Water Margins Record*—we are told that the hundred and eight brigands were originally divine deities in the celestial regions, who had been transformed into human beings. The *Chin Hua Yuan,* or *Romance of Mirror-Flowers,* is a romantic tale of fairies who descend to earth and turn into human beings with a taste for worldly pleasures and luxuries. Again the *Pei Yu Chi,* or *Record of Travels in the North* (parallel to the *Si Yu Chi,* or *Record of Travels in the West*), is a travesty on the journey of the Great Jade Ruler (*Yu Huang Tai Tai*), who, though the Supreme Master of the gods, descended to earth and became the companion of the people. These legends make clear that the various gods and spirits, though they enjoyed eternal life in heaven, yet became entangled in human affairs; as a result, they had a great affinity with humanity.

Just as gods descended to earth and were transformed into human beings, so men ascended to heaven and were deified. Parallel with the worship of ancestors [1] was the oblation of sages and heroes, which the people performed with profound reverence. They believed that sages and heroes, as divine beings, should be honored after death by deification. In fact, the system of posthumous distinction was not confined to sages and heroes. Any person whose conduct was meritorious would be duly canonized or deified. In the *Fong Shen Yin Yi,* or *Romance of Gods and Deities*, we are told that gods come of deities and deities come of men, and that by the process of turning men into divinities, sages, heroes, and meritorious persons are duly deified and worshiped until they reach the stage of godship. In this stage of belief, the Chinese people constructed for themselves "Jacob's ladders" between heaven and earth; man ascended to heaven and gods descended to earth. From time to time they might revise the list of local deities, striking out those whom they thought fit to remove, and filling up the vacancies by the deification of those recently deceased. All these illustrations

[1] See Chapter VI, Sec. 3.

point to the humanistic temperament of the Chinese people in the matter of religion.

To the Chinese people the invisible world was peopled with all kinds of gods, spirits, ghosts, and demons. The world of spirits was like the world of men; and, as in this life, it was impossible to live without eating, or to obtain comforts without money; therefore, in the life to come, the same state of things prevailed. Hence the custom was prevalent in China of setting out food for the departed and burning paper money for their expenses in the invisible world. This kind of belief perpetuated the fusion of the two spheres of existence, as well as the relationship between divinities and humanity.

The Chinese people believed that a person's soul on his death either ascended to heaven and became *shen*, a divinity, or descended to the underworld and became *kuei*, a ghost; this would depend upon his own merits. While the *shen* enjoyed all kinds of heavenly pleasures, the *kuei* suffered those of earthly tortures. Some of the *kuei* were condemned by Yen-lo Wang, the ruler of Hades; others hunted the graves where their former bodies were interred. All Souls' Day, or the Buddhist Festival of Departed Spirits (*Yun Lan P'en Hui*; lit., "the vessel to hold offerings") was celebrated on the fifteenth day of the seventh moon, chiefly for the purpose of saying Buddhist masses for the solitary souls of those who died away from home and had nobody to perpetuate their memories by ancestral worship. During the Ching-ming Festival or Festival of Visiting Graves, occasion was also taken for the worship of the departed spirits. These festivals were observed in all classes of society and in all geographical areas.

The Chinese people derived religious comfort from these superstitious beliefs. Man is a being with a soul, and that soul, which looks into the past and the future as well as the present, feels the need of understanding the mystery of the universe in which he lives. Religion lightens the burden of the mystery of the universe by giving him a sense of security and permanence. Religion gives man a belief in a divine power that can control the natural forces that threaten him, and a belief in a future state of being the condition of which is determined by his conduct in the present life. In China the superstitions and mythologies became a religion of the masses, providing for the people the same sense of security and permanence that religion affords mankind.

The religious beliefs of the Chinese people are concerned not, like those of Western cultures, with the omnipotence and supremacy of God and the assurance of immortality, but rather with the invisible world and the doctrine of providential retribution: the certainty of prosperity as the reward of virtue, and of calamity as the penalty of vice. The Chinese people have a common saying, which affords a key to the understanding of the popular beliefs: "Happiness follows in the footsteps of virtue, as shadow follows substance." This, as fortified by the Buddhist doctrine of the transmigration of souls, became the conviction that each individual soul, sooner or later, inevitably reaps the reward of its deeds—a conviction which took so strong a hold on the public mind as to become the foundation for the religion of the masses.

Now let us further illustrate the popular beliefs in China, by reference to the attitude of the Chinese people toward Christianity and Buddhism. Christianity came to China with the arrival of St. Francis Xavier, the first Jesuit missionary to the Far East and the founder of the modern mission to China, in 1583. Despite their contributions to Chinese education and culture, Christian missionaries failed in bringing about an early conversion of the Chinese people. There is a great divergency between the religion of the masses and Christianity. According to Christianity, the first two ancestors of mankind were most happy in the heavenly garden, and lost it afterward through their own sin. Man is born with a multitude of sins, which can only be purified by God, and he can never return to the lost paradise without God's grace. The Chinese people reject the theory of original sin, and believe that the sage, the saint, or the Buddha is similar to everyone else. Hence any man can become a sage, a saint, or a Buddha, if only he stores up good deeds; man can enter the heavenly paradise by his merits, or by his virtue. This feeling has been deepened by the belief that the invisible world is not a domain from which no travelers return, but rather a place where one changes forms. There is a constant interchange of forms in the two spheres of existence, mingling death with life and the divine with the human. The Chinese people, practical in their beliefs, were amazed at the offer of a religion that holds out only the assurance of immortality.

Buddhism took about three hundred years to obtain official recognition and many centuries more to establish a strong hold over the people. To adapt itself to the comprehension of the masses, Buddhism personified its abstract conceptions and converted them into divinities, and, by the theory of metempsychosis, seemed to reveal the link that connects man with the gods. In order to furnish the people with an object of worship more attractive than an unconscious deity, the Buddhists brought forward a Goddess of Mercy (*Kuan Yin* in Chinese), whose merit was that, having reached the verge of Nirvana, she declined to enter, preferring to remain where she could hear the cries and succor the calamities of human beings. To pave the way for its easier acceptance, Buddhism included the local gods and heroes in its pantheon. This is the way in which the "otherworldliness" of Indian Buddhism has been modified by the "this-worldliness" of Chinese thinking and made more acceptable to the popular mind. As a religion, Buddhism—in its modified system—seemed to enjoy more popular favor than Taoism, though the Buddhist faith counseled a withdrawal from the vanities of the world of affairs, while Taoism offered the blessings of health, wealth, and long life.

The various beliefs and worships were all jumbled together without regard to their distinct character and origin; not only did they coexist without conflict, but they exercised a joint sway over the minds and hearts of the Chinese people. It is impossible to apportion the people among the various creeds. They all reverenced Confucius and worshiped their ancestors; they all participated in the "feast of the souls" and employed the Buddhist burial service; and they all resorted to Taoist blessings of health and wealth. The inconsistency and multiplicity of the various beliefs and worships presented no administrative or intellectual difficulty to the Chinese.

With changing society, the religious beliefs change too. During the last fifty years, there has been a general decline in the folk religion. Many images and idols were demolished, temples and monasteries were converted into schools or storage depots, mystic beliefs and practices were curbed. The decline also affected the three great religious traditions. Confucianism, being stripped of its divine power and prestige, disappeared as a religion, and religious Taoism degenerated into the crudest superstition. Buddhism, assuring every man of an interest in a life to come, still excited the popular mind, but its revival was ephemeral. From what has been happening in recent years on the mainland, it seems clear that the

Chinese Communists cannot tolerate religious freedom. Their basic policy is to destroy all religious traditions, substituting a monolithic Communist ideology. They have taken drastic measures to bring the various religious groups under the control of the state and the Communist Party. The impact of these measures is, however, still difficult to determine. All we can say is that religious ideas and activities, which may be controlled or suppressed, can never be completely eradicated.

CHAPTER XII.   CHINESE LITERATURE

1. Literature and Philosophy

No one denies that literature is closely affiliated with philosophy. Philosophy is the soul of literature; literature is the expression of philosophy. They are alike in content, but different in purpose. The content of both is to criticize life. But the criticism of life presupposes a standard, ideal or actual, from which the life criticized is different; otherwise the criticism would be without much meaning. Here is the difference between literature and philosophy. Literature criticizes life by taking some standard of criticism for granted, and so its purpose is to point out the wrong and the false. On the other hand, philosophy builds up its own standard of criticism, and so its purpose is to tell the right and the true. In the West, literature and philosophy constitute two separate branches of culture, even though they are intimately associated.

One important feature of Chinese literature is its intimate alliance with philosophy. It is worth notice that Chinese literature and philosophical writings originated about the same time, in the ninth and eighth centuries B.C. And from the same sources, that is, the Five Classics, developed the great literature of prose and poetry, and also the divergent schools of philosophy. Their close association was further strengthened by the fact that in the early days, what literature meant was in fact learning and culture, in which philosophy occupies an important part.

Moreover, Chinese writers of general prose literature frequently thought of themselves as philosophers and attempted to make contributions to learning. For instance, Yang Hsiung (53 B.C.–A.D. 18), a well-known figure in

Chinese literature, regarded prose writings and poetry as "minor arts," and in glorification of the *Yi Ching* he wrote the *Tai Hsüan Ching* (*Book of Supreme Mystery*), and in exaltation of the Confucian *Analects*, he wrote a treatise known as the *Fa Yen* (*Model Speeches*). Han Yü (768–824), a great essayist of the T'ang dynasty, claimed to have a place among the great teachers of China. In his *Yüan Tao* (*On the Origin of the Tao*), Han Yü wrote: "Yao [a traditional sage-king of antiquity] transmitted the *Tao* to Shun [another sage-king]; Shun transmitted it to Yü [founder of the Hsia dynasty]; and Yü transmitted it to [kings] Wen and Wu and the Duke of Chou [the three founders of the Chou dynasty]. The latter transmitted it to Confucius, and Confucius transmitted it to Mencius. After Mencius, it was no longer transmitted." It clearly implied that he might be the one to whom the *Tao* was transmitted. Liu Tsung-yüan (773–819), a poet, essayist, and calligraphist, purported to be a philosopher by commenting on the meaning and significance of Confucian virtues. There were many other first-rate writers and great poets, such as Ch'u Yuan (340–295 B.C.), who originated the elegy (*ch'u tzu*); Szu-ma Ch'ien (b. 145 B.C.), the Herodotus of China, whose *Shih Chi* (*Historical Records*), was the prototype of all later dynastic histories, e.g., the *Twenty-four Dynastic Histories;* Tao Yüan-ming (365–427), a great poet of the Chin period; and Li Po (705–762) and Tu Fu (712–770), known as the Dryden and Pope of the T'ang period, who were not only well versed in literature, but also had profound philosophical ideas.

And again, just as the writers and poets claimed to be philosophers, so the philosophers cultivated a literary style and made their writings great works of literature. "If one's word is not well cultivated, one's action will not go far," is the maxim which Confucius followed in the expression of his own thoughts and taught to his disciples. Most of the Chinese philosophical writings are noted for purity of style and felicity of expression. In the Confucian *Analects,* the language is concise and rhythmical, each paragraph consisting of only a few words. The *Tao-te Ching* consists of about five thousand words and is cast in a semi-poetical mold; its dark pages, obscure and paradoxical, are illumined by many a flash of far-reaching light. Each of the two great philosophers impressed his own style of expression on the school which he founded. Mencius was less dogmatic and more vehement than Confucius, while the wild fancy of Chuang Tzu exaggerated the mystic features of Lao Tzu. In both, the current of diction flows like a river, and their works are noted for literary beauty.

Inasmuch as Chinese literature is associated with philosophy, it follows that one must be studied in the light of the other. The real, as Plato held, always strives to attain the ideal, but always falls short of it. History is conceived as the actual realization of philosophy, but it can never be as perfect as philosophy. It is literature through which philosophy finds its full expression. In China, Taoist philosophy has never been and perhaps will never be realized in history. But it has been realized in Chinese literature, particularly in poetry. It should be stressed that in China poets and philosophers do not live in isolation, but breathe a common air and catch light and heat from each other's thought. The unity of this spirit is, indeed, of the very essence of Chinese culture; and it is to this intimate alliance with philosophy that Chinese literature owes much of its dignity and influence.

2. The Character of Chinese Literature

Before attempting to illustrate by extracts the character of Chinese literature, it will be better to list some of the leading features which serve to distinguish it from Western literature. First, heroic literature, conspicuous in the West, was wanting in China. In Chinese history there were very few persons of distinction who deserved rightly to be called heroes. For instance, the Ch'in emperor Shih Huang Ti and the Han emperor Wu Ti might be called heroes in some respects, for the former abolished Chou feudalism and thus created a centralized Chinese empire under his rule and the latter extended the empire to the borders of China proper. But in the eyes of the Chinese people, they were but despotic tyrants. The general Hsiang Yu, a man of immense strength and courage who struggled for leadership with Liu Pang, founder of the Han dynasty, might deserve to be called a hero. He was much praised by the Chinese people throughout the ages. However, his biography can be found only in the

Shih Chi (*Historical Records*), and the poets even jeered at his tragic suicide. Here is a fragment of the verse:

> Victory and defeats are variable features;
> Prudence and patience are important virtues;
> Youths of Kiang-tung, brave and valorous, at hand,
> Taking up arms, might recover the lost land.

Kiang-tung was the hero's native place. It was the poets' opinion that his fellow countrymen would have helped him into power, had he not committed suicide.

In Chinese novels there are very few heroic characters. In the *San Kuo Yin Yi* (*Romance of the Three Kingdoms*), a historical novel based on the wars of the three kingdoms that fought for supremacy at the beginning of the third century, Kuan Yu, later canonized as Kuan Ti (God of War), might be called a war hero, but not in the sense of Western heroes. For the latter are characterized by the spirit of chivalry, whereas the former was noted for the virtue of loyalty. And even in the *Erh Ju Yin Hsiung Chüan* (*Biography of Heroine*—a popular novel of the Ch'ing dynasty), the female character is described as a girl of ability and courage, but the main emphasis is placed on the traditional feminine virtues; she is more good daughter and good wife than heroine.

Secondly, literature of romantic love was not much esteemed, though love stories and love poems are not wanting. For instance, in the *Shih Ching* (*Book of Odes*), a collection of popular songs and poems, there are many love songs and ballads. But Confucian scholars gave them ethical interpretations and read into them moral ideas. Confucius himself selected 305 songs out of more than 3,000 pieces and said of his work: "If I should try to sum up the 300 poems in one sentence, I would say that wayward thought was absent" (*Analects*, II, 2). In the *Hsi Hsiang Chi* (*Story of the Western Pavilion*) of the Yuan period, a popular dramatic elegy, we find many expressions about love, full of passion and intrigue, but tinged with the ethics of Oriental conjugal affection. Generally speaking, in Chinese novels and poems the love stories and love verses were motivated by sensual gratifications and conjugal relations. This became a conventional expression in the short stories of the T'ang period, popular tales of the Sung and Ming periods, and novels of the

Ch'ing period. The *Hung Lou Meng* (*Dream of the Red Chamber*) of the seventeenth century is a popular novel of domestic and love affairs, full of humorous and pathetic episodes of everyday life, and interspersed with short poems of high literary finish; however, the love represented in the novel is rather sensual and stresses conjugal union. The novelists seem to imply that the theory of love as its own reward is too refined for the popular mind; to the mass of mankind love has no charms aside from conjugal relations. This attitude, as we shall see, determines the ethical character of Chinese literature.

And thirdly, realistic literature—the reflection of man's real life and social conditions—did not flourish in China. There is virtually no Chinese poem that touches on social conditions. Chinese novels, which enjoyed great popularity in the early time, may be ranged under five heads; (1) historical anecdotes, such as *San Kuo Yin Yi* (*Romance of the Three Kingdoms*); (2) romances, such as the *Hung Lou Meng* (*Dream of the Red Chamber*), which as a tale of domestic life only indirectly reflects the social conditions of that time; (3) adventure tales, such as the *Shui Hui Chüan* (*Water Margins Record*) which deals with the adventures of the outlaw Sung Chiang and his comrades, who terrorized a couple of provinces in the twelfth century, but its stress is placed on the descriptions of the different characters; (4) supernatural tales, such as the *Liao-chai Chi Yi* (*Strange Tales of Liao-chai*), the superiority of which lies in the detailed and realistic descriptions of fairies, foxes, ghosts, and goblins and the fact that the supernatural beings appear human and approachable; and (5) satirical stories, such as the *Ju Lin Wai Shih* (*Anecdotes of Scholars*) of the eighteenth century, in which the writer portrays all sorts of scholars, including many strange types, in considerable detail. In this last the writer criticizes social abuses without any personal malice, directing his attack mainly on the literati. There are two more popular novels which attempted realistically to reflect the conditions of the times, but their descriptions of social evil were rather exaggerated and superficial. Both were written in the beginning of the twentieth century, when Western realism had invaded the Chinese literary world. However, there has not yet been a Chinese novel that contains such detailed and realistic description of social life as the works of Charles Dickens.

The foregoing review shows that Chinese writers did not praise heroes, or represent love, or describe social conditions. Then what did they do? They described natural scenery and illustrated virtues. Let us turn first to a consideration of the ethical character of Chinese literature. Heroic poems, conspicuous in the West, were wanting in China, but writings extolling gallantry and chivalry are abundant. When the Chinese speak of a person who is gallant and chivalrous, they mean that he has the virtue to offer his service to others and maintain fidelity to his professional ethics. Such a person was known as a *hsieh*, or knight-errant. In the *Shih Chi* there is a chapter on *hsieh* which says: "*Hsieh*'s words were always sincere and trustworthy, and his actions always quick and decisive. He was always true to what he promised, and without regard to his own person he would take up his sword and rush into the dangers threatening others" (Chap. 124). Such were his professional ethics, for the *hsieh* believed that "virtue is man's only jewel" and that loyalty and fidelity are the roots of virtue. To these ideals Chinese writers often gave elaborate expression.

Next, as we have seen, the literature of romantic love, very popular in the West, was not highly esteemed in China. To the Chinese people, conjugal affection is much superior to romantic love. In the West the people make love when they are lovers; they look forward and long for the future. But the Chinese nourish love when they are united in wedlock; so they look backward and recollect the past. In the West love poems and love letters are written during the time of wooing and love making. In China the poems express conjugal affection, sadness on the death of a spouse, longing for home when on a journey, and happiness at reunion. after a long separation. The elegy *Yee Pei Huai* (*Lines to Ease the Aching Heart*) written on the death of his wife by Yuan Chen, a poet of the T'ang dynasty, would serve as a good illustration, were it not too long for quotation here. We will, instead, give a short poem of four lines written by a poet of the Ch'ing dynasty, who had gone with his wife to Wuchang, where after a stay of many years she died. He wrote the poem on leaving Wuchang:

This grief is common to everyone,
One hundred years how many can attain?

But 'tis heartbreaking, oh the Yangtze River!
Together we came—but not we return!

And here are two lines of poetry from a wife to her absent husband:

The day when you think of coming home;
Ah! then my heart will already be broken.

Again, while Chinese writers were not given to the realistic description of social conditions, they sometimes expressed their resentment against political corruptions and social evils. But these writings had no perceptible influence on political or social reform. The works of Ch'ü Yüan, great patriotic poet, offer a good illustration. The poet, though he came of a royal family, steadfastly opposed the corrupt government of the state of Ch'u. His immortal *Li Sao* (*Falling into Trouble*), a poem of more than three hundred and seventy lines, is the exquisite expression of his love for his country and concern for his countrymen, ruthlessly exposing the king's folly and the treachery of evil ministers. Overwhelmed by social evils and political chaos, and caring no longer to live, Ch'ü Yüan went to the banks of the Mi-lo River, where he met a fisherman. Their conversation, as reported in his *Works,* ran as follows:

"Are you," asked the fisherman, "not His Excellency the Minister? What has brought you here?"

"While the world," replied Ch'ü Yüan, "is foul, I alone am clean. All men are drunk, but I alone am sober. So I am banished."

"Ah!" rejoined the fisherman, "the Sage does not quarrel with his environment, but adapts himself to it. If the world is foul, why not make it clean? If all men are drunk, why not teach them to be sober?"

Then the fisherman rowed away and Ch'ü Yüan plunged into the river and drowned himself. Tradition has it that the poet died on the fifth day of the fifth moon; ever afterward the people commemorated the day by the Dragon-boat Festival.

Ch'ü Yüan was a patriotic poet, but he could do nothing to save the ruin of his country. His twenty-five poems, however, are more lyric expression of his passionate love for his country than realistic reflection of the conditions of the times.

In this connection, we should like to quote four lines of poetry, written in political allegory by Tu Fu, great poet of the T'ang dynasty, when he was disappointed in a political career:

> As the spring flood overflows,
>   The torrent rushes on;
> The ferry-boat is away blown,
>   For the ferry-man is gone.

Chinese literature abounds in such expressions. A well-known satirical piece written by Liu Tsung-yüan (773–819), who was noted for his purity of style and felicity of expression, is entitled "Catching Snakes," and is directed against the hardship of taxation. Another piece, written by Liu Chi (1311–1375), a writer of the Ming dynasty, is entitled "Outsides" and is a light satire on the corruption of his day. From these writings and poems and others which might be cited, we conclude that Chinese writers were not always timid in denouncing corrupt government, even though they failed to give realistic representations of social conditions and to register their aspirations for improvement and reform.

Next, let us turn to another important quality of Chinese literature, that is, its power of expressing a delicate and intimate feeling for the beauty of nature. Chinese writers excel in the description of natural scenes and landscape. They have an eye for the picturesque in nature; and nature throws her varied charm over the pages of their literature with a profusion unknown among the Western writers. Love for nature pervades Chinese literature. Taoism was a naturalistic philosophy which from very early times had a great influence on men of culture, especially on poets. The Taoist ideal was to withdraw from the world of affairs and live in tranquil communion with nature among forests and streams and hills. Cultivated scholars and poets were tempted to retire to the mountains in search of contemplative solitude and they often gave exquisite expression to this urge in their writings and poems. Take, for instance, the writings of Tao Yüan-ming (365–427). A Taoist poet, he occupied himself with music and the cultivation of flowers, especially chrysanthemums. In his famous poetic prose work *Home-*

ward I Am Bound, he tells how he took his pleasure in his garden and contemplated the lovely scenes of the universe.

> Wealth, I want not; honor, I desire not; heavenly palace is beyond my hopes.
> Then let me enjoy the happy hours, and stroll about my garden among my flowers.
> I'll mount the spring hill and sing my songs; I'll visit the clear brook and verse my poems.
> Ah! By course of nature, all fade into infinity.
> Thus will I follow Nature and content myself with Fate.
> What else do I worry about?

Chinese critics speak of Tao Yüan-ming as "drunk with the fumes of spring." Much of his writing is picturesque and bristles with charming allegories and beautiful scenes, intermixed with Taoist thoughts. His *Peach-blossom Fountain,* which represents a form of literature much cultivated by Chinese writers, tells how a fisherman lost his way among the creeks of a river, and came to a dense grove of lovely peach trees in full bloom, through which he pushed his boat and discovered the Taoist Utopia—a tiny village-community, quiet, simple, contented, cut off completely from the rest of the world.

Another example of the Taoist ideal, and one in which the writer traces the strange, mystic sense of life as a part of nature, drawing strength and color and character from hills and streams, is *The Western-Hill Trip,* written by Liu Tsung-yüan:

> Spontaneously with Nature, I cannot comprehend how boundless it is; happily with Creation, I cannot know how fathomless it is. Take wine and drink the cup dry; in my cups, I am unconscious that it is drawing toward sunset. The gloomy dusk deepens from afar, but I still linger on till none can be seen. My mind is calm and my soul is serene; only then can I be completely absorbed in Nature.

Chinese literature has in its amazing diversity one aim: to seek harmony with nature. This is particularly true of Chinese poetry. The poet submerges his consciousness in the universe, and his own life is identified with the rest of creation. The barrier between external phenomena and internal feeling is broken down. This great ideal seems to be what

Chuang Tzu calls the "equalization of all things." Chinese poetry, as we know, came into being with the *Odes* (*Shih*), developed with the elegy of Ch'ü Yüan, burst forth and reached perfection during the time of the T'angs. Among the poets of the T'ang dynasty (619–907), the greatest was Li Po (701-762). He was most of his life a wanderer. For a time he lived in the mountains with five other poets, and they were known as the "Six Idlers of the Bamboo-grove." Li Po was also a moon lover; often he would bring wine and sit alone in the seclusion of a bamboo grove to enjoy the moon on a quiet night. His famous ode "On Drinking Alone by Moonlight" is considered one of the masterpieces of poetry. Here is an extract:

> An arbor of flowers
>   and a kettle of wine:
> Alas! in the bowers
>   no companion is mine.
> Then the moon sheds her rays
>   on my goblet and me,
> And my shadow betrays
>   we're a party of three.[1]

This poem is permeated with a feeling of serenity and harmony, a kind of quietism. Similar to the above verse in spirit and style is the following quatrain, written by Wang Wei (699–759):

> *My Hermitage in the Bamboo Grove*
> Deep in the bamboo grove, sitting alone,
> I play on my lute and sing a tune.
> There is no one in sight
> Save the moon glittering bright.

Wang Wei was a devout Buddhist, and his passionate love for the beauty of nature pervades his poems. The following quatrain offers a good illustration:

> *The Deer-fold*
> Among the empty hills no one is in sight,
> But faint voices can be heard to resound.
> Through deep wood thrusts the reflected sunlight,
> Which falls again upon the mossy ground.

[1] Cf. H. A. Giles's translation in his *History of Chinese Literature*, New York, D. Appleton, 1927, p. 153.

It is never fair to Chinese poetry to quote it in translation. It takes many words to express the terse, suggestive Chinese characters. It is difficult to match Chinese rhythm, which is peculiarly musical because of the tone and inflection. Chinese poetry is the essence of meaning and feeling, and passionate love for nature and solitude is exquisitely expressed in the verses of the leading poets.

And again, we shall turn to what we call the fundamental sentiment as expressed in Chinese literature. In their outlook on life, the Chinese are this-worldly and yet otherworldly, pessimistic and yet optimistic. This peculiar mixed sentiment pervades Chinese literature. For instance, the *Hung Lou Meng (Dream of the Red Chamber)*, as a panorama of Chinese domestic life, starts with an explanation of the supernatural origin of the story; then it runs smoothly along upon earthly lines, but overshadowed by spiritual influences; and finally it comes to the tragic end that Lin Tai-yu, the heroine, dies of a broken heart and Chia Pao-yu, the hero, escapes from the world of dust and turmoil. So the novel concludes:

> This is a tale of sorrow
> And yet of fantasy;
> Life is but a dream;
> Laugh not at man's folly.

The *San Kuo Yin Yi (Romance of the Three Kingdoms)* is a historical novel, but the story starts with the following lines:

> The mighty river flows east,
>   sweeping away countless heroes.
> Right and wrong, success and failure,
>   are all alike vanities.
> The green hills are still in sight,
>   but many sunsets have elapsed.
> The old fisherman, staying in the small island,
>   has experienced many "autumn moons and spring winds."
> Now we sup the wine for the pleasure of our reunion;
>   what has been passed is merely laughed away!

This speaks well for the dream of life.

We shall trace this peculiar mixed sentiment—sensitivity to suffering and capacity of fascination—in Chinese poetry. In the famous *Li Sao,* Ch'ü Yüan lamented:

> Just as heaven and earth are fathomless,
> So the toil of life is endless.
> The past cannot be held,
> Nor can the future be told.

Cheng Tzu-ang (656–598) was a poet of the T'ang dynasty, and the following extract exhibits him in a mood not far removed from the lamentation of Ch'ü Yüan:

Regrets

> The ancients cannot be seen;
> Newcomers are not yet in sight.
> For heaven and earth—ah! so uncertain,
> I weep and grieve at heart.

Now let us take leave of the pessimistic sentiment of Chinese literature and turn to its optimistic sentiment. In fact, the literary writings of a distinctively optimistic type are not so abundant as those that express pessimistic sentiment. However, they are not wanting. In the *Shih Ching*, we read:

> Why should we sigh at the change of "a date,"
>   When life's flowing on in a full, steady tide?
> Come, let us be merry with those that we love;
>   For pleasure in measure is no one to chide.

This is the oldest temperance ode in the world. The old-time theme of "eat, drink, and be merry" is exploited as follows:

> Here are food and wine;
> Why not play on lute in time,
> That you enjoy yourself, not to delay
> But to lengthen your day?
> By and by you will depart from the life,
> And someone, in your place, will revive.

The philosophy of Yang Chu, which represents the materialistic aspect of Taoism, has exerted some influence on the optimistic sentiment of the Chinese. His faith was in the present life, and he wanted the pleasure that could be immediately realized.

> When we have wine,
>   Let us drink it on time;

When we'll have sorrow,
Let us care not till tomorrow.

This is exactly what Yang Chu teaches: "Enjoy life and take one's ease." The poet has no faith in the past, no hope in the future, but will enjoy the blessing of life and quietly await death. This may be a good state, but it is a sad one. Under the surface of melancholy pleasure, there is a strong current of pessimism.

To those who seek out immortality
    Death is allotted;
To those who look for happiness
    Grief is awarded.
As we should live,
    What will life give to us?
As we should die,
    What will death bring to us?

These expressions of mixed sentiment are to be found scattered throughout Chinese literature. The Chinese, as we have noted, is not so impressed by the antagonism as by the continuity of the world. Hence to the Chinese people the difference between life and death is "shaded off as the day into night." To quote a Chinese saying:

If a man lives to a hundred years, his life is but a dream;
Glory and wealth pass away as wandering clouds.

3. The Literary Revolution

Not until the Literary Revolution of 1917 was there any marked change in Chinese literature. Since the beginning of the twentieth century, Western literary theories, particularly realism, have fostered the growth of a new literature in China. Living in a period of chaos, Chinese writers could no longer shut their eyes to the realities. They attempted realistically to reflect the conditions of the times in a simple and simplified language and literature. In 1915, Huang Yüan-yung, a well-known journalist of the day, wrote in a letter:

As to the fundamental salvation [of China], I believe a beginning must be initiated in the promotion of a new literature. We must endeavor to bring Chinese thought into direct contact with the contemporary thought of the world, for only then can it be stimulated and awakened. And also, it is essential that the basic ideals of world thought be affiliated to the life of the average man, by the use of simple and simplified language and literature for the wide dissemination of ideas. Have we not heard that the Renaissance laid the basis for the overthrow of medievalism in Europe?

However, the ideas of Huang Yüan–yung did not receive wide acceptance; nor had any concrete plan developed until Hu Shih formally launched a vigorous debate by publishing an article entitled "A Preliminary Discussion of Literary Reform" in 1917. In this article he suggested that literary reform must begin with these eight precepts: (1) Write with real substance; (2) Do not imitate the ancients; (3) Emphasize grammar; (4) Reject melancholy; (5) Discard stale, timeworn phrases; (6) Do not use classical allusions; (7) Do not use couplets and parallelisms; and (8) Do not avoid popular expressions or popular forms of characters. Hu Shih laid special stress on the last item because he believed that vernacular literature should be the main literary product of the times.

In support of Hu Shih's proposals, Ch'en Tu-hsiu, the founder of the Chinese Communist Party, wrote a more startling article entitled "On Literary Revolution." In this article, he expressed the following three principles:

1. The destruction of the painted, powdered, and obsequious literature of the aristocratic few, and the creation of a plain, simple, and expressive literature of the masses.

2. The destruction of the outmoded and showy literature of classicism, and the creation of a fresh and sincere literature of realism.

3. The destruction of the obscure and pedantic literature of the "hermit," and the creation of a clear and popular literature of a living society.

Writing in the vernacular came into vogue, in spite of the opposition of the traditional scholars. By 1919 many vernacular newspapers and magazines were published, and in 1920 the Ministry of Education ordered that, beginning in the fall of 1921, textbooks for the first two grades in the primary schools should be in the vernacular language.

This adoption of the vernacular soon spread to the middle and higher schools.

The leadership of this literary reform was in the hands of Hu Shih and Ch'en Tu-hsiu only for a short time; it soon began to separate into various literary groups. Special mention should be made of the Literary Research Society which at the beginning advocated a "literature of humanity," that is, a literature based on individualistic humanitarianism. But in further interpretations of the literature of humanity, the members of the society did not seem to take a uniform stand. While some identified the idea of humanity with idealism, others showed a tendency toward realism. Contemporary with the Literary Research Society was the Creation Society, which attached social value to literature and later advocated "proletarian literature." Generally speaking, the new literature, as fostered under the influence of the literary revolution, was essentially realistic and had a definite social message. This was evidenced by the emergence of the League of Leftist Writers under the leadership of Lu Hsün (d. 1936), the most outstanding author of that time. In opposition to the leftist writings and activities stood a group advocating "nationalist literature," led by the Nationalists. During the Sino-Japanese War (1937–1945), both the Nationalists and the Communists endeavored to use the new literature, developed since 1917, as an effective means for propaganda. In the years since 1949, socialist realism, as advocated by the early leftist writers, has been repeatedly stressed and expounded in the literary world of mainland China.

The practical aspects of the new-literature movement were successful; as a result the simplified *pai-hua*, or spoken-language style of writing, became the common medium of literary, scientific, and journalistic communication. But it would be a great mistake to consider the literary revolution against the archaic language and the old stereotyped literature as the extermination of classical literature, which is still active and is still manifesting vigor and resilience. The Chinese Communists have so far adhered to the policy of preserving what they believe to be the best literary heritage of China. Chou Yang, vice-minister of cultural affairs of the People's Government, made the following statement: "As socialist literature can only grow and flower on its own native soil, it must re-evaluate and carry forward the national tradition and evolve a national style." [2] This statement may be regarded as a summary of basic Communist policy concerning China's literary heritage. In accordance with this policy, many of the classical novels, dramas, and poems have been re-edited and re-evaluated. The *Hung Lou Meng (Dream of the Red Chamber)*, the *San Kuo Yin Yi (Romance of the Three Kingdoms)*, the *Shui Hui Chüan (Water Margins Record)*, and the *Ju Lin Wai Shih (Anecdotes of Scholars)*, for example, have appeared in new editions. On the other hand, in the re-evaluation of China's literary traditions, the Communists have rejected much as detrimental to the whole theory of realism. Many new themes and new characters have appeared in the Communist literary and artistic works. Here is an estimate, arranged according to topic, of the 177 works in the *Chinese People's Literature Series*, including operas, plays, novels, and poems: [3]

> The War of Resistance to Japanese Aggression, the People's War of Liberation, and life in the People's army—101
>> Land reform and other antifeudal struggles—41
>> Industrial and agricultural production—16
>> The history of the revolution—7
>> Other topics—12

In addition to these new themes and new characters, all forms of classical literature which the Communists deem worthy of preservation have undergone revision both in language and content in recent years.

[2] See Chou Yang, "The Great Debate on the Literary Front," *Peking Review*, Vol. 1, No. 4, March 1958, p. 12.

[3] Chou Yang, "The People's New Literature and Art," *China's New Literature and Art*, Peking, Foreign Languages Press, 1954, p. 53.

CHAPTER XIII

THE CHINESE LANGUAGE

The great majority of the people in China speak Chinese, but in the border regions there are numerous minorities that speak other languages. Some of these languages are related to Chinese, while others are of quite different origins and belong to various language families.[1] This chapter will trace the origin and development, of the Chinese language, and discuss the language reform advocated in recent decades.

1. The Origin and Development of the Chinese Language

The origin of a language must always remain a mystery; no one knows its precise details. Primitive men had no language at the start, but in working together, they had to exchange ideas, and so they gradually learned to make different sounds. Once these sounds were represented by symbols, writing was in existence. The Western alphabet is believed to have begun with picture-writing, but at an early period the system was changed so that the symbols stood not for objects or ideas, but for the sounds of the words used for these things. Thus Western language has specialized in the representation of sounds. This is a change which took place in most languages of the world. But the Chinese language has never become completely phonetic or alphabetic. Chinese has specialized in visual representation; the word is made so

---

[1] The Chinese spoken language may be classified into three main parent families: the Sino-Tibetan (or the Indo-Chinese) family, the Austroasiatic family, and the Altaian Family. For the description of these languages, read Tung Tung-ho, *Languages of China,* Taipei, China Culture Publishing Foundation, 1953.

suggestive to the eye that it immediately calls up ideas and vivid pictures without the interposition of sounds.

The origin of the Chinese language must be of great antiquity; it was capable of expressing complex thoughts with fine shades of meaning when Westerners were by comparison babbling mere baby sounds. The first system of writing employed *wen*, image-scripts of visible objects; these developed into *tzu*, ideographic characters. Hence the Chinese term for language is *wen tzu*. Generally speaking, the Chinese character began with pictographs, advanced through the stage of ideograms, and gradually reached its present development of combined symbols of sound and meaning. From the time of the Chou dynasty, the graphic symbols of Chinese have been divided into six main categories, known as *Liu Shu*: (1) Pictographs—conventional pictures of objects such as *jih* (日), "sun"; *yueh* (月), "moon"; *shan* (山), "hill." (2) Indicators—shapeless things, such as *shang* (上), "above"; *hsien* (下), "below"; *chung* (中), "middle." (3) Ideograms —combined images, such as *ming* (明), "sun-moon," or "bright"; *wen* (聞), "door-ear," or "to hear"; *hsien* (仙), "man-hill," or "hermit." (4) Phonograms, formed of a pictogram and a phonetic, the former supplying a guide to the meaning and the latter to the sound. (5) Derivative characters. (6) Phonetic loan characters. The last two categories are manifestly subordinate groups, and may well be included in the four other groups. Among these categories, the pictograms and the indicators are the basic forms from which the others are derived, but the phonograms, i.e., combined symbols of sound and meaning, make up the largest class of Chinese words.

Modern dictionaries are based on the principle of the phonetic-radical compounds—one part of the character (phonetic) gives the pronunciation, and another (radical) suggests the meaning. *Yu* (油), "oil," is made up of 由 *yu*, phonetic; and 氵 "water," radical. *Shen* (神), god: 申 *shen* phonetic; (礻), "omen," radical. *Chia* (駕), "ride:" 加 *chia*, phonetic; 馬 "horse," radical. There are about 214 radicals and 888 phonetics. The pronunciation of the written language depends upon the modern dialect of the reader. No one knows what the language originally sounded like. This does not mean that the Chinese have been unconcerned with the sounds of language, but because of the nonphonetic nature of the characters "they have had to deal chiefly in the abstract classification and relationship of sounds rather than with the phonetic values of the sounds themselves." [2]

Inscribed oracle bones, which were used for divination, are our chief source of information on the Chinese language of the Shang period. Some 4,000 different characters have been identified, among them representatives of the six main categories, although there are a considerable number of archaic characters now rare or obsolete. In the Shang period the Chinese language had passed the stage of pictographs, and an intricate writing system with graceful lines and curves had come into use.

2. The Classification of Dialects

China has only one written language. The spoken language, however, consists of various dialects, some of which are not intelligible to other Chinese.

1. *The Zone of the Mandarin Dialects.* This dialect zone can be divided into a northern group, eastern group, and southwestern group. The northern group consists of the people of North China, the Northwestern Provinces, and Sinkiang. To this group belongs the dialect of Peking, which is now the standard language of the whole country. Eastern Mandarin is spoken along the lower Yangtze River valley, mainly in the provinces of Anhwei and Kiangsu north of the river. Southwestern Mandarin is a fairly uniform dialect and is spoken throughout a large area covering Szechuan, Yunnan, Kweichow, part of Kwangsi, and part of Hupeh up to and including Hankow (Wuhan). All Mandarin dialects agree in having relatively simple sound-systems. They generally have four or five tones.

2. *The Zone of the Southeastern Coastal Provinces.* This is the zone of the greatest variety, consisting of six dialect groups—the Wu, Hsiang, Hakka, Kan, Cantonese, and Min. The Wu group of dialects is spoken south of the lower Yangtze in the provinces of Kiangsu and Chekiang and in a

[2] Yuen Ren Chao, *Mandarin Primer: An Intensive Course in Spoken Language*, Cambridge, Harvard Univ. Press, 1948, p. 4.

few districts in the eastern part of Kiangsi. There are generally six to eight tones in the Wu dialect. The Hsiang dialect is spoken principally in Hunan and resembles to some extent the southwestern Mandarin; in this group the number of tones varies from six to seven. The Hakka dialect is found principally over the area from Fukien to Kwangsi, including southern Kiangsi, northern Kwangtung, with offshoots in Taiwan and Hainan. Settlements of Hakka people can be found in the Philippines, Indochina, Burma, Thailand, Malaya, and Sumatra. The Kan group is much like Hakka, but differs from the latter in tonal system and final consonants. The Cantonese group is spoken principally in Kwangtung and Kwangsi. Settlements in which these dialects are spoken are found in large numbers in Indochina, Thailand, Burma, the Malay Peninsula, and the South Seas. These are the dialects used by Chinese residents in Chinatowns in the United States. There are eight, nine, or more tones in the dialects of this group. The Min or Fukien dialect can be divided into two groups: Northern Min as represented by the Foochow dialect, and Southern Min as represented by the dialects of Amoy and Swatow. This group of dialects is spoken chiefly in Taiwan, in the Hainan Islands, and in a district of northeastern Kwangtung. The tone system resembles that of the Wu and Hakka groups.

3. *The Zone of the Borderlands.* This zone, including the province of Sinkiang, covers more than half the area of all the others, but contains less than one-tenth of the population. In this zone, non-Chinese languages are spoken side by side with some form of Mandarin.

In the course of its evolution, the spoken language has undergone important modifications. Some of these modifications can be traced from early records. For instance, archaic Chinese, which had a very rich system of consonants and vowels, is known to us from the study of the rhyming patterns in the Shih Ching (*Book of Odes*). From archaic to ancient Chinese the most important change was that the pure-voiced initials had become semivowels; as a result, the phonetic system of ancient Chinese was much more complicated than any of the modern dialects. Ancient Chinese is known to us mainly from the rhyme books compiled in the Sui and T'ang dynasties around the seventh century. Since A.D. 600 there have been changes affecting most modern dialects, including Mandarin. Early Mandarin was represented in the Yüan dramas. On the whole, spoken Chinese has been more flexible than written Chinese and easily adaptable to the changes of time and geographical barriers, with the result that a number of dialects have developed. Dialects differ from one another not only in pronunciation but also in grammar. The most common dialect is that of Peking, the so-called "Mandarin" in the narrow sense, which varies the least from place to place and is spoken and understood by the greatest number of people. Hence the Peking dialect is recognized as the standard of pronunciation and is the chief basis of *kuo yü* (national language).

In recent years, the National Spoken Language Movement has made considerable progress in overcoming the difficulties caused by the dialectal differences. In 1919 a system of 39 National Phonetic Letters was devised; later the number was changed to 40, then to 37, and the name became "Phonetic Symbols." Under the auspices of the Ministry of Education, the Committee on the Unification of the National Language was formed, and machinery was set up to train teachers to teach the National Language in the schools. The Chinese government, as a whole, has been persistent in its efforts to unify the spoken language of the nation.

3. The Evolution of Chinese Characters

Chinese characters may be written in different ways, according to the styles of script. The oldest form is called the Ancient Script, as represented by the Shell and Bone inscriptions, *chia ku wen,* which date from the Shang dynasty. The characters inscribed on oracle shells and bones are varied in form; some are more complicated than others. On the whole, most of them are relatively simple and are often known as single-unit characters, *wen.* Later, when the number of characters increased, many combined characters, *tzu,* came into existence. As a result, the structure of characters became more complex. This tendency toward growing complexity, however, applied only to a small percentage of Chinese characters and occurred only during the period when the number of characters was sharply increasing.

The Ancient Script was soon superseded by the Seal

Script, *chuan shu,* as represented in the bronze inscriptions of the Chou dynasty. Although many of the characters inscribed on bronze objects show identity with the types found on oracle bones, on the whole the two forms of writing differed from each other both in form and style. With the exception of some new words in the ever-growing written vocabulary of the Chinese language, there was a tendency toward simplification in the style of writing.

By the Ch'un Ch'iu period (722–481 B.C.), two forms of writing had come into popular use. These forms are known in Chinese history as the "Westernland" and "Easternland" forms of writing, and were devised to replace the more cumbrous characters inscribed on bronze objects. These forms were in popular use until the third century B.C., when Li Ssu, prime minister of the first emperor of the Ch'in dynasty, modified them and introduced what was known as the "ornamental form" of writing. Cheng Miao, of the Ch'in dynasty, introduced the square form of writing known as *li shu,* which became the standard Han script.

By the end of the Han dynasty, in the second century after Christ, there was a new simplified form of writing known as the orthodox style, *ch'iai shu,* the pattern or plain character. This handwriting was devised to replace the *li shu,* and has been used ever since for official documents and ceremonial writings. Meanwhile, another simplified form of writing known as *chang tsao* (the "running style") came into fashion. This style gradually became a loosely flowing form with many of the characters connected, and is called *tsao shu* ("grass style"). Because it is easier to use than the other scripts, *tsao shu* is the most popular form for personal correspondence. The *ch'iai shu* (orthodox), the *chang tsao* (running style), and the *tsao shu* (correspondence) are the three main styles of writing in wide use throughout China today.

From the artistic point of view it is not the history of Chinese language, but the language itself that is facinating. Chinese characters picture actions as well as objects, and appeal to the eye as well as to the mind. Indeed, the Chinese language is a work of art, and only by looking at it as such can we grasp its significance.

There are two outstanding characteristics of the Chinese language. First, although the language originated in the form of pictographs, it soon became more abstract. So a character

EVOLUTION OF CHINESE CHARACTERS

Oracle Bone	Bronze work	East & Westland	Ornamental	Square Style	Running Style	Orthodox
				漁	漁	漁
				僕	傈	僕
				艱	報	艱
				尊	芎	尊

does not often picture a thing concretely, but gives only a general outline. For instance, in 土 "earth," the upper line represents the surface soil and the lower line the subsoil, while the straight line represents vegetation. In 米 "rice"; ∷ represents grains, divided by 十 representing the separation by threshing.

Second, curved lines are used to depict the outline of the object represented. This is a more convenient means than that of the Egyptian hieroglyphs, in which concrete images are used to represent objects. For instance, the hieroglyphic words for "ox" and "sheep" are written in the shapes of an ox and a sheep. Ancient Chinese pictographs as found in the oracle-bone and bronze inscriptions show the same characteristics, but later the literal images gave place to abstract suggestions; thus the Chinese words for "ox" and "sheep" even in ancient times were written 牛 and 羊, formed by a few lines only.

Representing the complex by means of the simple, and the concrete by means of the abstract, the Chinese language is a great achievement. Civilization is nothing more than the art of using simple means to symbolize the complexity of nature, and abstract ideas to represent concrete objects. In understanding how Chinese civilization spread and persisted over a vast area through the centuries, these characteristics of the language must be taken into consideration.

Moreover, because lines and curves are used to represent ideas and objects, Chinese characters can multiply indefinitely. Later an onomatopoetic element was added, and thus many more words were added to the language. The onomatopoetic element and the symbolic element were put together to form one word. Thus two simple words became one complex word, and again the number of words greatly increased. New objects and new ideas can be represented in Chinese by combining existing characters to form new terms. For instance, "electric light" is expressed in Chinese by putting together two words, *tien tung* (電 燈), (meaning "electric lamp"). "Locomotive" is *huo ch'eh* (火 車), meaning "fire vehicle."

The Chinese written language controls the spoken language. For instance, the character for "tiger" is *hu* (虎), which in some districts was spoken *wu tu* (於 菟). Because the monosyllabic *hu* was the standard written character, the vernacular *wu tu* went out of use. The Chinese character for pen is *pi* (筆), which in some districts was spoken *pu lu* (不 律). Because *pi* was the standard writter character, the vernacular *pi lu* was no longer used. The Chinese term for matches is *huo ts'a* (火 柴), meaning "firewood," which in some parts of China was known as *yang huo* (洋 火), meaning "foreign fire," or as *tze lai huo* (自 來 火), meaning "self-coming fire," or as *ch'u tung* (取 燈), meaning "light-bringer." Since *hu ts'a* was most widely used, the other terms were gradually dropped. Hence the written language has acted as a check to the spoken language, and its uniformity prevents too great a discrepancy between local dialects. In this way the conservative tendency of the Chinese written language has been a factor making for unity in Chinese civilization.

4. The Language Reform

The Chinese language is written largely in an ideographic script of great antiquity. Although this system involves a severe strain on the memory and takes much longer to learn than alphabetic scripts, it has two great merits: First, the written language is independent of sound and so it is not affected by dialect differences. There are many dialects, speakers of some of which can hardly understand those of the next, but all Chinese who can read and write can communicate with each other in that medium. Second, the Chinese written language has changed very little in the course of time. An ancient document, if legible, is no more difficult to read than a modern one written in the same style. The Chinese dynastic histories, written at periods between the first century before Christ and modern times, use the same style and are equally intelligible.

Chinese became a language of brevity, in which latent ideas play an important part. The reader himself must supply all the links that are necessary for the continuity of thought. As a result, the written language bears no close relation to the spoken language. Written Chinese became the preserve of a special and limited class—the scholars. This kind of language made education difficult, expensive, and exclusive.

Moreover, most of the Chinese characters are very clumsy and unwieldy, consisting of massive structures of strokes and containing a number of components which sometimes are individual ideographs in their own right. Of the two thousand most commonly used words, only 28 per cent have less than eight strokes, the rest containing from nine to twenty-seven strokes. Learning to read and to write the elaborate ideographic script is a very difficult process. The scholars either used the running hand for quick writing or adopted simpler variants for complicated words, but until recently, there was no revolutionary change in the language.

The movement of 1917 to adopt *pai hua,* or the spoken language, as a recognized style for literature and official writing, was undoubtedly a great advance, but no attempt was made for the adoption of a system of simplified characters. It is not only necessary but also possible to simplify the written language so that it can be used as an easier and more serviceable tool for cultural development and mass education. In January 1956, the Communist State Council published the three-part Scheme for Simplifying Chinese Characters. The first part consists of a list of 230 simplified characters, which came into use when the scheme was published; the second is a list of 285 simplified characters, of which 95 came into use on a trial basis; the third is a list of 54 simplified radicals, which will entail the simplification of more than a thousand words. A language project made experiments with the students of a normal school and found out that they could write simplified characters nearly three times as fast as they could write the more complex characters. The Communist

Committee for Reforming the Chinese Written Language then introduced the 515 simplified characters of the first and second lists of the Scheme. These characters averaged 8.16 strokes each against an average of 16.08 strokes each in their original forms. With the publication of books and periodicals in the simplified language, illiteracy in China should be overcome to a considerable degree.

There had been several proposals in recent decades to abandon the Chinese characters and to adopt a phonetic alphabet in their place, but they all failed to achieve the desired aim. Chinese Communist leaders have been persistent in their efforts to reform the language, declaring that the fundamental solution to the problem is to replace the ideographic system with a phonetic script. In 1956 a committee of linguistic experts appointed by the Communist regime decided to adopt the twenty-six-letter Latin alphabet for the Chinese written language. But they are aware that many problems must be met before Latinized writing can be considered a fully satisfactory substitute; they also think it better to allow a period of transition in which to make the necessary preparations for this change. As of now, the twenty-six-letter Latin alphabet is "not to replace Chinese characters," but "to give the pronunciation of these characters." [3]

[3] See Chou En-lai's "Current Tasks of Reforming The Written Language," a speech delivered at a meeting sponsored by the National Committee of the Chinese People's Political Consultative Conference, January 10, 1958.

CHAPTER XIV. BASIC IDEALS OF CHINESE ART

Of all the expressions of Chinese civilization, it is Chinese art that has made the lasting contribution to the culture of the world. Chinese science is not pre-eminent, although China has given the world many noteworthy inventions, such as paper and printing, gunpowder, the compass, silk, and tea. Even Chinese philosophy has not yet made any lasting impression on the West; its moderation, restraint, and pacifism hardly suit the exuberant Western temperament. It would be unfair to judge the Chinese as a nation without a consideration of their art. There are certain inherent qualities of the Chinese soul that can be known only through their reflection in Chinese art.

Our purpose in this chapter is to consider the basic ideals which distinguish Chinese art from that of the West—and, indeed, from that of the other Oriental civilizations.

1. Formalism—The Perfection of Form

Chinese culture, as we know, seeks the essence of life in intuitively apprehended values, in spiritual intimations, and in the abstract elements of linear rhythm and formal organization. What strikes one is the perfection of form shown in Chinese art. One striking difference between Western and Chinese art is that in the former stress is laid on content, while in the latter form is pre-eminent. Let us illustrate this by reference to Chinese calligraphy, painting, and poetry.

Chinese calligraphy is a most marvelous art. Painting must represent something, some object, or some scene; when one looks at a painting, one's mind is directed toward the fairness of representation, as well as the quality of the strokes which represent it. But calligraphy is the expression of rhythm, the pureness of form. It is calligraphy that has given the Chinese basic notions of line and form. In fact, from calligraphy came not only painting, but also a certain feeling for architecture. The flowing curves, the straight lines, and the graceful angles of temple roof or monument arch have their basis in the brush strokes of the Chinese script. This explains why the Chinese rank calligraphy as the very highest of the fine arts. But it is only after long and patient practice—practice of the arm and wrist and hand and finger—that one can master the technique of using the brush; and it is only its masterly use that gives Chinese calligraphy its special form and style. A stroke of the brush once made is there forever; alteration or revision would be out of the question. So the Chinese calligrapher will not set down a stroke unless he is completely assured of its beauty and perfection.

Chinese painting is closely related to calligraphy, in principle and technique. As to their relation, an early Chinese writer said: "When the people could not express their thoughts in painting, they made characters, and when they could not express shapes in writing, they made painting." Thus one supplements the other. Calligraphy and painting are considered twin arts in China. First of all, the materials used in writing—the brushes, ink, paper, and ink slab (known as the "Four Treasures of the Literary Apartment")—are the same as those used in painting. Eight fundamental strokes used in the formation of Chinese characters are also carried over into painting as the essential ways of handling a brush-pen. It is no wonder, then, that Chinese painting, like the calligraphy, is characterized by linear rhythm and formal vitality. Chinese monochrome painting, executed with a few simple but effective strokes of the brush, has a vital beauty. For instance, the monochromes of Wang Wei (A.D. 699–759), especially noted for his snow scenes,[1] suggest the reality of nature without the aid of shades. Chinese artists use Chinese ink, which is rubbed down with water on the ink slab until it reaches the required consistency for

[1] Wang Wei, founder of the southern school of Chinese painting, stressed the handling of the brush to secure harmony of tone. "There is poetry in his painting and painting in his poetry" was said of the poet-painter. See Chapter XII.

writing or drawing on paper or silk. A quality which ink sketches must possess, if they are to be works of art, is perfection of form. It is said that the natural aspect of an object can be beautifully conveyed in ink if one knows how to produce the required form, that is, the creative formal organization. In a Chinese painting the light and dark elements always make a pattern, governed by the structural requirement of the picture itself.

Chinese poems are deliberately tranquil and sober in tone, just as calm and harmony distinguish Chinese painting; there is no excitement, no ecstasy, little or no rhetoric. Hence the poems are generally deficient in range and splendor, but they are content with the charm of exquisiteness, intimacy, and sincerity. As a result, Chinese poetry seldom shapes itself into long and elaborate designs, but indulges in quiet subtleties and delicacies. The classical poems, for instance, are versed in five or seven monosyllabic words each with its corresponding character in the other seven lines; and there is a rhyme in terminal sounds and by alternative tones or pitches. This artifice relies on showing the perfection of form and phrase, and unity of mood.

To the Chinese artist, the form of an artistic image is constructed on reality. And yet the form can only be comprehended in its harmony, by which is meant the compromise of odds, regularity of movements, melody of tune, and unity of mood. To the Chinese, art is the mirror of the artist's mind, and expressive of his personality or even his idiosyncrasy. To produce a masterpiece an artist must first saturate himself with the spirit of his subject and strive through the medium of form to bring out the very soul of the person, or the very essence of the particular object which he has selected as his theme. The great T'ang poet Tu Fu (712–770) once wrote that he worked "in pensive search for the design," and also: "I'll not stop until I find that line that moves the soul of man."

2. Symbolism—The Economy of Means

Side by side with formalism, there is a kind of symbolism very evident in Chinese art. In this respect, the Chinese language offers a good illustration. The Chinese language is a work of art, and its ideographic script is very symbolic, full of implications and suggestions. As we have seen, the Chinese character does not often depict a thing concretely, but rather gives a general outline that suggests it. This is the product of the same genius that invented the eight trigrams in the *Book of Change*, which are supposed to represent the complexity of nature by means of a few symbols. However, the trigrams only have sixty-four combinations, whereas the Chinese written character is capable of an infinite variety of forms. All that happens in the universe, natural or human, is incorporated into the strokes of a Chinese pen. A single Chinese character often condenses the meaning of many words in English. Take the character 閒 (*hsien*), for instance: the symbol is made of two parts—two doors open at the center (門) and the moon (月) comes between them; moonlight streaming in through the closed doors suggests "at ease, leisure, calm."

Another important quality of Chinese is brevity. One may think that the Chinese language is too allusive and too obscure, but to the Chinese, obscurity is a lesser fault than redundancy. The Chinese language, in its written form, has become a secret code of subtle suggestions. There is nothing quite like this language elsewhere, nothing to match it in the simplicity and brevity of phrases conveying so many ideas.

This is also true of Chinese painting, which follows the same tradition, portraying ideas or objects by abstract lines. Chinese painting pays great attention to empty space. "Making space serve as color" has been the important principle of Chinese painting. This does not weaken the effect but emphasizes the salient points of a picture and so brings them out in sharper relief. It is well said: "An inch of canvas is worth an inch of gold." Complex subjects should be organized and arranged so that the picture most pregnant with meaning is achieved with the minimum strokes and the largest image is created on the smallest piece of paper. In painting it is essential always to maintain such economy of means while expressing to the full the feelings and thoughts of the artist.

Yet another illustration. Chinese drama appears to the eyes of Occidentals as difficult of comprehension as the mystic smile of the sphinx. Chinese drama is not in the least realistic. The traditional stage has no scenery whatsoever; the properties used in the drama are as simple as the stage is bare. Nothing can equal the humor of a Chinese actor, who on a stage bare of scenery gallops across the floor, dismounts and passes his horse to a groom, flirts with a young lady or hides behind a battlement to attack his enemy. Nothing is there but the man, and yet one sees it as clearly as if there were a hundred scenes and endless props.

There is symbolism in every detail of the play; in signs and make-believes, in the movements and costumes of the actors. Everything has its implications and suggestions, for the Chinese audience does not go to the theater to see the play; it goes there to see how well the actor renders it. In almost every play a complicated story is told by the actor's singing and dancing, and it is by the aid of symbolic movements that the actor can suggest the objects which are supposed to appear in the development of the story.

Symbolism consists of two fundamental elements, namely, simplicity and suggestiveness. Because of its simplicity, Chinese art is intelligible; because of its suggestiveness, it is full of imagination and feeling.

3. Naturalism—The Beauty of Nature

The third important ideal of Chinese art is naturalism. In the West art is a deliberate work of man, in which nature has no part; it is a matter of human choice and invention. Western art rises out of sensitive observation, and its ideal lies in the perfection of proportion, structure, and coloring. Western paintings, for instance, deal with persons and objects; their delineations are clear, but they do not exist as a distinct, natural art. Western skyscrapers stand out in blocks against the sky, without arches and curves; they have little relation to nature. The attitude of the Western artist mirrors that of Western religion and philosophy. Western culture can be envisioned as a gigantic struggle between man and nature; its history is the history of the human ego battling for domination over the "materialistic" forces of the universe.

The Chinese have not suffered from this peculiar destructive dichotomy. Centuries before the emergence of landscape painting as a distinctive art, the Chinese venerated nature. Confucius said as early as the fifth century B.C.: "The wise man delights in water; the good man delights in mountains" (*Analects*, VI, 21). The Chinese term for "landscape" combines the same two concepts which Confucius mentioned, for it consists of the characters for mountain and water. This in itself is deeply meaningful, suggesting as it does the very elements which were considered the most important in representing nature. The sacred mountains had been worshiped in China from time immemorial. Water also was of prime importance to an agricultural people like the Chinese, and it was worshiped in the form of rivers, clouds, mist, and rain, and symbolized by the dragon, one of the most ancient and popular of the Chinese sacred animals. In the earliest recorded documents, on the oracle bones, and in the *Shin Ching* (*Book of Odes*), there is a keen sense of the beauty of nature and, what is equally important, a deep sense of man's relationship to nature. Chinese art conceives nature as animated by an immanent force, and the object of the artists is to put themselves in communion with this force, and then to give exquisite expression to it in their works.

Compare, for example, Chinese landscape paintings with those of the West. It strikes one immediately that the Western painters have been trying to give clear, realistic representations of a particular scene, that is, to be faithful to what their eyes see; therefore behind Western landscapes is the implication of visual experience. The Chinese painting suggests an aspect of nature that the artist has absorbed into his system and expressed in his brushwork. That is, he is faithful to what he feels. Behind Chinese landscapes is the implication of a mood. Chinese landscapes represent the intuitive expression of man in communion with nature.

That is not to say that the Chinese painter does not observe nature as closely as the Westerner. He sees nature in essence, in spiritual significance, and attempts to express in his work the harmony of the universe, instead of trying to represent natural appearances. Chinese landscapes vary in mood depending upon the time of day, the state of the weather, and the season of the year. Kuo Hsi (1020–1090), the great landscapist of the Sung period, in his *Essay on Landscape Painting* wrote:

> The spring mountain is wrapped in an unbroken
> stretch of dreamy haze and mist, and so men are joy-

ful; the summer mountain is rich with shady foliage, and so men are at leisure; the autumn mountain is serene and calm, with withering leaves and dying plants, and so men are solemn; the winter mountain is gloomy with storm-clouds, and so men are forlorn.

Kuo Hsi was famous for his landscapes, and his landscapes were of course the product of careful observation. But his art was more a product of the feeling evoked by natural phenomena than a mere representation of natural appearances. The Chinese artist addresses his art to the mind instead of trying to please the eyes by clever imitation.

The Chinese as a whole have an eye for the picturesque in nature. Even the ordinary implements, tools, and utensils in China are often painted or carved with flowers and birds, mountains and rivers. Westerners are familiar with the artistically decorated Chinese parasols, beautifully painted Chinese fans, and skillfully embroidered kerchiefs.

At this point, reference might be made to Chinese architecture. For instance, the exteriors of the early palaces were covered with colorful scenes; the buildings were roofed with picturesque arches and curves; pillars were beautifully carved; gardens and yards were dotted with hills, ponds, and pagodas, and shadowed by the luxuriant foliage of pines, cedars, and willows. The houses, with their curved, thatched roofs, stood under trees that were left to twist themselves into any fanciful shapes that pleased nature. Bridges arched gracefully across the canals and the teahouses on piles along the river edge were intricate with lattices.

The Great Wall does not fail to represent the beauty of nature. It climbs the steepest slopes, creeps along sheer precipices, and springs from height to height, leaving a square crenelated tower on every crown; and then it zigzags from crest to crest, dips into ravines, and emerges mounting the ranges beyond. The grand work of man is thus harmonized with the beauty of nature.

Most of the Buddhist temples were built on gorges or on the slopes of hills, where the solitude is as complete as the most devote hermit can desire. The only means of access to these temples are the narrow, serpentine passages along which the worshipers from the great cities and scattered villages wound in and out on festival days to make offerings to the enshrined Buddha. The shrines were lavishly decorated with carvings in which the sacred lotus, the flower of Nirvana, predominated. Sculptural works were carved on the cliffs and precipices, so as to match human skill with the beauty of nature.

The love of nature was emphasized by the Taoist philosophers. The Taoist ideal, as enhanced by Buddhism, is to withdraw from world affairs and to live in tranquil communion with nature. It had a special appeal for artists and poets, who returned to nature in search of contemplative solitude. We often find the delicate and intimate feeling for the beauty of nature in their paintings and poems. This escape from worldliness is not merely to absorb impressions from the varied forms of nature, but also to search for moral and aesthetic elevation. From the mountaintops the artist surveys the world with a calm expansion of the spirit, and this spirit goes into his art. It is this spirit of calm and harmony, this flavor of mountain air always tinged with the recluse's passion for leisure and solitude, which characterizes all forms of Chinese art. Consequently, the ideal of Chinese art is not supremacy over nature, but harmony with nature.

4. Romanticism—The Spirit of Creation

"Romanticism" is meant here in the sense of the creative spirit that works by taking impressions and reflections from all that man hears and feels and sees. The artist begins to paint when he is inspired; in other words, he paints because he must. Inspiration originates in the sense of romanticism. Before he takes up his brush, the artist must submerge his consciousness in the universe, and the beating of his heart is identified with the pulsation of all life; only then is he at peace and communion with nature. This is the peak of art. For instance, Wu Tao-tze (c. 700–760), the greatest painter of the T'ang dynasty, was once sent by the emperor to paint the scenery of the Chia-lin River. He returned empty-handed. When asked about it, he replied, "I have it all in my heart." Like many other Chinese artists, he made no preliminary sketches; but he was so inspired by the scenery that, within a few hours, he executed a landscape that is one of the greatest and most beautiful paintings ever made of a river.

If the Chinese painter wished to depict a landscape, he would ascend a high mountain, where he would sit and think of the picture he was to paint, preparing himself mentally for the undertaking, much as a poet meditates on the thought he wishes to express. The essence had to be discovered before work could begin.

We have spoken of the delicate and intimate feeling for the beauty of nature in Chinese poetry. The great poet Li Po was most of his life a wanderer, and spent his time in drinking, writing, and reciting poems in the seclusion of forests and mountains. His *On Drinking Alone by Moonlight*, a magnificent Bacchanalian rhapsody, was written when he was alone with a kettle of wine under the bright moon. Here the poet, his shadow, and the moon—a party of three—are all equally parts of nature, in which the poet has allowed his own consciousness to dissolve.

Generally speaking, Chinese painting is never far from poetry. Painters see and feel as poets do. As there is lyric poetry, so there is mental painting. What we call mental painting is really a painting which comes from the inner sources of the artist's own tradition. But no one has ever given a good definition of this tradition. To attain it will depend much upon the artist's own cultivation and his mental power. The artist is a man of double activity. He has to portray in his mind what he is going to make; and he must also have the power to translate through his brush what he has felt and sensed in his mind. So the saying goes: "When a man has read ten thousand books and traveled ten thousand miles, then he may seize the brush and try his hand at painting." The Chinese artist does not learn painting by shutting himself in a room. He must travel and visit famous mountains and rivers, in order to absorb impressions from the myriad forms of nature and to feed his inspiration. Once his mind feels the approach of inspiration his hands instinctively have the urge to paint; then by making use of his highest mental power to portray what he has absorbed and express it through his brush, he reaches his artistic goal, that is, the creative spirit.

Now, what is this thing called creative spirit? We take it

to be a synthesis of the external scene [1] and the artist's sentiments. It seems that in any genuine art both elements—external scene and internal sentiment—are present. In depicting a scene, the artist also communicates his sentiments. For instance, landscape painting must involve, of course, the natural elements of the scene, but it is essential that it communicates the artist's sentiments and inspiration aroused by the sight of nature, the feeling and emotion stirred by the scene. A painting which consists entirely of a mechanical description of physical objects can at best be a decorative picture but can hardly be considered genuine art. Insofar as the painting is genuine, it will transport us into its special "state of mind" and make us see and feel something new, or make us see and feel something familiar in a new way; that is, the artist's sentiments expressed in the description of external scenes. When a creative spirit is embodied in a poem or a painting, then that poem or painting can be said to have a soul.

"Depict the scene to convey sentiments"—this is something that the great artists have always understood. When he was about to paint, the great Sung artist Kuo Hsi would wash his hands and rinse his ink slab, and he would put his desk in order and burn incense, thereby calming his spirit and composing his thoughts.

Perfect absorption and intense concentration are necessary for artistic creation. Whatever subject or theme an artist may choose becomes the center and the whole of his being. He sees the subject already in his mind's eye and then sets out to work. Thus he brings the talent in him into harmony with nature; the barrier between the external world of phenomena and the internal world of feeling is broken down. Is this the reason why the great art of China seems to be supernatural?

[1] The word "scene" used here includes not only natural scenery but any physical object. Moreover, the "scene" in a painting or a poem may not be actual; when the artist uses concrete images to express his sentiment, they also constitute a "scene," though of an imaginary order.

Part Three: Reform and Revolution

CHAPTER XV. SOCIAL CHANGES IN THE PAST
            HUNDRED YEARS

The history of China since 1842 might be looked upon as a tragic story of the breakdown of the traditional society based on the Confucian social norm. Let us first examine the foreign influences and domestic conditions, and then trace the economic and intellectual developments which were responsible for eventually toppling the traditional order. The history of China in the past hundred years, insofar as social changes are concerned, may be divided into two major stages. The first begins with the Opium War (1839–1842) and ends with the first Sino-Japanese War of 1894. The second covers the period from the year 1895 up to the present. The first period was a time of Western encroachments and the collapse of the imperial rule. The second was a time of economic difficulties, political chaos, and ideological conflicts, all leading to the total destruction of the old order. It is best that we examine the social changes of the past hundred years in some detail.

1. Western Encroachments

For centuries prior to the Opium War of 1839, China had lived in lofty isolation, with a belief in her superiority. In the ancient days, there was a sharp distinction between Hua-Hsia (Chinese) and the *Yi Ti* (barbarians). (See Chapter II.) The regions surrounding China were either held under military control or treated as satellite areas. It was the rule that those barbarians who wished to "come and be transformed," and so participate in the benefits of Chinese civilization, must recognize the imperial supremacy of the Middle Kingdom. This supremacy was acknowledged either in the performance of the *kowtow*—the three kneelings and nine prostrations—or by the bringing of tributes.

When the Chinese first came in contact with Westerners in the beginning of the seventeenth century, they regarded them as barbarians and their special envoys as tribute bearers. The Manchu government frequently rejected the proposals that official missions be exchanged to negotiate a commercial treaty. The British, determined to achieve free trade in China, started the Opium War of 1839–1842. It ended in a complete victory for the British and marked a decisive turning point in the history of China.

After the Opium War a number of treaties were made between foreign powers and China. The British made two treaties, in 1842 and 1844; the French and American treaties were also concluded in 1844. By these agreements, Western nations secured "settlements" or "concessions" in different localities, over which the Chinese government had no administrative jurisdiction. This was tantamount to the establishment of many foreign states within the territory of China. Moreover, resident aliens and corporations enjoyed extraterritorial status exempting them from Chinese law and authority. Other areas were later leased outright, the leases ranging from twenty-five years up to ninety-nine years. These foreign encroachments led to the dividing of China into several "spheres of special interest." Manchuria belonged to Imperial Russia's sphere of interest, Shantung to that of Germany, the areas along the Yangtze River to that of Great Britain, and so forth.

With the Opium War and the subsequent treaties, the traditional order disintegrated rapidly. In the course of a few decades the Western "barbarians" who had forced their way into China brought about a reversal of the old relationship: at the mercy of Western military occupation, political aggression, and economic exploitation, China became in effect a tributary to the Western powers.

Thereafter foreign encroachments on China increased. The effect was immediate. The Chinese were for the first time convinced that they had something to learn from the Western countries. The following passage, taken from *Suggestions On Foreign Affairs,* submitted by Hsüeh Fu-ch'eng (1838–1894) to the Tsungli Yamen (Office in General Charge of Foreign Affairs), offers a good illustration:

> Western nations rely on intelligence and energy to compete with one another. To come abreast of them, China should plan to promote commerce and open mines; unless we change, the Westerners will be rich and we poor. We should excel in technology and the manufacture of machinery; unless we change, they will be skillful and we clumsy. Steamships, trains, and the telegraph should be adopted; unless we change, the Westerners will be quick and we slow. The advantages and disadvantages of treaties, the competence and incompetence of envoys, and the improvement of military organization and strategy should be discussed. Unless we change, the Westerners will cooperate with each other and we shall stand isolated; they will be strong and we shall be weak.[1]

The Manchu government introduced a few reforms to imitate Western methods in building steam gunboats, manufacturing military weapons, and training soldiers. Such, indeed, was her proficiency in the arts of war that China supposed herself able to cope with the Western powers, until the war with Japan dispelled the illusion.

2. Collapse of the Imperial Rule

With the Sino-Japanese War of 1894–1895, the defeat of China was complete. The weaknesses and corruption of the Manchu government were fully exposed to the world. This display of weakness and corruption stirred many scholar-officials. These men, understanding that China's humiliating defeat in the Sino-Japanese War was due not only to military inferiority, but also to political degeneration, began the organization of reform clubs in the capital and throughout the country. They sought the advice of missionaries and were

[1] See W. T. De Bary and others, eds., *Sources of Chinese Tradition,* New York, Columbia Univ. Press, 1960, p. 715.

also encouraged by the viceroys and governors. In 1893 the eminent Cantonese scholar, K'ang Yu-wei (1858–1927), convinced that to revive China must follow the example of Meiji Japan, launched a reform movement with the support of the young emperor Kuang-hsü. The movement advocated a basic change from absolute monarchy to constitutional rule, but it resulted in precipitating the *coup d'état* executed by the empress dowager. The emperor was imprisoned and the reforms abandoned. (See Chap. XVI.)

The failure of the reform movement intensified the reaction of the conservative forces. These conservatives, bigoted by their traditional conceptions, still considered the Westerners as identical with the early barbarians. They were convinced that even though China suffered many defeats in war, Chinese culture would eventually dominate the world. The following passages are taken from the works of Yeh Te-hui (1864–1927):

> Of all countries in the five continents China is the most populous. It is situated in the north temperate zone, with a mild climate and abundant natural resources, and its culture leads the world. The boundary between China and foreign countries, between Chinese and barbarians, admits of no argument and cannot be discussed in terms of their strength or our weakness. . . .
> An examination of the causes of success and failure in government reveals that in general the upholding of Confucianism leads to good government while the adoption of foreignism leads to disorder. If one keeps to the kingly way [relying on virtue], there will be order; if one follows the way of the overlord [relying on power], there will be disorder. . . .
> Confucianism represents the supreme expression of justice in the principle of Heaven and the hearts of men. In the future it will undoubtedly be adopted by civilized countries of both East and West. The essence of Confucianism will shine brightly as it renews itself from day to day.[2]

Such expressions reveal the attitude of the conservatives. Rallying around the imperial court, they rejected foreign learning and opposed new reforms. They fostered antiforeign feeling and sponsored the *I-ho-t'uan* (Righteous and

[2] *Ibid.*, pp. 742-743.

Harmonious Society) generally known as the Boxers. These reactionary activities led to the invasion of the Chinese capital by an expeditionary force of the eight Allied Powers in 1900. China was forced to sign the Hsin-Ch'ou (the Chinese name for the year 1901) Peace Treaty in 1901, which not only discredited the Manchu government once and for all, but also resulted in the continuous decline of the national economy.

Then the Manchu government, promulgated a reform program in order to pacify the Chinese people. Consequently, five high officials were sent to foreign countries to investigate constitutional government. Meanwhile, Sun Yat-sen (1856–1925), convinced that the Manchu regime was beyond the hope of reforming, organized the *Tung-meng hui,* or the League of Common Alliance, out of which later grew the Kuomintang, or the Nationalist Party. Thereafter two great movements, one preparing for a constitutional monarchy and one advocating revolution, operated simultaneously. It was Sun Yat-sen who appealed to the Chinese youth, and his revolutionary movement grew in strength. (See Chapter XVII.) In the autumn of 1911, the revolution exploded in Wuchang and soon brought the overthrow of the Manchu dynasty.

These historical facts serve to explain that Chinese society at the time, owing to external encroachments and internal weaknesses, had already undergone some fundamental changes. The conditions upon which the old social order depended were gradually losing ground and would eventually collapse. In the 1870's and '80s, the scholar-officials sought to preserve the old social order through the adoption of Western technology, but in the end they were not only unable to resist social changes, but contributed further to the processes of disintegration which marked the last years of the Manchu government. After the defeat of the Taipings in 1864, able statesmen like Tseng Kuo-fan (1811–1872), Li Hung-chang (1823–1901), and others had encouraged the manufacturing of arms, the building of ships, the construction of railways, and improvements in telegraphic communication, by means of which many of the commodity industries, such as weaving and silk-reeling, were developed. Unfortunately, many of these enterprises, for one reason or the other, not only ended in failure, but also undermined various handiwork and home industries, which were essential to

agrarian economy. It was this failure that led to demands
for more drastic changes.

3. Breakdown of Agrarian Economy

For the economic difficulties which began to plague the
country from the late nineteenth century on, the Chinese
people could blame the inept and predatory government, the
drainage of profits from the enormous foreign investment in
China, and the special rights to foreign nations granted by
the unequal treaties. The economic development of China
started from the Yellow River basin, then gradually was fo-
cused in the Yangtze Valley, and finally moved to the coast
in the Southeast. China was an agricultural country, and the
great majority of the Chinese depended upon the
agrarian economy. The age-long superiority of the "root"
(agriculture) over the "branch" (commerce), the principle of
"fair distribution of wealth," the ideal of the "well field"
system, and the various measures for limiting the ownership
of land adopted by the various dynasties, all were intended
to rehabilitate the traditional agrarian economy and maintain
agricultural lands in due proportion all over the country,
with the exception of the outlying areas. For this reason,
there was never any marked disparity in the density of population anywhere. Although economic development changed
from the river basin to the sea coast, there had been no
great tendency toward overlocalization.

After the opening of China, foreigners had seized local
points along the southeastern coast and made them trade
ports for the penetration of the interior. Under the Inland Nav-
igation Regulations of 1898, foreigners could travel freely
along a sea coast of 5,000 nautical miles and through inland
rivers as long as 10,000 nautical miles. During the period
1895–1926, an overall length of 7,671 miles of railroads was
built mostly with foreign capital, cutting the major portion
of the mainland from north to south as well as east to west.
From then on, foreign trade readily penetrated to the rural
areas. Consequently, the traditional social order disintegrated and new groups emerged. Urban development spread
from the city to the village and changed ways of life and

patterns of values. Rural communities were affected to a degree that was deep and far-reaching.

But urbanization brought no significant increase in industrialization. The total foreign investments in China increased from $500,000,000 in 1902 to $1,000,000,000 in 1914 and up to $2,000,000,000 in 1931, of which foreign trade amounted to about 72.7 per cent and industries and mining only 21.3 per cent.[3] From urbanization, therefore, China derived no benefit of the kind that could in any way help the development of her industry or agricultural production. Moreover, the foreign goods, under the protection of the unequal treaties, were dumped on the Chinese market, and native products could not successfully compete with them. The existing handicraft industries, once an important source of supplementary income, began to disappear; and yet, at the same time, the newly founded industries failed to prosper, owing to foreign competition. Consequently, the ever-increasing excess of imports over exports, together with the imbalance between the high market value of manufactured goods and the low market value of agricultural products, caused the bankruptcy of China's agrarian economy.

During the last fifty years, China remained an essentially agricultural country, and the peasant's produce remained the chief source of revenue. However, no effective remedy or relief was devised for the plight of the peasant. The Nationalists, who came to power in 1927, had an elaborate rural program based on the equal distribution of land and government control of capital, but its implementation was delayed until the threats from the Chinese Communists and from Japan could be eliminated. Meanwhile, the Communists, after the break with the Nationalists in 1927, began a series of land-reform experiments; and during the civil war of 1946–1949 they succeeded in using land reform as a major political and military weapon. As stated earlier, there have been many peasant-led uprisings throughout the history of China. These historical precedents were neglected by the Nationalists, but not by the Communists, who were able successfully to enlist the support of the peasants for their revolution.

[3] For all the investment figures quoted, see C. F. Remer, *Foreign Investment in China,* New York, Macmillan, 1933.

4. Traditionalism versus Modernism

Another disruptive force was represented by the intellectuals who attempted to destroy the age-old traditions as detrimental to new ideas and the forces of progress. This revolt started with the Reform Movement and reached its climax in the New Culture Movement. It won the support of the younger generation, and provoked the traditionalists to virulent opposition. Scholar-officials like Chang Chih-tung (1837–1909) and others had dwelt upon "Chinese learning for substance, Western learning for function" in the hope that they might preserve the established traditions intact and at the same time provide a sanction for needed reform. The formula served somewhat to ease the conflict between old and new, but it was not able to prevent change. At the beginning of the Russo-Japanese War in 1904, the *Shanghai Times,* then published for the first time, said in its first editorial: "The cream of our culture is to be honored, but things that do not fit in with our contemporary thought should be shelved; likewise, Western civilization is to be respected, but those features that cannot be adopted for our present purpose should be deferred to a future time." [4]

From this statement, we can see how far the drift toward Westernization had progressed. In 1905 came the abolition of the age-old civil-service examination system, from which most government officials had been selected. At the same time the traditional educational system, strictly confined to the Confucian classics, was supplanted by a modern school system. Such a change was contrary to the "ancestral institutions" and had no precedent in Chinese history. It was tantamount to doing away with the unification of thought, and it hastened the disintegration of the learned class.

From then on, the Chinese mind, long confined to tradition, seemed to burst forth with current ideas and modern doctrines. With this liberation there arose a new type of Chinese intellectual, trained in the knowledge of the West and anxious to liberate the Chinese mentality from traditionalism.

[4] *Shanghai Times,* February 10, 1904.

But another group of scholars, still devoted to the preservation of China's traditional culture, reacted against the complete Westernization advocated by the new intellectuals. In the end those who spoke for progress and modernism prevailed against the neo-traditionalists. As has been said earlier, the latter exerted their best efforts for the preservation of China's national culture, but in the long run they could find no way to arrest the turbulent social changes.

An examination of social changes in the last hundred years should make two points clear: First, the old foundations of Chinese society had been gradually eaten away. Second, the traditional concept of a social norm has been gradually collapsing. From the policy of "Enrich the nation and strengthen the army" to that of "Chinese learning for substance, Western learning for function," from the Reform Movement of 1898 to the advocacy of complete Westernization, the old value system had been ever deteriorating and the old order proceeding toward disintegration.

CHAPTER XVI. K'ANG YU-WEI AND THE REFORM MOVEMENT

1. K'ang's Political Views and Activities

After the Sino-Japanese War of 1894, a movement for avenging the national humiliation and strengthening the nation sprang up among the Chinese people. This culminated in the work of two great leaders, K'ang Yu-wei (1858–1927) and Sun Yat-sen (1866–1925). Both of these two leaders lived in Kwangtung, where the Western influence upon China's economic and cultural life was strongest. With this common stimulus, both accepted at an early age the vocation of political reformer. Both of them became convinced that China's weakness was due not so much to her military inferiority as to her political decadence, which in turn could be traced to monarchic despotism. However, at the outset of their careers, they differed widely in their theories of political reform. As early as 1885 Sun Yat-sen had made up his mind to overthrow the Manchu government, and in 1905 he organized the *T'ung-meng hui* (League of Common Alliance) to advocate the Nationalist revolution. (See Chap. XVII.) But K'ang Yu-wei favored safe-guarding the sovereign position of the monarch, and he formed various clubs and groups, such as the *Ch'iang-hsüeh hui* (Society for the Study of National Strengthening) and the *Pao-kuo hui* (National Protection Society), to pursue his program. The family backgrounds and early education of the two leaders will help to explain their political differences.

Sun Yat-sen came of an old agricultural family and spent his early years in a peasant household. He was cut off from the official tradition and Confucian orthodoxy and would naturally follow the Taiping leader Hung Hsiu-ch'üan's steps. By contrast K'ang Yu-wei came from a family of Confucian scholars and prepared himself for entry into the old elite. Moreover, Sun Yat-sen received a modern Western education and had direct contact with Western culture. Consequently he was inspired by a belief that China could be quickly and easily modernized by the adoption of Western ideas and institutions. On the other hand, K'ang Yu-wei received a traditional education and his acquaintance with Western culture was only indirect. K'ang's political ideas mostly derived from the Confucian classics, which had been traditionally respected as a criterion of good government. He claimed that what he was doing in his reform program was not the adoption of Western institutions and ideas, but rather the realization of the Confucian scheme. The reason why K'ang Yu-wei could become a reform leader and win the support of many high officials and scholars was simply that his theories suited the tempo of the times.

Now let us turn to the consideration of K'ang's political activities and his reform program. As early as 1888, when he was in Peking, he sent to the emperor his first memorial on the reform of government. But the memorial never reached the emperor, and K'ang returned to Canton. In 1895, after the Sino-Japanese War, he was back in Peking, together with over 1,200 young scholars who were candidates for the metropolitan examination. K'ang submitted another memorial to the emperor, in which he called for a repudiation of the treaty, a move of the capital to the interior of the country, and the total reform of the government. This demand had no effect, but in 1898 he was admitted into the emperor's presence and submitted another critical memorial in which he set forth a whole program of reform, including the development of agriculture and industry as well as a total revision of the educational system. K'ang Yu-wei was a man of strong and persuasive personality, and he convinced the emperor that these reforms were essential if China was to survive.

In the summer of 1898, the emperor began to issue a series of reform edicts, based on the program spelled out by K'ang Yu-wei, and instituted what was later known as "the Hundred Days' Reform." [1] What K'ang Yu-wei had in

[1] The movement lasted from June 11 to September 16, a span of about a hundred days.

mind were basic political and constitutional reforms, similar to those of the Meiji era in Japan. He wanted a constitutional monarchy supported by a new type of official. The traditional education and the examination system were no longer producing men of ability for the service of the state. K'ang Yu-wei proposed, therefore, the abolition of the state examination and a complete renovation of the educational system in which Western sciences and practical arts would be studied together with the Chinese classics. He also proposed the establishment of common schools, for which Buddhist temples were to be thrown open, and the creation of a modern university in the capital, which should gather in the provincial graduates and train them for the civil service. A bureau of translation was to be established, and newspapers were to be encouraged.

K'ang's general economic plans were to encourage commerce and industry through the construction of railways and factories. Steps were also to be taken to develop mining and to promote agricultural improvements. A modern budget was to be introduced, so that the government would be able to balance revenue and expenditure. There were many other measures, aimed at social and institutional reforms. To clear the way for his reform program, K'ang Yu-wei tried to reorganize the government machinery and eliminate the old officialdom.

The reforms were not at all bad in themselves; they would have paved the way for the modernization of China. But they aroused a storm of opposition from those who by conviction or interest were wedded to the old order. The situation was complicated by the rivalries of two factions at court, one of them disposed to countenance reforms, and the other taking the conservative side. The conservatives looked to the empress dowager for support and leadership. She had always kept closely in touch with the developing situation and at the same time kept a vigilant eye on the emperor. When the empress saw that the emperor was actually launching reforms, she went to work with lightning speed. Very soon the reformers had to flee; those who failed to make good their escape were arrested and executed. The emperor was made a prisoner, and remained a captive until his death in 1908. The empress dowager resumed her regency in his behalf and annulled all the reform edicts.

After the failure of the reform movement, K'ang Yu-wei

went abroad and continued to write and raise funds in behalf of the movement. However, he no longer played any important part in Chinese politics and his place was soon taken over by Sun Yat-sen, who turned the reform movement into a revolution.

2. K'ang's Writings and Philolosphy

Politically the contribution of K'ang Yu-wei was less important, but culturally he did much to stimulate the thinking of the Chinese people and teach them a critical attitude toward the Confucian classics. His significance as a thinker lies in his attempt to provide a Confucian justification for his basic reform ideas. In his opinion, what he was advocating in his reform program was not the adoption of Western civilization, but rather the realization of Confucian teachings. He wrote many commentaries on the Confucian classics and read his new ideas into them. Before 1894 K'ang wrote two books, one entitled *Hsin-hsüeh wei-ching k'ao* (*The Forged Classics of the Hsin Dynasty*) and the other *K'ung-tzu kai-chih k'ao* (*Confucius as a Reformer*). In the first book, he charged that the so-called Confucian classics of the Old Script School, which was defended by Liu Hsin (46? B.C.–A.D. 23), one of the most remarkable scholars of the Han period, were forgeries, while the books of the New Script School, headed by Tung Chung-shu (179?–104? B.C.), the greatest of the early Han scholars, were the really authentic texts.[2] K'ang Yu-wei, as a Confucian scholar of the *Kung-yang* school,[3] attempted to break down the prestige of the

[2] In Chapter X, we saw that the Han scholars divided themselves into two schools of Confucianism: one known as the New Script School, and the other the Old Script School. During the Ch'ing dynasty, the scholars, in reaction against Neo-Confucianism, turned to the Han learning, and hence the battle of the two schools revived. As was natural, the adherents of the New Script School would rally around Tung Chung-shu and his *Kung-Yang Commentary* for academic research.

[3] There are three important commentaries written on the *Ch'un Ch'iu*, namely, the *Tso Commentary* (*Tso Chuan*), and *Kung Yang* and *Ku Liang* commentaries. Among the three commentaries, the *Kung Yang*, particularly, interprets the *Ch'un Ch'iu* in agreement with the theories of Tung Chung-shu.

popular Han School interpretation of Confucian classics and to open a whole new realm of thought.

In the second book, K'ang Yu-wei presented Confucius in the role of a great reformer, a man of social vision, who laid down all the principles and institutions needed to change the old customs. Moreover, according to K'ang Yu-wei, the greatness of Confucius lies in his having written all the Six Classics—the *Yi* (*Change*), the *Shih* (*Odes*), the *Shu* (*History*), the *Li* (*Rites*), the *Yüeh* (*Music*), and the *Ch'un Ch'iu* (*Spring and Autumn Annals*)—to promote reform in his own time. In his book on Confucius, K'ang said: "Only when a scholar recognizes that the Six Classics were written by Confucius can he understand why Confucius was the great sage, the founder of the doctrine, and the model for all ages; and why Confucius alone was called the Great Master." While these two books stirred up a great storm in scholarly circles, their real objective seems to have been to furnish a Confucian sanction for the author's reform ideas. As K'ang's disciple Liang Ch'i-ch'ao said in 1902: "In China today a majority of the people would still be terrified at the mention of constitutional or republican government; but unless such ideas can be quoted from the early sages as a basis, how can we set up a fortress to fight against the formidable enemy with a tradition of two thousand years?" [4]

More significant than his attempts at reconstructing Confucianism is K'ang Yu-wei's conception of a new world Utopia. This he called *Ta Tung,* the Grand Unity, from a passage in the "Li Yün," one of the sections of the *Li Chi* (*Book of Rites*), generally attributed to Confucius. In this connection, this passage is worth quoting:

> When the great *Tao* was pursued, a public and common ruled over the world; men of talents, virtue, and ability were selected; sincerity was emphasized and harmony was cultivated. Therefore, men did not love their parents only, nor did they treat as children only their own sons. A competent provision was secured for the aged till their death, employment was given to the able-bodied, and the means of growing up was provided for the young. Kindness and compassion were

shown to widows, orphans, childless men, and those who were disabled by disease, so that they were all sufficiently supported. Men had their proper work, and women had their homes. They developed the wealth of natural resources, disliking that it should be discarded under the ground, but not wishing to keep it for their own use. They labored with their strength, disliking that it should not be exerted, but exerting it not for their own benefit. In this way, all cunning designs became useless, and theft and banditry did not show themselves, so that the outer doors remained open, and were not shut. This was called Ta Tung.[5]

This passage provided K'ang Yu-wei with inspiration for a concrete picture of the ideal world, which he depicted in his famous book Ta T'ung Shu (Book of Grand Unity) written in 1884.[6] Before we proceed to examine the text, let us first present the author's theory of historical progress based upon the concept of the Three Ages, as found in the Kung-Yang Chuan (Commentary on the Ch'un Ch'iu), the Li Yün section of the Li Chi, and illustrated in the writings of the Han scholars Tung Chung-shu (179?–104? B.C. and Ho Hsiu (A.D. 129–182). According to this theory, there were three Ages, namely, the Age of Disorder, the Age of Approaching Peace, and the Age of Great Peace. In the Age of Disorder, Confucius devoted himself to his own state of Lu, and took Lu as the center of his reforms. In the Age of Approaching Peace, having given good government to his own state, Confucius took China as the center of his reforms so as to bring peace and order to other states. And in the Age of Great Peace, having brought peace and order to all states within China, Confucius, finally took the world as the center of his reforms in order to civilize all the surrounding barbarians and unite humanity into one harmonious whole. Believing that Confucius was a teacher with divine personality, K'ang Yu-wei now revived this theory. He said, in the Ta T'ung Shu:

[5] Li Chi, Bk IV, Sec. 9.

[6] Its English translation, under the title The One-World Philosophy of K'ang Yu-wei, by Laurence G. Thompson, London, Allen & Unwin, 1958.

Having long considered [the problem of attaining happiness and doing away with suffering] and grieved over it, the sage-king Confucius, with divine enlightenment, set up the law of Three Systems [represented by the Three Dynasties, Hsia, Shang, and Chou] and the Three Ages: following [the Age of] Disorder, [the world] will change to [the Ages of] Approaching Peace and Great Peace; that is, following [the Age of] Small Tranquillity, [the world] will advance to [the Age of] Grand Unity.[7]

K'ang Yu-wei further maintained that the growing communications between East and West, and the political and social reforms in Europe and America, showed that the world is evolving from the Age of Disorder toward the Age of Approaching Peace. And this in turn will be followed by the Age of Great Peace, the last stage of human progress, in which "there will be unity of the world irrespective of the size of countries and distance between them; with the national states abolished, and racial distinctions eliminated, and traditions and cultures all in harmony, there will be one world of peace and happiness." Then K'ang Yu-wei added, "Confucius had long known all this in advance." [8]

Of these three ages, the most significant one is the Age of Great Peace, in which, according to K'ang Yu-wei, his utopian scheme can be realized. K'ang Yu-wei maintained that the evolution from the Age of Disorder to the Age of Great Peace is a long and gradual process. He provided for the transition from one stage of human civilization to the other, rather than for any sudden, unaccountable change. During the Age of Disorder, Confucius considered his own state as the center, while in the Age of Approaching Peace, he considered China as the center. Only in the Age of Great Peace did Confucius "consider everything, far or near, large or small, as if it were one. In doing this he was applying the principle of evolution." [9] In following the Confucian scheme, K'ang Yu-wei insisted that his program of a united world could not be put into practice except in the last and highest stage of human progress.

[7] Part I, Introduction.

[8] K'ang Yu-wei's *Lun-Yü Chu* (*Commentary on the Analects*), *chüan* 2.

[9] *Ibid.*

What engrossed him most was the formation of a united world of peace and happiness, i.e., *Ta T'ung.* Here the problem is one of execution rather than of planning. Back of the formation of a united world must be the establishment of a world government built on the concept of unity, equality, and brotherhood. K'ang Yu-wei made a very detailed study of the world as it was and is. In this study, he tried to analyze the causes of the disorder and decay of the world, whence came all the miseries and sufferings of human life. According to his analysis, the sources of all suffering "lie only in nine boundaries." What are the nine boundaries?

The first is called nation-boundaries: [this is] division by territorial frontiers and by tribes.

The second is called class-boundaries: [this is] division by noble and base, by pure and impure.

The third is called race-boundaries: [this is] by yellow, white, brown and black [skin types].

The fourth is called sex-[literally, "form"] boundaries: [this is] division by male and female.

The fifth is called family-boundaries: [this is] the private relationships of father and son, husband and wife, elder and younger brother.

The sixth is called occupation-boundaries: [this is] the private ownership of agriculture, industry, and commerce.

The seventh is called disorder-boundaries: [this is] the existence of unequal, unthorough, dissimilar, and unjust laws.

The eighth is called kind-boundaries: [this is] the existence of a separation between man, and the birds, beasts, insects, and fish.

The ninth is called suffering-boundaries: [this means] by suffering, giving rise to suffering. The perpetuation [of suffering] is inexhaustible and endless—beyond conception.[10]

K'ang Yu-wei's scheme for attaining the global utopia calls for the abolition of these nine boundaries. With the abolition of these nine boundaries, there will be One World, in which a world government, with no national barriers and divided into a number of local units, will be es-

[10] See *Ta T'ung Shu, The One World Philosophy of K'ang Yu-Wei,* trans. L. G. Thompson. London: G. Allen & Unwin, 1958, p. 74.

tablished. Within these units life will be completely communal and completely equal, without distinction as to race or sex. Even the age-old institutions of clan and family will be abolished, since they can no longer serve any valid social function. With the disappearance of family, traditional marriage will be replaced by the marriage contract which is valid for not more than a year, and at the same time women will no longer be burdened with the age-old duties of caring for children. And in the One World the emphasis is on the constant betterment of material conditions and the greater manifestation of *jen* (human-heartedness).

Such, in the outline, are the major ideas discussed in the great book *Ta T'ung Shu*. K'ang Yu-wei gave us a concrete picture of a kind of ideal world. He also embodied the picture in his philosophy and told us the way to attain it. Whether this ideal world is really practicable or whether his theory is sound are questions still to be answered.

CHAPTER XVII.   SUN YAT-SEN AND THE
                NATIONALIST REVOLUTION

1. The Evolution of the Kuomintang (Nationalist Party)

In order to understand Chinese political development after the overthrow of the Manchu dynasty, it is necessary to review the life and work of Sun Yat-sen, with emphasis on his Kuomintang and *San Min Chu I*, or Three Principles of the People. In contrast to K'ang Yu-wei, Sun Yat-sen was not only a republican revolutionary, but also a man of magnetic political personality. He came of a poor peasant family, and received his education in Western schools. Hence he was not bound to conventional Chinese scholarship and became an ardent believer in Western culture and science.

In 1879, at the age of twelve, Sun Yat-sen joined his brother in Honolulu, where he learned about Western democracy, the influence of which was later to play an important part in the formation of his own political philosophy. From 1884 to 1886, he continued his education in Hong Kong, where he studied Western medicine, and after graduation he practiced medicine in Macao. But his professional career did not last long, for he soon took active part in the revolutionary movement.

Sun Yat-sen's revolutionary ideas might be traced back to 1885, when China was defeated by France. He then believed that a revolutionary movement might be brought about to replace the decadent Manchu dynasty and the entire imperial system with a republican government. From then on, as he said in his autobiography, "I [used] the school as the place for propaganda and [used] medicine as a medium for entering the world [that is, for the purpose of overthrowing the Manchu dynasty]." [1]

---

[1] Li Chien-nung, *The Political History of China, 1940–1928*, 2nd ed., Taiwan, Commercial Press, Vol. I., p. 172. See also Teng and Ingalls' translation, Princeton, Van Nostrand, 1956 p. 145.

In 1894, just after the calamities of the Sino-Japanese War, Sun Yat-sen founded the *Hsing-Chung Hui* (China Regeneration Society) in Honolulu for the purpose of overthrowing the Manchu dynasty. His early efforts were not very successful. We have already seen how the thinking of the early reformers was often influenced by the West, but these reformers, in most cases, attempted to graft Western ideas onto the base of Chinese culture. This explains why Sun Yat-sen's radical ideas, derived largely from Western sources, were little adapted to traditional Chinese attitudes. But after 1905 attitudes changed. Japan's victory over Russia had a strong impact on the Chinese people, especially Chinese students abroad. They were then convinced that the only solution lay in outright revolution and the establishment of a new order. Meanwhile Sun Yat-sen reorganized his *Hsing-Chung Hui* into the *T'ung-Meng Hui* (League of Common Alliance) in Japan, in order to express his political philosophy through an organized political movement. His program was as follows:

1. The expulsion of the Manchus and the restoration of China. This was later formulated as the Principle of *Min-tsu* (People's Rule), translated as "Nationalism."

2. The establishment of a republic—later formulated as the Principle of *Min-ch'üan* (People's Authority), translated as "Democracy."

3. Equal distribution and nationalization of land—later formulated as the Principle of *Min-sheng* (People's Livelihood), translated as "Socialism."

The program included the main points which served as the basic text of the Nationalist movement, and was later known as the Three People's Principles. After the founding of the *T'ung-meng Hui,* in the essay published in the first issue of his party organ *Min-pao (People's Tribune)* Sun Yat-sen wrote of the three principles:

I consider that the progress of Europe and America was based on three major principles, namely the People's Rule, or Nationalism, the People's Authority, or Democracy, and the People's Livelihood, or Socialism. . . . These three major principles were all concerned with the people, and through the development of these principles, the Europeans were well governed. . . . Now, China has been plagued by despotism for over a thousand years. She has been further afflicted with alien races, encroached upon by foreign nations. The principles of nationalism and democracy are indispensable for us, while the principle of people's livelihood or socialism, which the Europeans and Americans are worrying about, has not yet affected China very much and it is easy for her to remove its defect.[2]

However, the majority of the *T'ung-meng Hui* members were most concerned with the overthrow of the imperial government and the establishment of a republic.

Despite many reverses, persecutions, and rebuffs, the revolution broke out in October 1911, and succeeded in the overthrow of the Manchu dynasty. After the establishment of the Republic, Sun Yat-sen could have accomplished much to bring peace and order to China, had the other forces not got the better of him. Political power very soon passed into the hands of Yuan Shih-kai, a political opportunist and militarist. As a result, China was engaged in civil wars among the warlords for thirteen years. During these years of trouble Sun Yat-sen continued his work, though ignored by the Western powers. In 1912, his *T'ung-meng Hui* was reorganized, together with other political groups, into the Kuomintang (Nationalist Party), as an open political party with open membership, with the purpose of implanting the foundation of the Three People's Principles in the minds and lives of the people. Sun Yat-sen's leadership in the revolutionary organizations was based on his ability to bring together men of widely divergent views, theories, and personal interests, and to convince them to work together in accordance with what they had in common. In the meantime, he wrote a series of books on the general theme of national reconstruction and completed the following works: *The Philosophy of Sun Wen* (Sun's original name), 1919; *The Preliminary Step to the Practice of People's Authority*, 1919; *The International Development of China*, 1921; *Fundamentals of National Reconstruction*, 1921; and *Lectures on the Three People's Principles*, 1921.

Sun Yat-sen was greatly influenced by the success of the Bolshevik Revolution in Russia. In 1923 he accepted offers of assistance and guidance from the Soviet government and invited a host of Soviet advisers to help reorganize the

---

[2] Li Chien-nung, *op. cit.* Vol. I, p. 242; see also Teng and Ingalls' translation, pp. 204-205.

Kuomintang and train its troops. During 1924 the Kuomintang was completely reorganized on the model of the Russian Communist Party, and a military school under Russian auspices was established at Whampoa. Members of the Chinese Communist Party, which had been formed in 1921, were admitted into the Kuomintang on an individual basis. All these measures were approved by the first party congress, which met in January 1924. These measures marked the influence of the Communist Party on the policies of the Kuomintang, which were in turn formulated on the political doctrines of Sun Yat-sen.

At the end of 1924, Sun Yat-sen with some of his followers went to Peking to negotiate a reconciliation between the North and the South. Before any definite results had been attained, he died in Peking on March 12, 1925, leaving a last testament urging his followers to continue to work for the solution of China's problems along the lines that he had laid down in his writings. His teachings formed the basic political doctrine of the Kuomintang. The new China, he believed, was to be achieved through three stages: military operations to unify the nation; political tutelage to train the people in representative government; and finally, a constitutional form of government.

2. The Political Doctrines of Sun Yat-sen

The political doctrines of Sun Yat-sen were embodied in a number of lectures which he gave in 1924, and were collected and edited under the title *San Min Chu I,* or *The Three People's Principles.*

The Principle of Nationalism.   The principle of nationalism was directed mainly against the Manchus before the fall of the monarchy and embraced the doctrine of self-determination for all the races living in China. When the principle was formally proclaimed in 1924, it was extended to include opposition against foreign imperialism. Manchu domination had been disposed of in 1911, but foreign imperialism still persisted. In his first group of lectures on nationalism, Sun Yat-sen stressed two major issues. First was the Chinese people's need for national solidarity; that is, "consolidation of the deep-rooted sentiment prevailing in the family and clan into a powerful national spirit." Second was the freedom of China from foreign domination, especially from foreign economic imperialism. As regards the first issue, Sun Yat-sen said:

> . . . the Chinese people have only family and clan solidarity, but they have no national spirit. Therefore even though there are four hundred million people gathered together in one China, in fact they are just a heap of loose sand. That is why at present we are the poorest and weakest nation in the world, and occupy the lowest position in the international community. "Other men are the carving knife and serving dish; we are the fish and the meat." Our position at this time is most perilous. If we do not earnestly espouse nationalism and consolidate our four hundred million people into one strong nation, there is danger of China's being lost and our people being eliminated. If we wish to avert this catastrophe, we must espouse nationalism and bring this national spirit to the salvation of the country.[3]

As regards the second issue, Sun Yat-sen stressed that China could develop as a nation only by shaking off the imperialistic yoke, and especially foreign economic imperialism. He pointed out to the Chinese people that "economic oppression is even worse than political oppression. . . . Political oppression is apparent to all, but economic oppression is not usually seen or felt. China has already experienced several decades of economic oppression by the foreign powers, and so far the nation has for the most part shown no sense of irritation. As a consequence, China is being transformed everywhere into a colony of the foreign powers." [4] According to Sun Yat-sen, China was in fact a "hypo-colony," a colony of many countries. Hence the principle of nationalism was aimed at achieving both political unity within China and independence from foreign domination.

In the last of his series of lectures on nationalism, Sun Yat-sen also stressed the fact that if the Chinese people

---

[3] San Ming Chu I, Lecture I; see also W. T. De Bary and others, eds., Sources of Chinese Tradition, New York, Columbia Univ. Press, 1960, p. 769.

[4] San Ming Chu I, Lecture IV.

wanted to restore their standing, they must first restore the traditional national spirit and morality. That China has been able to rise up more than once after periods of national eclipse and never fall under the foreign domination for good must be attributed to the traditional national spirit and morality. Here we note that Sun Yat-sen, searching for an ethical basis for his political philosophy, chose Confucianism. He adopted as the ethical norm of his political movement the eight cardinal Confucian virtues: loyalty and filial piety, humanity and love, faithfulness and righteousness, harmony and peace. He contended that the Chinese people must recover and restore these eight cardinal virtues.

The Principle of Democracy. The principle of democracy was directed mainly against constitutional monarchy, as advocated by K'ang Yu-wei, which Sun Yat-sen identified with "absolutism." In his lectures he had elaborated this principle and developed what he called the "Four Powers of the People" and the "Five-Power Constitution." His aim was to achieve a centralized government on a popular basis. According to Sun Yat-sen, the best government is that which ensures popular control through electoral processes, and yet gives a strong executive wide powers to manage all the nation's business. Therefore, the principle of democracy was recognized by the Kuomintang as supporting not only the Swiss doctrine of initiation, referendum, election, and recall, but also the Soviet idea of democratic centralism.

Sun Yat-sen believed that there must be a distinction between sovereignty and ability; that is, a distinction between the sovereign power of the people and the ruling power of the government.

> . . . the political power of the reconstructed state will be divided into two parts. One is the power over the government; that great power will be placed entirely in the hands of the people, who will have a full degree of sovereignty and will be able to control directly the affairs of state—this political power is popular sovereignty. The other power is the governing power; that great power will be placed in the hands of the government organs, which will be powerful and will manage all the nation's business—this governing power is the power of the government.[5]

[5] Lecture VI. See De Bary, *op cit.,* p. 773.

Sun Yat-sen compared his government system with an automobile owned by a man—the people—who does not know how to drive and so engages a driver—a man of ability. The people have the sovereign power, but do not have the ability. So he concludes:

> Let the great political force of the state be divided into two: the power of the government and the power of the people. Such a division will make the government the machinery and the people the engineer. The attitude of the people toward the government will then resemble the attitude of the engineer toward his machine.[6]

This distinction between the people's sovereign power and the government's ruling power was accepted as the basis of government under the Kuomintang. According to Sun Yat-sen, the popular sovereignty is to be expressed by the four popular rights of suffrage, recall, initiative, and referendum. "Only when the people have these four rights," said he, "can we say that democracy is complete." [7] However, the people's right of sovereignty is to be separate from the government's power to rule. As to the government system, Sun Yat-sen advocated that in addition to the three Western governmental powers—the executive, legislative, and judicial —there should be the Chinese powers of examination and censorate, so as to make "a perfect government of five powers." He worked out his theory of the five-power constitution on two assumptions: first, the people are ignorant and so must allow able men to run the government; secondly, the men who run the government should have no limitations placed on their power. This is the theory which laid the foundation for the so-called May Fifth Constitution draft.[8]

The Principle of Socialism. This principle embraces a variety of social and economic theories, but its meaning is rather vague. As defined by Sun Yat-sen, the term *min-sheng* means "people's livelihood," "society's existence," "the nation's economy," and "the life of the masses." He tried to give the term a meaning which would satisfy all of his

[6] Lecture VI, on the Principle of Democracy.

[7] *Ibid.*

[8] See Chap. IV, Sec. II, of this book.

followers, and consequently this principle has been given various interpretations. To carry out this principle, he made two concrete proposals: the equalization of landownership and the regulation of capital. The declaration issued by the First National Congress of the Kuomintang in 1924 says in part:

> The Principle of the People's Livelihood comprises two essential objectives: equalization of landownership and regulation of capital. Economic inequality is primarily traceable to the fact that land is monopolized by a few. It is, therefore, imperative that the state regulate the ownership, use, and purchase of the land as well as the assessed value of the land. The value of lands privately owned, after having been properly assessed by their owners, must be reported to the government, which will either tax them or, if necessary, buy them, according to their assessed value. Such regulations are the essentials with respect to equality of the right to land.
>
> All enterprises, owned both by Chinese citizens and foreigners, which partake of the nature of monopoly, or assume proportions incommensurate with the financial resources of the individual enterpreneurs, such as all banks, railroads, and ship lines, will be undertaken by the state, so that private capitalism will be prevented from controlling the people's livelihood. These are the fundamentals of the regulation of capital. With the equalization of landownership and regulation of capital, the principle of socialism may be said to have been placed on a secure foundation.

From the above passage, it can be seen that the *min-sheng* principle, as the Communists claim, has much in common with Marxism. Sun Yat-sen had great respect for Karl Marx, but he was never subservient to Marxism. He was in fact opposed to the materialistic theory of history and sought another interpretation of human development. He stressed that *"min-sheng* is the central force in social progress, and social progress is the central force in history; consequently, *min-sheng,* not material forces, determines the course of history." Moreover, Sun Yat-sen disagreed with Marx's theory of the class struggle. According to Sun Yat-sen, man by nature has a "sense of humanity" or "the consciousness of kind" and knows how to avoid conflicts in social relations

and to achieve progress through compromise and conciliation. Hence he concluded that the brutal class struggle is un-
necessary and impracticable, especially in China, where industry was not yet well developed.

CHAPTER XVIII

CHIANG KAI-SHEK AND
NATIONALISM

1. The Nationalist Collapse on the Mainland

The part which Chiang Kai-shek (born in 1886) has played
in the history of modern China will be a subject of controversy for a long time. In the 1920's he was the leader of
the Northern Expedition against the warlords to bring China
under unified control. In the 1930's he accepted the United
Front and stood forth as the leader of national resistance
against Japanese aggression. In the 1940's when he was the
leader of China as a world power, he was at the height of
his power and prestige. But in the 1950's he was defeated
by the Communists and withdrew to Taiwan, where he sur-
vives on the assistance of the United States. It is not for us
to assess the whole picture of the Nationalist collapse. We
would like only to point out the share which Chiang Kai-
shek and the Kuomintang contributed to the fall of the mainland.

The history of modern China is clearly inseparable from
the history of the Kuomintang and its two leaders, Sun
Yat-sen and Chiang Kai-shek. But the Kuomintang was not
a mass party, and drew its support chiefly from businessmen,
intellectuals, and soldiers. There was an inherent weakness
in its organization which was responsible for the instability
and lack of unity within the ranks of the party. The death of
Sun Yat-sen in 1925 had been followed after a time by ten-
sion between the right and left wings of the party. In 1923
Sun Yat-sen had invited a number of Russian advisers to
assist in remodeling the Kuomintang and in building up a
revolutionary army. This change had been advocated by
the members of the Left, but was strongly opposed by those

of the Right. In the meantime, the Whampoa Military Academy was set up for the training of an officer corps. The president of this military academy was Chiang Kai-shek, who from the time of his appointment played a decisive role in the Kuomintang and in the Nationalist government.

Under the supreme command of Chiang Kai-shek, the Kuomintang armies, officered by cadets of the Whampoa Military Academy, set out in the summer of 1926 on the long-planned Northern Expedition. In this force were many Communists who had joined the revolution on the promise that they would support the principles of Kuomintang. The Kuomintang and its government were then fairly radical in politics. With the continued success of the Northern Expedition, Chiang Kai-shek had to make a decision. Should the left wing be allowed to gain the upper hand and the capitalists and "landlords" be expropriated? Or should the right wing prevail and an alliance be made with the gentry? At the siege of Shanghai, Chiang Kai-shek and his closest colleagues decided on the second alternative. As a result Shanghai came into his hands without a struggle, and the capital of the Shanghai financiers and industrialists was placed at his disposal, so that he could pay his troops and finance his administration. At the same time the Russian advisers were dismissed and the Communists were expelled. The latter established themselves as a guerrilla force in rural areas, where they remained an archenemy of the Kuomintang and its government.

The decision arrived at by Chiang Kai-shek and his friends secured him the party leadership and at the same time deepened the party schisms. In addition to the warlord forces and the Communists, Chiang Kai-shek faced opposition and a struggle for power within the party itself. In order to strengthen his position he tried to consolidate his control over the party machine. His struggle for supremacy revealed not only his strength, but also his weakness. He is undoubtedly a good strategist and skillful in politics as it was played in the Kuomintang; but he is not a man who abides by law or believes in the rule of law. He has always made the first criterion for his support of a subordinate the quality of personal loyalty, rather than ability or devotion to any particular political program. Chiang Kai-shek has always allowed the Kuomintang to be segmented into rival cliques that he can play off one against the other. It is essential not to conceive of these cliques as if they were organized political bodies. Basically any clique or group is the combination of a leader and his personal following. Most of the cliques, it must be noted, are extremely conservative in outlook and stupidly repressive in action. Personal rivalry and clique antagonisms paralyzed the Kuomintang in the struggle with the Communists.

The Reform Movement of 1950–1952, inaugurated in Taiwan after the fall of the mainland, brought some new and younger members into the party, but it failed to rejuvenate its organization by reducing the animosities of the rival cliques. Some changes in the pattern of cliques might nevertheless have resulted from the Reform Movement, but this is simply the same old package with a cleaner wrapping. Indeed, the Kuomintang lost the vitality and resourcefulness that characterized it in the early revolutionary days.

Another important factor that contributed to the collapse of the Nationalists was Chiang Kai-shek's persistent conviction that political, social, and economic reforms must be delayed until threats from the Communists and from Japan could be removed. But he failed to realize that so long as the opposition had just grievances and the government lost popular support, he would find it difficult to deal with the Communists and Japan. Through all these years, Japanese aggression was closely related to the inner conflicts between the Nationalist regime and its political opponents. The Japanese attack that led to the Sino-Japanese War of 1937 blocked the program of the National government and paved the way for the victory of Communism.

In general, the Kuomintang made little effort to present to the Chinese people an attractive postwar political, social, and economic program. In particular, during the civil war, 1946–1949, the Kuomintang was not prepared to take any drastic steps to alleviate the plight of the rural areas. The Chinese American Joint Committee on Rural Reconstruction aimed to improve agrarian technology in the hope that, with an increased harvest, the plight of the peasants could be alleviated without damage to the interests of the landowners. As a general rule, no technological change can be brought about without institutional change; without social reform, agrarian technology offers no advantage to the peasants.

The land reform carried out by the Kuomintang in Taiwan

has brought about no bloodshed, no class struggle, no broken homes, but a larger degree of social stability, an increase in food production, an improvement in the livelihood of the peasants, and an added impetus to industrial reconstruction. The success of the program is largely due to the soundness of the land-to-the-tiller policy, which was originally incorporated in the elaborate rural program advocated by the Kuomintang, but its implementation was unfortunately delayed until after the retreat to Taiwan.

There remains one supreme question concerning the future of the Kuomintang and its leader, Chiang Kai-shek. The policy and administrative decision of the Nationalist government in Taiwan are suspended between two considerations: realistically, it cannot anticipate recapture of the mainland, either by its own efforts or in a future global war; politically, it must rule nobly and hopefully as the legitimate government of all China. Taken either way, the military factor is a very important one. The Nationalists stress that their early revolutions in 1911 and 1926 were consummated only after many years of failure. With these historical precedents, they believe that the present may be merely another period of temporary eclipse. This is the Nationalist view of the future, but it is at best a mere wishful conjecture. The time is as yet premature to predict what chances there are for the Kuomintang and its government under Chiang Kai-shek to regain control over the mainland.

2. The Political Thought of Chiang Kai-shek

Chiang Kai-shek is a devoted follower and admirer of Sun Yat-sen, but his mental outlook is different from that of his mentor. Sun Yat-sen had a cosmopolitan outlook and cosmopolitan ideals, and took all mankind as his province. But Chiang Kai-shek is a nationalist in his outlook and confines himself to China's problems, particularly those of the last hundred years. Consequently his ideas begin by stressing the principle of nationalism and from it tracing back to the national heritage to draw his inspiration for the gigantic task of resisting Communist aggression and building up a new China. As Chiang Kai-shek himself has put it in his

Basic Principles Underlying Our Anti-Communist and Anti-Aggression Struggle: "What we rely upon now cannot be sheer armed force, but is our national sense of righteousness and our revolutionary principles." By "revolutionary principles" Chiang Kai-shek means the Three People's Principles of Sun Yat-sen, particularly the first principle—Nationalism.

To understand his thought, it is essential to know that Chiang Kai-shek is not a political philosopher, but a man of action who turns to creative thinking as a matter of convenience. His political thought is reflected in his responses to the problems confronting him. For instance, in 1934 when he was engaged in a campaign against the Communists, he launched his New Life Movement to tighten discipline and build up morale, in the Kuomintang and the nation as a whole, through a revival of the traditional cardinal virtues of moral conduct. In his *Essentials of the New Life Movement*, Chiang Kai-shek emphatically declares:

> The New Life Movement aims at the promotion of a regular life guided by the four virtues, namely, *li* [regulated attitude or propriety], *i* [right conduct or righteousness], *lien* [clear discrimination or integrity], and *ch'ih* [conscience or sense of shame]. These virtues must be applied to ordinary life in the matter of food, clothing, shelter, and action. The four virtues are the essential principles for the promotion of morality. They form the major rules for dealing with men and human affairs, for cultivating oneself, and for adjusting to one's surroundings. Whoever violates these rules is bound to fail; and a nation which neglects them will not survive.[1]

Here we note that in tackling China's problem of social regeneration, Chiang Kai-shek has turned to the Confucian view, which lays primary emphasis on the cultivation of the personal life. According to Confucian tradition, only when one's personal life is well cultivated can one be expected to do anything for the welfare of others. Tradition-bound, Chiang Kai-shek sought intellectual sanction for a new stability in the classical doctrine, and hence he stressed Confucian self-cultivation, a life of frugality, and dedication to the nation in his New Life Movement.

[1] W. T. De Bary and others, eds., *Sources of Chinese Tradition*, New York, Columbia Univ. Press, 1960, p. 801-802.

In 1943, Chiang published his chief work, *China's Destiny,* as a formal statement of his political ideas. This book was written during the time of China's greatest isolation, for the purpose of drawing spiritual strength from the greatness of China's past. Its publication brought acute criticism from Western readers. In this volume Chiang laid the blame for the misfortunes of China principally upon the Western powers, which had imposed the unequal treaties, but he rejoiced in the recent abrogation of those treaties by Britain and the United States. He regarded the end of the unequal treaties and foreign concessions as the beginning of a new era in the Chinese Revolution.

> . . . we are justified in saying that the failure of our Revolution and national reconstruction had been mainly due to the existence of the unequal treaties. During the last century China had been suffering from the manifold oppressions of the unequal treaties, and this has resulted in political disunity, backwardness of economic development, and evil social tendencies. The cumulative effect of these factors is to make moral cowards of our people who have forgotten even how to save themselves while the lowering of their ethical standards has deprived them of their sense of honor. Up to the present, therefore, the Chinese people's moral degradation and loss of self-confidence may be said to have reached their nadir. Directly or indirectly this is entirely due to the influence of the unequal treaties. The foreign Concessions and Garrison Areas have been the breeding ground of decadent customs and evil habits.[2]

In effect, Chiang Kai-shek attributed to the unequal treaties and foreign concessions all social evils and economic backwardness.

What was in Chiang Kai-shek's mind was still political and military unification. To achieve this great goal, he outlined a five-point program of national reconstruction. First, there must be psychological reconstruction, based on the development of an "independent ideology" and emphasizing pride in China's culture. Second, there must be moral reconstruction, stressing a return to Confucian virtues such as

[2] Chiang Kai-shek, *China's Destiny* tr. Wang Chung-hui, New York, Macmillan, 1947 pp. 90-91.

benevolence, sincerity, loyalty, and filial piety, which were to be based on the supremacy of the state and nation. Third, there must be social reconstruction, based on the New Life Movement, "having the modernization of the Chinese people as its object" and restoring the traditional system of joint responsibility and mutual aid. Fourth, there must be political reconstruction, which, Chiang Kai-shek claimed, had begun in accordance with the "Plan of Resistance and Reconstruction." But he stressed that "China's democratic institutions will not be a mere copy of nineteenth century European and American democratic institutions which are based on individualism and the class consciousness." Lastly, there must be economic reconstruction along the lines laid down by Sun Yat-sen—industrialization, land acquisition, and state capitalization in a planned economy. In support of his view of economic reconstruction, Chiang Kai-shek published in 1943 another book (restricted to official circles), entitled *Chinese Economic Theory,* in which he berated Western liberalism and derived from ancient philosophers a sanction for the state control of economic life and for the conscription of China's farmers onto collective farms. This was reminiscent of what the ancient Legalists called "the acts of agriculture and war."

His views as expressed in the two books are those of an intensely nationalistic military man, who would have military control of China and wanted to achieve social order, political stability, and economic prosperity according to a traditional pattern—a kind of moral rearmament based on self-cultivation and tightened social discipline. After he retreated to Taiwan, Chiang Kai-shek turned more and more to traditional values. In 1952 he wrote and published a booklet under the title *Chapters on National Fecundity, Social Welfare, Education, and Health and Happiness,* as a supplement to Sun Yat-sen's writings on the Principle of People's Livelihood. In it Chiang Kai-shek acknowledges the importance of modern science in buildings up a new society in which all aspects of the people's life other than food and shelter—health, education, recreation, and social welfare—shall be adequately provided for. This merely echoed the nineteenth-century slogan "Chinese learning for substance, Western learning for function."

The ideas of Chiang Kai-shek made no contribution to Chinese thought but were significant because they were held by his followers, who occupied important positions in government and party. It was in leadership, rather than the institutions, that they placed hope. They had not been able to modernize their own thinking, and they sought intellectual sanction in the traditional Confucian doctrine—rule by leaders of moral virtue, and obedience by a people disciplined in Confucian virtues, especially loyalty and filial piety, in support of the central power. From such an outlook came the strength of Chiang Kai-shek as well as his weakness, his successes as well as his failures.

CHAPTER XIX. MAO TSE-TUNG AND COMMUNISM

1. The Rise of Chinese Communism

It is our purpose in this chapter to assess the forces and factors which contributed to the triumph of Communism on the mainland of China. As we have seen above (Chap. X), the dominant trend of thought in the New Culture Movement was toward Westernization. This movement led to a general attack on the Confucian tradition and a popular demand for political and social reform. It was against this background that the Chinese Communist Party came into being. The party was a creation of the Communist International and was closely controlled by Moscow from the first. In the early formative years it joined the Kuomintang in a short-lived coalition, with the purpose of gaining strength, ultimately capturing the Kuomintang machinery, and thereby seizing total power in China. The alliance abruptly ended in 1927, when Chiang Kai-shek expelled all Communist members from the Kuomintang and declared the party illegal. The Communists then established themselves as a guerrilla force in the mountains of south central China, and there followed a series of bloody and unsuccessful uprisings in the cities. The early period was also characterized by frequent shifts of party line and party leadership, which always followed tactical failures in the Communist movement.

However, the Chinese Communists learned many lessons from their early failures. The party began placing emphasis on the consolidation of the Red Army and upon the use of rural bases—a policy which inevitably brought the peasant leader Mao Tse-tung into the leadership. The Communists depended upon their Red Army for turning back a series of "extermination campaigns" directed against them by Chiang Kai-shek. Mao Tse-tung explained later:

> Following out the tactics of swift concentration and swift dispersal, we attacked each unit separately, using our main forces. Admitting the enemy troops deeply into Soviet territory, we staged sudden concentrated attacks, in superior numbers, on isolated units of the Kuomintang troops, achieving positions of maneuver in which, momentarily, we could encircle them, thus reversing the general strategic advantage enjoyed by a numerically greatly superior enemy.[1]

Since then, the Red Army has become well known for its guerrilla warfare.

> When the enemy comes forward, we withdraw;
> when the enemy withdraws, we go forward.
> When the enemy settles down, we disturb him.
> when the enemy is exhausted, we fight him.

Because of these basic principles, the Communists had managed to hold the mountainous area of South Kiangsi as their base and to evade the Nationalist attacks.

Meanwhile, the Chinese Communists looked upon the policy of land reform as the most vital feature of their revolution and made this policy an indispensable part of their guerrilla tactics. In 1931, when the "Chinese Soviet Republic" was established in Kiangsi, the Communists published their first land law, emphasizing land confiscation and land distribution. Another important document concerning the Communist agrarian policy is Mao Tse-tung's report to the Second All-China Soviet Congress (January 22, 1934), in which he said:

> Our class line in the agrarian revolution is to depend upon the hired farm hands and poor peasants, to ally with the middle peasants, to check the rich peasants, and to annihilate the landlords. The correct practice of this line is the key to the success of the agrarian revolution and the foundation for all other policies of the Soviet government in the villages.

However, in the course of 1936, the political and military situation was changed when Chiang Kai-shek was forced

[1] See Edgar Snow, *Red Star over China*. New York: Random House, 1944.

to seek a compromise with the Communists and to establish the United Front against Japan. It was in the interest of the Communists that Chiang Kai-shek committed his military resources against the Japanese rather than devote them to the destruction of the Red armies. Therefore the Communists promised to accept the Three People's Principles as the code of the land, to give up their policy of overthrowing the Kuomintang by force, and to abandon their campaign against landlordism. The Soviet government was to be incorporated into the National government and the Red Army to become a part of the National Revolutionary Army. This agreement was of course to be understood as a tactical truce, agreeable to both sides for different reasons, in the face of the situation posed by Japanese invasion.

As a matter of fact, the Communists never intended to abolish their Soviet government in the border region and to place their armed forces under the control of the National government. Meanwhile they made the most intensive efforts in preparation for the postwar struggle for power in China. They presented their moderate land-reform program to mobilize peasant support, and at the same time built up a disciplined cadre of party members from the many recruits who joined the Communist Party in this period. Their primary objective throughout the war years was the pursuit of power in China. It is essential to know that their relations with the Kuomintang, their limited military operation against Japanese forces, their posture toward the Western powers, and their proclaimed program for the future were all geared to this overriding tactical objective. By the end of World War II, the Chinese Communists had succeeded in laying the foundation for their victory on the mainland.

The United Front between the Nationalists and the Communists began to crack in 1939–1940, as the Japanese pressure on China lessened and the war became an endurance contest. The year of 1943 saw a sharp turning point in both Russian and Chinese Communist policies, which served as a dual program, culminating in their conquest of the mainland in 1949. During this period, the Soviet Union maintained its official policy of diplomatic support for Chiang Kai-shek, while the Chinese Communists pressed terms which they never expected the Nationalists to accept. Meanwhile they made certain maneuvers, such as the Russian dissolution of the Comintern and the Chinese Communist demand for "agrarian reform" and "democratic liberty," which led many observers to believe that Mao Tse-tung and his comrades were not really Communists, but rather "mere agrarian reformers." This unrealistic appraisal began figuring as an element in world politics and a factor in the American attitude toward China.

In 1945 the United States government announced a new formation of its policy, stressing that "a strong, united and democratic China is of the utmost importance to the success of the United Nations organization and for world peace." The United States urged a cessation of civil war and a convention of the major political elements in China. The course of negotiation was affected by the failure to reach an effective truce. On the one hand, in the light of his knowledge of Communist purposes, Chiang Kai-shek saw no possibility of an acceptable solution without complete elimination of Communist military strength. On the other hand, Mao Tse-tung, knowing the Kuomintang military strength, might have accepted a minority status in a unified government, but was never prepared to consider any formula which would deprive him of his own armed forces. And this ruled out, of course, any meaningful unification of China. Then the Chinese Communists moved gradually into a general military offensive until they completed the occupation of the mainland in 1949.

To speak of the Communist triumph as a "popular revolution" is not only to mislead many observers, but also to misinterpret the Communist movement. The key to their victory is the organization by means of which they built up a very powerful army and a highly disciplined party, capable of quick and sustained political action to mobilize and control the mass of the people.

2. Mao Tse-tung's Early Activities and Writings

When the Comintern agents organized the Chinese Communist Party, Mao Tse-tung was one of its first members. Like other Communists, he accepted the doctrine of the proletarian revolution. The Comintern emphasized that the Chinese revolution must inevitably be led by the Chinese proletariat. However, since 1925, when he was sent to

Hunan to organize peasant associations for the party, Mao Tse-tung had been convinced of the enormous revolutionary potential of the peasantry. In his Report on an Investigation of the Peasant Movement in Hunan, published early in 1927, Mao seemed to ignore the proletariat and predicted the triumph of the peasant movement. As he said in his report:

> In a very short time, in China's central, southern, and northern provinces, several hundred million peasants will rise like a tornado or tempest, a force so extraordinarily swift and violent that no power, however great, will be able to suppress it. They will break all trammels that now bind them and rush forward along the road to liberation. They will send all imperialists, warlords, corrupt officials, local bullies, and bad gentry to their graves. All revolutionary parties and all revolutionary comrades will stand before them to be tested, and to be accepted or rejected as they decide.[1]

Mao Tse-tung also allotted the peasants seven out of ten points in the accomplishments of the democratic revolution. By making the peasantry the main revolutionary force, he diverged from the orthodox Marxist-Leninist doctrine, which regards the peasantry as only an auxiliary force in the "proletarian revolution." But in his report Mao Tse-tung was speaking not of the "proletarian revolution," but of the "democratic revolution" or the "national revolution." The "national" and "democratic" revolutions are synonymous, and, according to Mao Tse-tung, represent the goal to which "Sun Yat-sen devoted forty years." The significance of his report is that he realized the importance of peasant support. His prediction of the rising of "several hundred million peasants" might be full of exaggerations. But China is an agrarian country where land is the primary basis of the people's livelihood, and by the third and fourth decades of the twentieth century it could no longer keep them alive without radical changes, which only Mao Tse-tung and his comrades offered.

However, Mao's ascendancy came slowly after his life-and-death struggle against Chiang Kai-shek's "extermination campaigns." During the war years he had developed his peas-

[2] W. T. De Bary and others, eds., *Sources of Chinese Tradition*, New York, Columbia Univ. Press, 1960, p. 867.

ant army and built up a disciplined party organization loyal to him personally. Meanwhile he acquainted himself with the writings of Lenin and Stalin, and in 1940 published his *On New Democracy*—based on Leninist and Stalinist doctrines—a persuasive propaganda document, justifying the united front as a temporary measure and reaffirming the party's long-term mission. The Chinese revolution, he maintained, would be divided into two stages—the democratic and the socialist. The two stages, though different in nature, can be blended into a continuous process, as conducted by a coalition of all revolutionary classes.

> The first stage of the Chinese revolution (itself subdivided into many minor stages) belongs, so far as its social character is concerned, to a new type of bourgeois-democratic revolution, and is not yet a proletarian-socialist revolution; but it has long become part of the proletarian-socialist world revolution and its great ally. The first step in, or the first stage of, this revolution is certainly not, and cannot be, the establishment of a capitalist society under the dictatorship of the Chinese bourgeoisie; on the contrary, the first stage is to end with the establishment of a new-democratic society under the joint dictatorship of all Chinese revolutionary classes headed by the Chinese proletariat. Then, the revolution will develop into the second stage so that a socialist society can be established in China.[2]

There was nothing essentially new in this concept: Marx had differentiated between the two revolutions, and Lenin had described how revolutionary masses could move toward communism without passing through all the various stages of capitalist development. But Mao Tse-tung's technique was aimed at seizing political power by collaborating with all who were willing to work along with the Communists. In political form, the New Democracy envisages a system of government known as "Democratic Centralism"—a system of government in which all power is centralized, but it is democratic, Mao Tse-tung claimed, because it is jointly ruled by the various "revolutionary classes" and based on elections in which all participate through suffrage that is "real, popular, and equal." In economic terms, Mao Tse-tung conceived of the New Democracy as a "new-democratic"

[3] De Bary, *op. cit.*, pp. 885-886.

economy. Three types of enterprise—private, cooperative, and state—would exist side by side, with the first strictly controlled and the third dominant. "All big banks, big industries, and big commercial enterprises shall be state-owned." However, "the state will not confiscate other forms of private property, or forbid the development of capitalist production so long as it is taken for granted that it 'does not dominate the people's livelihood.'" In developing these political and economic doctrines, Mao Tse-tung was careful to relate them to Sun Yat-sen's Three People's Principles, and he claimed for the New Democracy a direct descent from Sun Yat-sen. All this was designed to make Communist leadership acceptable and to prepare the way for isolating the Nationalists.

Mao Tse-tung thus used his New Democracy as a cloak for his personal dictatorial power. His claims to doctrinal authority and infallibility were further expressed in his *On Contradiction*, which was produced in the early Yenan period (about 1937) for inner party use. This essay became supremely important in Chinese Communist ideology after his speech *On the Correct Handling of Contradictions Among the People* was published in 1957. Taking Communist doctrine as a base, Mao Tse-tung insisted that conflict is inherent to human relations, and must therefore govern politics. According to Mao, there are two types of contradictions: The first type, called antagonistic contradictions, exist between hostile classes and hostile social systems, such as the contradictions between landlords and tenants, between capitalism and socialism. These are "between the enemy and ourselves," and are the very substance of the inexorable process of history. The second type is called nonantagonistic contradictions, which exist within the socialist society, such as "the contradictions between the interests of nation as a whole and those of the inviduals, the contradictions of democracy and centralism, the contradictions between leaders and led, between the government and the people." Mao Tse-tung stated that "it is of paramount importance for us to understand concretely the law of contradictions in things," and, that, on the basis of such analysis, we may "find out the methods of solving these contradictions."

As there is a distinction in the character of the two contradictions, there must be a difference in the mode of resolution for each of them. For the first type—antagonistic—it is essentially violent; these contradictions can be resolved only by force. For the second type of contradictions—nonantagonistic—it is essentially nonviolent; these contradictions can be resolved through the process of "discussion, criticism, and education." In his book, Mao Tse-tung stressed on the one hand the universality of these contradictions, and on the other their particularity as determined by the needs of time and place. Anyone who fought an issue at the wrong time or in the wrong place would be a deviationist from the party line. For every contradiction there can only be a single correct resolution, which springs out of what Mao Tse-tung calls "the fundamental consensus as to the interests of the People." The decision as to what this consensus is, is left to the party; the party acts as the infallible and supreme interpreter. The theoretical authority and infallibility of the party has been used by Mao Tse-tung to tighten discipline and consolidate his personal leadership. Only in this sense can we understand the emphasis placed by the Communists on the various "ideological remolding movements."

"Contradictions are universal, absolute, existing in all processes of the development of things, and running through all processes from beginning to end," the ideology of Mao Tse-tung teaches. Not only has he stressed the day-to-day programs of orderly "resolution of contradictions," but also he has launched many periodical large-scale movements—"mass movements"—to indoctrinate and train his party membership down to the lowest cadres. With his theory and tactics of "contradictions" Mao has built up a very powerful army and a highly disciplined party, and he has succeeded in imposing organization on the disorganized masses.

CHAPTER XX. THE CHANGING CHINESE IN A
CHANGING SOCIETY

1. The Chinese Type of Humanity

Once everything changed except China; now there is nothing in China that does not change. The most conservative nation in history has become the most radical, and has determined to destroy the time-honored traditions, whether in the form of institutions, classics, or social and moral norms. From what has been happening in recent years all over the mainland of China, it seems clear that the Chinese Communists are working hard to replace the Chinese type of humanity—the real Chinese, who has learned how to be a good man in his relations with others—by the Communist Chinese, treacherous, hideous, and ferocious. It may not be out of place to take a good look at the real Chinese, and see what distinguishes his mind, temper, and sentiment from the Communist type that we see rising up in China.

We can say with assurance that in the Chinese type of humanity there is nothing treacherous, hideous, or ferocious. A real Chinese may be coarse, but there is no ferocity in his coarseness; a real Chinese may be ugly, but there is no hideousness in his ugliness; a real Chinese may be cunning, but there is no treachery in his cunning. What we mean to say is that even in the physical and moral faults of a real Chinese there is nothing that revolts other people. We once read somewhere a statement made by an American missionary that the longer a foreigner lives in China, the more he likes the Chinese.

The fundamental impression that the Chinese makes on the world is that he is moderate. By moderation we do not mean softness, timidity, or submissiveness. By the word "moderate" we mean absence of harshness, vehemence, or violence. Moderation as here conceived is a way of action that avoids going to extremes, or a state of mind in which human reasoning and feeling reach a perfect harmony of calmness and soberness. The quality of moderation in the Chinese people is the product of faithfulness and sympathy—of what may be described as true and unselfish love or singleness of mind, leading to positive efforts for the good of others.

The Chinese have this love because they live a life of the heart, a life of feeling—not feeling in the sense of sensation that comes from the bodily organs, but feeling in the sense of human affection that springs spontaneously from the deepest part of the heart. Indeed, the Chinese people live such a life of feeling, a life of heart, that they naturally overlook material wants. This explains why they are insensible to physical discomforts and bear hardships with little complaint. Even in their present sufferings, they are still "happy, gregarious, noisy, curious, hospitable." The secret of their happiness is found in their life of feeling, the life of human affection.

Let us give some illustrations of what we mean by a life of the heart. First, take the Chinese love of home. Everyone loves his home, but the Chinese have shown more intense love of their ancestral home than any other people. Approach a Chinese anywhere and ask him where he is from. He will answer that he is from a certain part of China, although his family may have left there long ago and he himself may never have been in that place. The Chinese regard their ancestral homes as still theirs, to be loved and honored and supported, and to be visited as soon as they find an opportunity. This attitude grows out of the true and unselfish love for one's parents, family, and friends.

Next, take the Chinese ancestor worship, which started, in the opinion of many sociologists, as an extension of filial piety. The cult of ancestor worship in China is founded on the feeling of affection. A Chinese, when he dies, is consoled not by a belief that he will be immortal, but by his underlying sentiment for the coming generations, which will remember him, think of him, and love him, to the end of time.

Then take Chinese marriage. In the traditional Chinese marriage there was no ritual of lovemaking, wooing, and romance; yet, all things considered, a surprising degree of happiness often reigned in the family. What is the secret of this marital happiness? Again it lies in true and unselfish love. Even love, no matter how it starts, is something that must be consciously nourished. The Chinese people, living a life of feeling, have learned how to create and nourish love, for marital security and happiness.

And finally, let us take another well-known fact in the life of the Chinese people—their politeness. They are generally acknowledged to be a peculiarly polite people. The essence of true politeness is consideration for the feelings of others. The Chinese people are polite because, living a life of the heart, they know their own feelings and are thus able to show consideration for the feelings of others. The politeness of the Chinese people, although not elaborate like that of the Japanese, is pleasing, because it is a politeness that comes from the depths of the heart, not one learned for the purpose of social ceremonies.

Such illustrations could be multiplied, but these are sufficient to illustrate the point that the real Chinese people live a life of feeling, and this way of life has made them moderate, faithful, sympathetic. It is important that the Chinese, who are primitive in many of their ways, have yet a power of mind and rationality that we do not find in primitive people, a power that has enabled them to deal with the complex and difficult problems of human relations with a sense of justice and fairness, a spirit of tolerance, and a tie of mutual affection, all of which are contained in the significant word *jen* (humanity).

2. The Communist Type of Humanity

Will the Chinese people be transformed by the alien ideologies to which they are now subjected? As we stated earlier, during the 631 years from 1280 to 1911 China was under alien rulers for 355 years. When the Mongols and Manchus conquered China they had already to a considerable extent adopted the culture of the Chinese. Thus though they dominated the Chinese politically, the Chinese dominated them culturally. Therefore they did not create a marked break or change in the continuity and unity of Chinese culture and civilization. The present Communist regime, however, has been determined, since its seizure of power, to strike at the foundations of traditional Chinese culture and society, to put an end to the family with its old widespread functions, and to destroy the humanist social norms and moral virtues by ideological purges and "brainwashing" campaigns. The youngsters have been encouraged not only to break away from their family ties, but also openly to repudiate their parents and relatives. The Communist regime is now further strengthening its grip over the populace by its "People's Communes." Children are being delivered to communal nurseries; families are moving into barracks; even graveyards are being communalized.

But it would be a great mistake to consider the revolt against the traditional society with its institutions and morals as the extermination of Chinese culture and civilization. The Chinese Communists do not intend this; the traditional virtues and Confucian ethics are by no means entirely wiped out. Communism, like Westernism, is not the natural growth of the Chinese traditions, but something that is forced upon the Chinese people against their will. In the completely new situation that they have to face, they have been much bewildered. In the beginning of the twentieth century, many of the more forward-looking officials and scholars had tried to find the ways and means to graft Western ideas onto the base of Chinese culture; as a result, they had made the new situation more acceptable and more readily adaptable to the themes of Chinese humanist thought. Thus Western civilization was connected with Chinese civilization, and both of them were made intelligible to each other.

But the Chinese Communist leaders and theoreticians have attempted to modify Chinese culture and humanist thought and make them more acceptable and more readily adaptable to the themes of Marxian ideology. Hence they have not only interpreted the traditional ideas and ethics in terms of Marxism, but also criticized the former in the light of the latter. The interpretation and criticism of Chinese civilization is what has interested the Chinese Communists and has constituted the main current of Chinese thought during the last ten years. Liu Shao-ch'i, a veteran Communist and a theoretician, sees much in common between Communism and Confucianism. In his *How to Be a Good*

Communist, he points out that "our Communist Party did not drop from the heavens but was born out of Chinese society, and . . . every member . . . came from this squalid old society of China and is still living in this society today. Hence, our Party members have more or less brought with them the remnants of the ideology and habits of the old society." According to him, it is not only possible for the Communist party members to renovate themselves through self-cultivation, but also necessary that they do so. Marx had insisted that man is capable of basic change, and so have Confucian scholars. Was it not said in the works of Mencius that "any man can become a Yao or a Shun"? (*Mencius,* V-B, 2). (Yao and Shun were the two legendary sage-rulers.) Liu Shao-ch'i is urging that the Marxist "sages," such as Marx, Engels, Lenin, and Stalin, be used as models in the Confucian manner. Hence every Communist can become a Marxist "sage," if he gives full development to his "consciousness" by self-cultivation. This is just one example of the use that the Communist ideologues are making of Confucian tradition to elucidate Marxist doctrines.

The Chinese Communists have up to the present time adhered to the policy of appropriating traditional ideas for the uses of Marxian ideology. The first requisite for a good Communist, according to Liu Shao-ch'i, must be the possession of Communist ethics. What is the content of the Communist ethics? In his *How to Be a Good Communist,* Liu Shao-ch'i stated that the Communist undertaking is "to reform mankind into the completely selfless citizenry of a Communist society." Being "good" for a Communist means the utter subordination of individual interest to that of the party, and ultimately, to that of mankind. His description of a good Communist who exemplifies such ethics is studded with Confucian maxims and moral idioms. The good Communist "can both love and hate people"; he can deal with comrades in a "faithful and forgiving" spirit, and "put himself in the position of others. . . . He will never do to others anything he would not like others to do to him. . . . He will grieve long before the rest of the world grieves and he will rejoice only after the rest of the world has rejoiced." Being selfless, he can bear hardships and overcome difficulties. Therefore, "he is able to possess the greatest firmness and moral courage, which riches cannot corrupt, poverty cannot alter, and force cannot suppress." Liu Shao-

Studies, Vol. I, Hong Kong, Univ. of Hong Kong Press, 1956; Vol. II, London, Oxford Univ. Press, 1958.

Lamson, Hervert Day, *Social Pathology in China,* Shanghai, Commercial Press, 1934.

Lang, Olga, *China Family and Society,* New Haven, Yale Univ. Press, 1946.

Levy, Marion J., Jr., *Family Revolution in Modern China,* Cambridge, Harvard Univ. Press, 1949.

Linebarger, Paul, *Government in Republican China,* New York, McGraw-Hill, 1938.

Liu, Hui-chen Wang, *The Traditional Chinese Clan Rule,* Locust Valley, J. J. Augustin, 1959.

Meiger, Marinus J., *The Introduction of Modern Criminal Law in China,* Batavia, De Unie, 1950.

Tang, Peter S. H., *Communist China Today,* rev. ed., Washington: Research Institute on the Sino-Soviet Block, 1961.

Tsao, V. Y., *The Constitutional Structure of Modern China,* Melbourne, Melbourne Univ. Press. 1948.

Thomas, S. B., *Government and Administration in Communist China,* New York, Institute of Pacific Relations, 1953.

Walker, Richard L., *China Under Communism,* New Haven, Yale Univ. Press, 1955.

Wang Kan-yu, *The Local Government of China: A Study of the Administrative Nature of Local Units,* Chungking, China Institute of Pacific Relations, 1945.

Ward, J. S. M., and W. G. Sterling, *The Hung Society,* 2 vols., London, Baskerville, 1925–1926.

Wu, John C. H., *Juridical Essays and Studies,* Shanghai, Commercial Press, 1928.

Wu, Yuan-li, *An Economic Survey of Communist China,* New York, Bookman Associates, 1956.

Yang, C. K., *The Chinese Family in the Communist Revolution,* Cambridge, Technology Press, 1959.

Yang, C. K., *A Chinese Village in Early Communist Transition,* Cambridge, Technology Press, 1959.

Yang, L. S., *Studies in Chinese Institutional History,* Cambridge: Harvard University Press, 1961.

III. Thought and Learning

Chai, Ch'u, "Chinese Humanism: A Study of Chinese Mentality and Temperament," *Social Research,* Vol. XXVI, No. 1, 1959.

————, "Neo-Confucianism of the Sung-Ming Periods," *Social Research,* Vol. XVIII, No. 3, 1951.

————, and Winberg Chai, *Essential Writings of the Chinese Humanism,* New York, Bantam, forthcoming.

————, and Winberg Chai, *The Story of Chinese Philosophy,* New York, Washington Square, 1961.

————, Winberg Chai, and Thomas Horet, Jr., *The Wisdom of Tao from Lao Tzu,* New York, Western Publications, 1961.

Chan, Wing-tsit, *Religious Trends in Modern China,* New York, Columbia Univ. Press, 1953.

Chang, Carsun, *The Development of Neo-Confucian Thought,* New York, Bookman Associates, 1957.

Creel, H. G., *Chinese Thought from Confucius to Mao Tse-tung,* Chicago, Univ. of Chicago Press, 1953, Mentor Book ed., New York, New American Library, 1960.

De Bary, W. Theodore, and others, eds., *Sources of Chinese Tradition,* New York, Columbia Univ. Press, 1960.

Fairbank, John K., ed., *Chinese Thought and Institutions,* Chicago, Univ. of Chicago Press, 1957.

Fung, Yu-lan, *A History of Chinese Philosophy,* tr. by Derk Bodde, 2 vols., Princeton, Princeton Univ. Press, 1952, 1953.

————, *A Short History of Chinese Philosophy,* paperback ed., New York, Macmillan, 1960.

————, *The Spirit of Chinese Philosophy,* tr. by E. R. Hughes, London, Kegan Paul, 1947.

Giles, Herbert A., *A History of Chinese Literature,* New York, Appleton, 1927.

Grousset, René, *Chinese Art and Culture,* New York, Orion, 1959.

Hsia, C. T., *A History of Chinese Fiction, 1917–1957,* New Haven: Yale University Press, 1961.

Hu Shih, *The Chinese Renaissance,* Chicago, Univ. of Chicago Press, 1934.

Hughes, E. R., *Chinese Philosophy in Classical Times,* rev. ed., London, Dent, 1954.

Karlgren, Bernhard, *The Chinese Language,* New York, Ronald, 1949.

Levenson, Joseph R., *Confucian China and Its Modern Fate,* Berkeley and Los Angeles, Univ. of California Press, 1958.

Lin, Mousheng, *Men and Ideas: An Informal History of Chinese Political Thought,* New York, John Day, 1942.

Lin Yutang, *The Wisdom of China and India*, New York, Random House, 1942.

Liu Wu-Chi, *A Short History of Confucian Philosophy*, Harmondsworth, Penguin, 1955.

Needham, Joseph, and Wang Ling, *Science and Civilization in China:* Vol I, *Introductory Orientations*, 1954; Vol. II, *History of Scientific Thought*, 1956; Vol. III, *Mathematics and the Sciences of the Heavens and the Earth*, 1959; Cambridge, Cambridge Univ. Press.

Nivison, David S., and Arthur F. Wright, eds., *Confucianism in Action*, Stanford, Stanford Univ. Press, 1959.

Schyns, Joseph, and others, *1500 Modern Chinese Novels and Plays*, Peiping, Catholic Univ. Press, 1948.

Scott, A. C., *The Classical Theatre of China*, London, Allen and Unwin, 1957.

Silcock, Arnold, *Introduction to Chinese Art and History*, London, Faber & Faber, 1935.

Suzuki, D. T., *A Brief History of Chinese Philosophy*, London, Probsthain, 1914.

Sze, Mai-mai, *The Tao of Painting*, 2 vols., New York, Pantheon, 1956.

Tung, Tung-ho, *Languages of China*, Taipei, China Culture Publishing Foundation, 1953.

Waley, Arthur, *Three Ways of Thought in Ancient China*, London, Allen and Unwin, 1939. Anchor ed., New York, Doubleday, 1956.

Willetts, William, *Chinese Art*, 2 vols., Harmondsworth, Penguin, 1958.

Wright, Arthur F., *Buddhism in Chinese History*, Stanford, Stanford Univ. Press, 1959.

————, ed., *Studies in Chinese Thought*, Chicago, Univ. of Chicago Press, 1953.

Yang, Y. C., *China's Religious Heritage*, New York, Abingdon-Cokesbury Press, 1943.

IV. Reform and Revolution

Brandt, Conrad, and others, *A Documentary History of Chinese Communism*, Cambridge, Harvard Univ. Press, 1952.

Cameron, M. E., *The Reform Movement in China, 1898–1912*, Stanford, Standford Univ. Press, 1931.

Chang, Carsun, *The Third Force in China,* New York, Book-man Associates, 1952.

Chapman, H. Owen, *The Chinese Revolution, 1926–27,* London, Constable, 1928.

Chiang, Siang-tseh, *The Nien Rebellion,* Seattle, Univ. of Washington Press, 1954.

Chiang Kai-shek, *China's Destiny,* New York, Macmillan, 1947.

Chiang Monlin, *Tides from the West,* New Haven, Yale Univ. Press, 1947.

Chow, Tse-tung, *The May Fourth Movement,* Cambridge, Harvard Univ. Press, 1960.

Fitzgerald, C. P., *Revolution in China,* New York, Praeger, 1952.

Holcombe, A. N., *The Chinese Revolution,* Cambridge, Harvard Univ. Press, 1930.

Hu Sheng, *Imperialism and Chinese Politics,* Peking, Foreign Languages Press, 1955.

Isaacs, H. R., *The Tragedy of the Chinese Revolution,* rev. ed., Stanford, Stanford Univ. Press, 1951.

K'ang, Yu-wei, *Ta T'ung Shu: The One-World Philosophy of K'ang Yu-wei,* tr. by L. G. Thompson, London, Allen and Unwin, 1958.

Levenson, Joseph R., *Liang Ch'i-chao and the Mind of Modern China,* Cambridge, Harvard Univ. Press, 1953.

Li Chien-nung, *The Political History of China: 1840–1928,* tr. by S. Y. Teng and J. Ingalls, Princeton, Van Nostrand, 1956.

Linebarger, Paul, *The Political Doctrines of Sun Yat-sen,* Baltimore, Johns Hopkins Press, 1937.

Liu Shao-ch'i, *How to Be a Good Communist,* Peking, Foreign Languages Press, 1951.

Mao Tse-tung, *Selected Works,* 4 vols., New York, International Publishers, 1954–1956.

North, Robert C., *Moscow and Chinese Communists,* Stanford, Stanford Univ. Press, 1953.

Schwartz, Benjamin, *Chinese Communism and the Rise of Mao,* Cambridge, Harvard Univ. Press, 1951.

Sih, Paul K. T., *Decision for China: Communism or Christianity,* Chicago, Regnery, 1959.

Snow, Edgar, *Red Star Over China,* New York, Random House, 1944.

Tan, Chester C., *The Boxer Catastrophe,* New York, Columbia Univ. Press, 1955.

T'ang Leang-li, *The Inner History of the Chinese Revolution,* London, Routledge, 1930.

Teng, Ssŭ-yü, *New Light on the History of the Taiping Rebellion,* Cambridge, Harvard Univ. Press, 1950.

———, and John K. Fairbank, *China's Response to the West,* Cambridge, Harvard Univ. Press, 1954.

Tong, Hollington K., *Chiang Kai-shek: Soldier and Statesman,* 2 vols., Shanghai, China Publishing Company, 1937 (the authorized biography).

V. General Reference on Modern China

Bibliography of Asian Studies, published in September each year by the Association for Asian Studies, Ann Arbor, Michigan.

Chan, Wing-tsit, *An Outline and an Annotated Bibliography of Chinese Philosophy,* New Haven, Yale Univ. Far Eastern Publications, 1959.

Chao, Kuo-chun, *Selected Works in English for a Topical Study of Modern China: 1840–1952,* Cambridge, Harvard Univ. Regional Studies Program on East Asia, 1952.

———, *Source Materials from Communist China,* 3 vols., Cambridge, Harvard Univ. Russian Research Center, 1953.

Davidson, M. A., *A List of Published Translation from Chinese into English, French and German,* 2 parts, Ann Arbor, American Council of Learned Societies, 1952, 1957.

Fairbank, John King, and Kwang-ching Liu, *Modern China: A Bibliographical Guide to Chinese Works, 1898–1937,* Cambridge, Harvard Univ. Press, 1950.

Thomas, S. B., *Recent Books on China, 1945–51,* New York, Institute of Pacific Relations, 1951.

U. S. Consulate-General, Hong Kong, *Current Background.*

———, *Extracts from China Mainland Magazines,* published weekly.

———, *Survey of China Mainland Press,* published daily from Monday through Friday.

Yuan, Tung-li, *China in Western Literature,* New Haven, Yale Univ. Far Eastern Publications, 1958.

———, *Economic and Social Development of Modern China: A Bibliographical Guide,* New Haven, Human Relations Area Files, 1956.

Epoch	Division	Date	Capital	Major Events
Hsia		c. 2205–c. 1766 B.C.	?	Hsia was the first Chinese dynasty, but the period still lacks documentary evidence.
Shang (or Yin)		c. 1766–c. 1122 B.C.	Anyang	King ruled the nation by "mandate of Heaven," with limited control over his feudal states.
Chou	Western Chou	c. 1122–771 B.C.	Hao (Sian)	This is known to historians as the Classical Age. However, at about 900 B.C. the feudal empire of Chou began to show symptoms of decay. The princes of individual states defied the authority of the emperor. In 771 B.C. the Chous moved their capital from Hao to Loyi, and the dynasty was known as the Eastern Chou. The overlord was reduced to a figurehead with the states playing a dominant role. The period from 6th through the 3rd century B.C. saw the flowering of ancient Chinese philosophy and gave rise to the so-called "hundred schools of thought," among which Confucianism and Taoism were very important.
	Eastern Chou	771–255 B.C.	Loyi (Loyang)	
	(Ch'un-Ch'iu)	722–481 B.C.		
	(Chan-Kuo)	403–221 B.C.		
Ch'in		255–206 B.C.	Hsien Yang (west of Sian)	Shih Huang Ti founded the Ch'in and unified China for the first time. The empire was divided into many military areas and feudalism was abolished. Legalists were in power and Shih Huang Ti burned books so as to unify political thinking. The government built magnificent palaces, roads, and the Great Wall.

Han	Western Han	205 B.C.–A.D. 8	Changan (Sian)	This is known as the "Imperial Age." The empire was extended and the government centralized. The civil-service examination was introduced. Confucianism was elevated at the expense of other schools of thought. Government levied taxes, issued a reformed calendar, and extended system of grain storage. Ssu-ma Ch'ien (145–97 B.C.) wrote the first *Historical Records*.
	Hsin	A.D. 9–23	Changan	Wang Mang revolted (the Red Eyebrows Uprising) and made himself "Emperor of Hsin." He nationalized land and redistributed large holdings.
	Eastern Han	A.D. 25–220	Loyang	Liu Hsiu restored the Han empire and extended his authority to Central Asia. This was a time of many cultural developments, including the invention of paper by Tsai Lun (A.D. 105), the introduction of Buddhism from India (65–170), and the establishment of Taoism as a religion (130–190).
Three Kingdoms	Wei Shu Wu	220–265 221–263 222–280	Loyang Chengtu Nanking	Taoist priests and the Yellow-Turban bandits revolted, with the breakup of Han Empire. Despite economic and social insecurity, there came many high monks from every Buddhist region to China. Buddhist sutras was also translated.
Tsin	Western Tsin	265–316	Loyang	Ssu-ma family reunified the three kingdoms and founded the Tsin. However, there was a period of political anarchy with the rebellion of princes, uprisings of the Tanguts, and the invasion of Hu (Tartar) tribes. Buddhism and Taoism became popular, and Confucianism was misused by usurpers.
	Eastern Tsin	317–420	Nanking	

Epoch	Division	Date	Capital	Major Events
Southern and Northern Dynasties	SOUTH Sung Ch'i Liang Ch'en NORTH N. Wei E. Wei W. Wei N. Ch'i N. Chou	420–479 479–502 502–557 557–589 386–534 534–550 535–557 550–577 557–581	Nanking Nanking Nanking Nanking Pingcheng (Loyang) Yeh(Honan) Changan Yeh(Honan) Changan	This was again a period of political disunion, with frequent wars between southern and northern dynasties. There were great migrations from north to south and increased pilgrimages abroad. Northern barbarians gradually became Chinese in manners and habits. But aristocrats in the south lived on their estates like kings and enjoyed special privileges. Buddhist art was introduced and sculptured Buddha figures were made in cave temples.
Sui		581–618	Changan Loyang Yangchow	Yang Ti reunified the empire and improved internal administration by codifying criminal law. Great Wall repaired and extended; Grand Canal and other canals constructed; many palaces and parks were built with forced labor.
T'ang		619–907	Changan Loyang	Chinese culture reached its highest development during this period, which is known as the Golden Age of Poetry. There were some 2,000 minor and major poets including Wang Wei (699–759), Li Po (8th c.), Tu Fu (8th c.) and Po Chu-i (9th c.). Block printing was invented. Governmental system was also highly developed; provinces governed by governors appointed by emperor; civil-service examination system was improved; various institutions of higher learning were established. While Taoism received imperial favor, Confucianism and Buddhism were also honored. Islam and Nestorianism were introduced.

Wu Tai "Five Dynasties"	Late Liang Late T'ang Late Tsing Late Han Late Chou	907–923 923–936 936–947 947–950 951–960	Kaifeng Loyang Kaifeng Kaifeng Kaifeng	After the downfall of Tang, there was a period of political anarchy. Five military leaders made themselves kings in Kaifeng and Loyang. There were some 12 kingdoms in various parts of the country. During this period some 30,000 Buddhist monasteries were demolished.
Sung	North Sung	960–1127	Kaifeng	Chao K'uang-yin reunited the empire and founded the Sung dynasty. While he consolidated all the authority in the central government, the neighboring states (Khitan, Tangut, and Juchen Tungus) were becoming a constant threat. In 1127, Juchen Tungus invaded Kaifeng and captured the artist-emperor, Hui-tsung. Kao-tsung then established the South Sung in Hangchow and never succeeded in recovering the lost territories. Despite unsettled political conditions, the Sung was the period of Neo-Confucianism, with such outstanding philosophers as the two Chengs, Chang, and greatest of all, Chu-Hsi. Other noted achievements: printing by wooden blocks and by movable type, and the reform measures by Wang An-shih (1021–1086).
	South Sung	1127–1279	Hangchow	
Yüan		1279–1368	Peking	After conquering Tangut (1126), Juchen Tungus (1234), Kublai Khan, grandson of Jenghis Khan, declared himself emperor of China (1260). He later named his dynasty the Yüan (1271). Kublai employed men of all races in his government. Taoism was not in good favor, but Buddhists and Confucians were honored. Great developments in dramatic art and fiction took place.

Epoch	Division	Date	Capital	Major Events
Ming		1368–1644	Nanking Peking	Chu Yüan-chang, who restored the empire to Chinese rule, named his dynasty Ming (bright). Political system was modeled after that of Han-Tang, with 13 provinces. This period is not remarkable for any intellectual movement except the steady growth of an already enormous literature, the compilation of encyclopedias, and the codification of the laws. However, there was increasing communication with foreign countries. Cheng Ho's seven naval expeditions (1405–1431) sent him to Java, Sumatra, Ceylon, India, Arabia, and other nations. Portuguese and Spanish traders began to arrive at China coastal cities (1517, 1575). But the Japanese pirates invaded coastal cities (1370–1563), which caused much resentment toward foreigners.
Ch'ing		1644–1911	Peking	The Manchu Tartars, a small tribe called Juchen in the Chang Pai Mountains, gradually got possession of the Liaotung area, and with it acquired the civilization of China. At first there were many restrictions on the Chinese population: the men were required to shave their heads, to wear queues, and to adopt the Manchu costume. Eventually, however, the Manchus were absorbed by the Chinese culture. During the K'ang Hsi regime, culture began to flourish again. There were many studies made of classics, geography, history, law, etc. The Dictionary of K'ang Hsi contained 44,439 characters, and is still in use today. During this time progress was also made in all the minor arts, especially porcelain making. In the 18th and 19th centuries European influence became more marked; Christian missionaries taught the Chinese much about natural

				science; on the other hand, the Portuguese and Dutch brought in opium from India. The disastrous Opium War (1839–1842) with England forced China to open trade with foreign nations, and thus she was placed at the mercy of Western imperialism. The Chinese began to revolt against the Manchu regime—the Taiping Rebellion took place in 1851–1864. It paved the way for future revolutions.
Republic	Republic of China (Nationalist)	1912–	Nanking Taipei, Taiwan	Dr. Sun Yat-sen (1866–1925) and the Kuomintang (Nationalist Party) established the Chinese Republic and overthrew the Manchu government in 1911–1912. In 1920 occurred the first of five civil wars. The Nationalists reorganized in Canton, and with the death of Sun, the Nationalist government found a military leader in Chiang Kai-shek. Before the completion of a successful northern expedition, the Japanese attacked Manchuria in 1931. In 1937 Japan started a full-scale invasion, and the Nationalist government retreated to Chungking until the end of the war in 1945. The government returned to Nanking and the National Assembly elected Gen. Chiang president of the new constitutional government in 1948. In 1949, after many years of civil war, the Nationalist government abdicated to Taiwan (Formosa) where Chiang continues as its leader.
	People's Republic of China (Communist)	1949–	Peking	Mao Tse-tung proclaimed the establishment of the People's government at Peking in 1949 after capturing the ancient city. In 1954 the National People's Congress adopted a new constitution and elected Mao as first chairman of the republic. In 1959, Mao resigned to become chairman of the Communist Party while Liu Shao-ch'i succeeded him as chairman of the republic.

Index

Agrarian society and economy, 61, 62, 87, 192
Agriculture, importance of, 21
Analects, 21, 121, 122, 142, 152
Ancestor worship, 78, 79
Anecdotes of Scholars (*Ju Liu Wai Shih*), 166
Art, Chinese, 177-186

Babylonia, culture of, 16
Barbarians, 34
Biography of Heroine (*Erh Ju Yin Hsiung Chuan*), 154
Black Pottery culture, 14
Board of Censors, 48
"Body-laborers," 68
Buddhism, 20, 120, 134-138, 143, 144, 147, 148, 149, 184

Censorate system, 47, 48
Ch'an School, 135
Chang Tsai, his writings, 115
Cheng Tzu-ang (poet), 162
Changing Chinese Society, 230-236
Chiang Kai-shek, 214-221, 223
Ch'in dynasty, 31, 35, 132
China Regeneration Society, 206
Chinese art, 177-186
Chinese attitude toward life, 118
Chinese culture, 12, 21-24, 110, 111
Chinese government, 42-59
Chinese history, 11
Chinese language, 167-176
Chinese Law, 101-109

Chinese literature, 151-166
Chinese people, origin of, 25, 26
Chinese philosophy, development of, 126-141
Chinese Religion, 142-150
Chinese society, structure of, 66, 67, 70, 85
Chinese thought and learning, 110
Chinese (type of humanity), 230
Christianity in China, 148
Chou dynasty, 12, 30, 35, 126
Chou Li (*Ritual of Chou*), 27
Chou Tung-yi, his writings, 114
Ch'u Chai, 24
Chuang Tzu, his writings, 119, 128
Chung Yung (*Doctrine of the Mean*), 80, 123, 142
Ch'un Ch'iu (*Spring and Autumn Annals*), 17
Ch'ü Yüan, writer, 152, 157, 161
Commune, People's, 90, 92-100
Communism (and Mao Tse-tung), 222-229
Communist Agrarian Policy, 87-93
Communist government, structure of, 56
Communist (type of humanity), 232
Communists and religion, 150
Confucius and Confucianism, 21, 38, 43, 75-81, 102, 105, 113, 119-122, 128, 133, 142, 190

Constitution, 49, 52, 57
Constitutional government, 51, 52
Cosmic conception, 110
Cosmological philosophers, 114

De Bary, W. T., and others, 44
Dialects, 169, 170
Doctrine of the Mean (Chung Yung), 38, 142

Egypt, early civilization of, 15
European culture, origin of, 17
Examination system, 47

Family, 74-76, 83
Feudalism, 17, 62, 63, 67
"Five classics," 143
Formalism (in art) 177

Geographic background of China, 11
Government, Chinese, 42-48
Grand Terminus, Diagram of, 114
Great Appendix, The, 119, 124
Great Learning (Ta Hsüeh), 142
Greece, early culture of, 17, 18, 22

Han dynasty, 18, 31, 132, 133
Han Fei Tzu (Legalist school), 131
Han school of thought, 117
Han Yü, Chinese writer, 152
Happiness, Chinese conception of, 121
"Headman," 49, 107
Homeward I Am Bound (poem), 159
Hsai culture, 12
Hsiang Yu, general, 153
Hsi Hsiang Chi, 154
Hsiung Nu (Huns), 31
Hsun Tzu, his teachings, 128, 129
Hu Shih (writer), 165

Hua-Hsia people, 27, 35
Huang Ti (clan), 28
Huang Yuan-yung (journalist), 164
Hung Lou Meng, The *(Dream of the Red Chamber)*, 155, 161
Humanism, 40, 41

Imperial College, 50
India, early civilization of, 15

Ju Liu Wai Shih (Anecdotes of Scholars), 155

K'ang Yu-wei (and the Reform Movement), 196-204
Kuan Tzu (Legalist school), 131
Kuo Hsi (artist), 182, 183, 186
Kuomintang, 51, 191, 205, 208, 214
Kuo Yu (Records of Ancient States), 27

Land reform, 223
Language, Chinese, 167-176
Lao Tzu, his writings, 113, 119, 127
Law, Chinese, 101-109
League of Common Alliance, 191
Learning, Revival of, 132
Legalists, Teachings of, 131
Legends, 146
Li (Ceremonies), 17
Li Chi (Book of Rites), 22, 124, 200
Li Po (poet), 160, 185
Li Sao (Falling into Trouble), 157
Liang Ch'i-ch'ao, scholar, 140
Liao-chai Chi Yi, 155
Literature, Chinese, 151-166
Literary Revolution, 163, 164
Liu Pang, 153
Liu Tsung-yüan (poet), 152, 158
Local government, 48, 55
Love (Human-hearted), 120
Lung Shan culture, 14

Manchu dynasty, 139, 188, 189, 205-207
Manchus, 31-32
Marxism, 212
Mao Tse-tung, 96, 222-229
Marriage, institution of, 81
Marriage Law of 1950, 84
Mencius, his teachings, 38, 100, 104, 128, 129, 143
"Mind-laborers," 68
Ming dynasty, 32
"Minority nationalities," 35
Mohist school, 116, 130, 131
Mongols, 20
Mongol dynasty, 31
Mo Tzu, writings, 116, 117, 130, 131
Mythical period, 117

Nationalism (and Chiang Kai-shek), 214-221
Nationalist revolution, 205-212
Naturalism (in art), 181
Nature, Love for, 158, 159
Neo-Confucianism, 136-139
Neolithic Age, 29
New Culture Movement, 139, 194
New Democracy, 277
New Script school, 133
Nirvana, 123

Odes, Book of, 154
Old Script school, 133
Opium War, 187

Paleolithic Age, 29
Peasant revolts, 64
Peking Man, 29
People's Political Council, 51
Philosophy, Chinese, 126-141
Political thought, 37-39
Power, delegation of, 44-46

Racial amalgamation, 30-31
Reform and Revolution, 187
Reform Movement, 190, 196-204, 216
Religion, Chinese, 36, 142-150
Revolts of the Chinese, 64
Rites, Book of (Li Chi), 22, 38, 39, 124, 200

Roman culture, 18, 19, 22
Romance of the Three Kingdoms (San Kuo Yin Yi), 154, 161
Romanticism (in art), 184
Royce, Josiah, Spirit of Modern Philosophy, 127

San Kuo Yin Yi (Romance of the Three Kingdoms), 154, 161
San Miao people, 35
Secret Societies, 71-73
Shang dynasty, 13
Shao Yung, his writings, 115
Shen Nung (clan), 28
Shih Chi (book), 156
Shi Ching (Book of Odes), 12, 16, 28, 36, 154
Shih Huang Ti, Emperor, 132
Shui Hui Chüan (Water Margins Record), 155
Sui dynasty, 31
"Sophism," School of, 125
Sources of Chinese Tradition, 44
Spring and Autumn Annals (Ch'un Ch'iu), 200
Story of the Western Pavilion, 154
Strange Tales of Liao-chai, 155
Sun Yat-sen, 51, 52, 196, 205-212, 214
Szu-ma Chien, writer, 152

Ta Hsüeh (Great Learning), 38
Taiwan, 65, 216
Taoism, 118, 119, 127, 128, 134, 143, 144, 159, 184
Ta-tung, 39
T'ang dynasty, 31
Tao Yüan-ming, poet, 152, 158
Treaties with foreign powers, 188
Tseng Tzu, 22
Tu Fu, poet, 158
Tung Chung-shu, teachings of, 43
Tungus Manchus, 20

Upper Cave Man, 29

Wang Wei (poet, painter), 160, 178
Warring States, Period of, 128
Water Margins Record, 155
Western-Hill Trip (poem), 159
Western encroachments (on China), 187
Wu Tao-tze (artist), 184

Yang Chu, his writings, 118, 119, 128, 162, 163

Yang Hsiung, Chinese writer, 151
Yang Shao culture, 13
Ye Pei Huai (*Lines to Ease the Aching Heart*), 156
Yi Ching (*Book of Change*), 17, 37, 110, 111, 113, 123, 124
Yi Ti (barbarians), 34
Yin-Yang school, 126
Yin dynasty, 13
Yu culture, 12
Yüan (Mongol) dynasty, 31
Yueh people, 35

MENTOR Books of Related Interest

The White Pony *edited by Robert Payne.* A rich collection of Chinese poetry spanning more than three thousand years and covering every mood and subject. (#MT301—75¢)

A Treasury of Asian Literature *edited by John D. Yohannan.* The literary classics of the Orient: a collection of poetry, stories, and scriptures from Arabia and the Far East.
(#MT340—75¢)

A Treasury of Modern Asian Stories *edited by William Clifford and Daniel L. Milton.* The cream of contemporary fiction from China, India, Pakistan, Arabia, Israel, Persia, Malaya, Japan, and Korea. (#MD329—50¢)

The Travels of Marco Polo. The enduring record of a medieval Italian's journey to the fabulous East, as far as Cathay. Edited with an Introduction by Milton Rugoff.
(#CD97—50¢)

The Teachings of the Compassionate Buddha *edited with commentary by E. A. Burtt.* The best translations of the basic texts and scriptures, early discourses, the Dhammapada, and later writings. (#MP380—60¢)

The Way of Zen *by Alan W. Watts.* A modern American's interpretation of Zen Buddhism as a means of living serenely and fully in a confused and frustrating world.
(#MD273—50¢)

The Origins of Oriental Civilization *by Walter A. Fairservis, Jr.* An archaeological and anthropological study of the beginnings of culture in China, Korea, Japan, Mongolia, and Manchuria. Illustrated. (#MD251—50¢)

The Island Civilizations of Polynesia *by Robert C. Suggs.* An anthropologist reveals the origin and culture of primitive peoples of the South Seas. (#MD304—50¢)

A Short History of India and Pakistan *by T. Walter Wallbank.* This comprehensive and readable history is a revised, abridged, and up-dated edition of *India in the New Era.*
(#MD224—50¢)

Other MENTOR Books of Related Interest

How To Build
A Low-Cost Library

You can build a personal library of the best books for as little as 35 or 50 cents a volume. Choose from thousands of the classics and best sellers in literature, biography, poetry, art, history, religion, reference, and science as listed in a new catalog:

Paperbound books in print

If you've often had trouble finding the paperbacks you want—here are over 14,500—with information on how and where to get them. Here you can locate all the low-priced paper books available either by checking the thousands of titles listed alphabetically by author and by title, or by looking under any of the 90 categories where selected titles are grouped under helpful subject classification.

Order your copy of this unique buying guide today—either from your dealer or direct from RRB, New American Library of World Literature, 501 Madison Avenue, New York 22, N.Y.

If you order from New American Library please make checks payable to: R. R. Bowker Company. Single copies are $3 net prepaid, or you can subscribe to the 4 quarterly issues for just $8 a year and automatically be kept up to date on available paperbacks.